THE THINGS I'VE SEEN

First published in 2010 by
Liberties Press
Guinness Enterprise Centre | Taylor's Lane | Dublin 8
Tel: +353 (1) 415 1224
www.libertiespress.com | info@libertiespress.com

Distributed in the United States by
Dufour Editions | PO Box 7 | Chester Springs | Pennsylvania | 19425

and in Australia by
James Bennett Pty Limited | InBooks | 3 Narabang Way
Belrose NSW 2085

Trade enquiries to Gill & Macmillan Distribution
Hume Avenue | Park West | Dublin 12
Tel: +353 (1) 500 9534 | Fax: +353 (1) 500 9595
sales@gillmacmillan.ie

ISBN: 978-1-907593-04-8
2 4 6 8 10 9 7 5 3 1
A CIP record for this title is available from the British Library.

Cover design by Sin É Design
Internal design by Liberties Press
Printed in Ireland by Colour Books

THE THINGS I'VE SEEN

Nine Lives of a Foreign Correspondent

Lara Marlowe

For Michel and Chantal Déon

Contents

II LEBANON & ALGERIA

III YUGOSLAVIA

IV IRAN

'*There is such a thing as truth and it can be told.*'

– Seamus Heaney

(to Dennis O'Driscoll
in *Stepping Stones*,
Faber and Faber)

Acknowledgements

Journalism is a lifelong apprenticeship. Though it's usually a matter of trial and error, and especially a school of hard knocks, colleagues and editors have taught me a great deal.

I am grateful to *The Irish Times* for underwriting my reporting for the past fourteen years, and for giving permission for my articles to be reproduced in this book. There's a special place in my heart for Paul Gillespie, the *Irish Times'* retired foreign policy editor, who hired me and most of my generation of foreign correspondents.

I've had five fine foreign editors at *The Irish Times*. Over the years, they have been the umbilical cord that tied me to the paper, providing moral support, guidance and a degree of freedom that few publications grant their journalists.

In January 1988, Patrick Comerford commissioned 'Going West in Beirut', the first article I published in *The Irish Times*; it is reproduced in this book.

At my request, Seamus Martin sent me to Afghanistan after the atrocities of September 11, with the blessing of then editor Conor Brady.

Also at my request, the paper's current editor, Geraldine Kennedy, allowed me to cover the 2003 invasion of Iraq, and to return to the country repeatedly thereafter.

When he was foreign editor, Peter Murtagh saw me through NATO's bombardment of Serbia in 1999, the Iraq war, and Lebanon in the wake of Rafik al-Hariri's assassination.

Paddy Smyth sent me to cover the Israel-Hizballah war in 2006, the Georgian war two summers later, and the aftermath of Israel's January 2009 assault on the Gaza Strip.

In my present post as Washington correspondent, I have benefited from

Denis Staunton's vast knowledge of the US. With his rapid, infallible news sense, Denis dispatched me to Haiti to cover the earthquake, to Louisiana for the oil spill, and to Arizona for the battle over immigration.

For my first thirteen years at *The Irish Times*, Paris was my bread and butter. My foreign editors, but also editors from other sections, particularly Patsey Murphy in the Weekend section, and later the Saturday Magazine, received my copy with enthusiasm.

There is a terrific sense of collegiality on *The Irish Times*, and I've been encouraged and helped by secretaries, switchboard operators, copy-takers, sub-editors, computer technicians and accountants too numerous to name.

Long ago, the television producer Barry Lando gave me my first break in journalism when he hired me as a researcher-associate producer for CBS News' *60 Minutes* programme. Barry and I did some great stories together. On one of them, in Damascus in 1983, I met Robert Fisk, to whom I was married for twelve years. Robert was, *malgré tout*, the best journalism teacher.

Unless otherwise stated, all articles which appear in this collection were originally published in *The Irish Times*.

Preface:
A Life in Journalism

On a spring morning in 1981, I handed over a coin at the kiosk on the avenue Hoche, picked up a copy of the *International Herald Tribune* and turned to the back page. There was a photograph of Alain Robbe-Grillet, the 'father of the *nouveau roman*', whom I had just interviewed. I didn't know then that sub-editors, not reporters, write headlines. The title on the article was different from the one I had thought up before posting my copy to Neuilly. *The bastards*, I thought; *they ran an article by somebody else.*

Then my eyes fell to the byline, where I read, for the first time ever in a daily newspaper: 'by Lara Marlowe'. I yelped for joy, leapt in the air and ran around in circles. My life as a journalist had started.

I wrote another article, another and another. Some were rejected. There were setbacks. Nearly three decades and several thousand articles later, I am still pleased to see my byline.

I turned thirty, then forty, then fifty. Middle age did not creep up on me; it jumped out and said 'boo'. But two filing cabinet drawers full of articles were proof of the passage of time. They confirmed the breadth of my French experience, chronicled eight years in Beirut, recounted nearly a decade of blood letting in Algeria. From the siege of Sarajevo to NATO's punishing bombardment of Serbia, I had seen the breakup of Yugoslavia.

Without my realising it, my life fell into neat, historic segments. France and Ireland were my home base and refuge, and I often found their footprints in the regions where I travelled. But Lebanon, Algeria and Yugoslavia dominated the 1990s; Afghanistan, Iraq and the United States the first decade of the new century. I watched the Americans bomb Kabul, then Baghdad. 'Vietraqistan', as the American journalist Mort Rosenblum calls it, was the recurring theme of the noughties.

Much of my work was done from the safety of Paris. But without ever intending to be a war correspondent, I reported from frontlines in Central America, the Horn of Africa, the Caucasus and, especially, the Middle East and Iraq. The wars I covered, big and small, short and long, added up to some fifteen conflicts, depending how you counted.

Among the images that swarm through my mind is a narrow, monastic room in a retirement home in Bourj Hammoud, the Armenian quarter of Beirut. An icon of the Virgin hangs between two beds, in which lie a husband and wife, aged one hundred and five and ninety-seven respectively. Both are blind. They listen to Radio Yerevan in their waking hours. The old man bears a scar on one cheek, etched by a sabre at the Battle of Tannenberg, where he fought on the side of the Tsar's army in 1914. The following year, when the Turks began the first genocide of the twentieth century, he made the long march to what was then Mesopotamia, and across the desert to Lebanon, where he met his wife.

Had his life been happy, I asked him. 'I hate my circumstances now,' he said. 'But the things I have seen, no one has seen.'

I once asked my dear friend the French academician Michel Déon whether I should write fiction or non-fiction. 'Anyone can write a novel,' Michel replied. 'You have seen things no one else has.'

Writing novels remains the mirage that tantalises one through the slog of daily journalism. Yet I have loved this profession as one loves a place or a person. No adventure matches that paring down of belongings to a single suitcase and heading for the airport. Journalism, I realise now, has given me a far more pungent taste of life than any ivory tower.

Indeed, journalism has given me many lives. Each time I have moved on to a different country or conflict, the world has seemed new. And every time I have escaped a close call, I've wondered whether, like the cats who have been my companions, I am exhausting my nine lives.

In my reporting, I strive for authenticity: to freeze the fleetingness of time, to preserve people and situations in all their intensity. It is a paradox, for ours is a transient medium. As a French colleague liked to remind me, newspapers are meant to wrap fish the next day.

Like the proverbial fisherman, some of my best stories 'got away'. I searched fruitlessly through archives and old diskettes for three articles that fell victim to last minute confusion, rivalry among editors, and the dictates of political correctness at TIME Magazine, which employed me for eight years.

I loved the story of the Kuwaiti newspaper editor Faisal al-Marzouk, because it had a happy ending. On the day Iraqi forces fled Kuwait City in February 1991, a wealthy woman pleaded with me to find her brother, who had been taken to Basra by the Iraqis, along with hundreds of Kuwaiti civilians. Eventually, in the middle of a cold night on the Iraq–Kuwait frontier, I stuck my head into a dozen coaches filled with newly released prisoners. In each one I shouted: 'Is Faisal al-Marzouk here?'

From the photographs I had seen, I would not have recognised the grimy, dishevelled man who fell into my arms, weeping, when I told him: 'Faisal, I am a friend of Salwa, Jassem and Siham. They asked me to look for you. They are waiting for you.'

In 1994, I worked for weeks on a story slugged 'Tale of Two Cities', about Beirut recovering from civil war, just as Algiers plunged into darkness. I wrote thousands of words on the Arab capitals, but a dream recounted by Aliya Saïd, an upper middle class Beirut matron, taught me that wars never end for those who lose loved ones. Aliya's late husband, Rafik, had come to her in her sleep a few nights before, and said: 'Hurry up, Aliya. Get ready. We are going to see Fouad.'

The Saïds' son had been killed years earlier, in crossfire between Kurdish factions near Beirut's 'green line'. Rafik died of grief. Aliya lived like a zombie, playing bridge and holding dinner parties, trying to fill the void where her family had been. Eventually her liver gave out, destroyed by the amphetamines and tranquillisers she took to get up in the morning and sleep at night.

Another story, the text of which I have also lost, was entitled 'Family Saga'. It recounted the history of a Palestinian family who had been scattered by the creation of the state of Israel in 1948. Some clung to their native Galilee; others fled to Lebanon and Jordan. My editors at TIME thought that the problems of this Palestinian family should be solved by the 1993 Oslo Accords. When that turned out not to be the case, they lost interest. But I shall never forget Abu Ahmad, the patriarch of the Amman branch of the family, seated at a table in his prosperous restaurant, burying his head in his hands when he spoke of his childhood village, saying: 'Mirun, Mirun, I cannot forget you.'

I visited Mirun with Abu Ahmad's Arab-Israeli cousins. Their family's graceful stone houses had been transformed into a Yeshiva, for the study of Jewish sacred texts. I spoke in French with one of the inhabitants, a Talmudic scholar who had emigrated from Morocco. As the Palestinians hung back, fearing confrontation, I asked the Jewish man from Morocco what had happened to Mirun's Arab inhabitants. 'There were never any Arabs here,' he said curtly, ending our conversation.

Suffering is the lot of mankind; if my reporting sometimes strikes a chord in readers, I believe it is because I feel tied to the people whose pain I describe. As T. S. Eliot wrote: 'I am moved by . . . The notion of some infinitely gentle/ Infinitely suffering thing.' Some, like the parents of children who died violently in Ireland and France, became friends. Most have been swallowed up by distance and time. But I do not forget them.

There is Leila Behbehani, the three year old Iranian girl whose body I saw in a cold storage warehouse in Bandar Abbas, one of 290 civilians killed when the USS *Vincennes* guided missile cruiser shot down an Iranian airliner in 1988. Leila was on her way to a wedding, and was wearing a turquoise party dress. She died with the contorted face of a child who is crying. Captain Will Rogers III, the commander of the Vincennes, was given a medal.

There is the woman in the smouldering, blood spattered ruins of UNIFIL's Fidjian Battalion headquarters in Qana, southern Lebanon, on 18 April 1996, less than an hour after Israel had bombarded the post, killing 106 Lebanese civilians. She squats on the ground, her arms laced around her father's torso, rocking on her ankles and sobbing 'Abi, abi' ('My father, my father'). He cannot hear her, for his body has been cleaved diagonally by a proximity shell.

Nothing happens in isolation. Sometimes the link is obvious. The cancellation of elections won by Islamists in Algeria precipitated years of bloodshed. I still believe that the Lockerbie bombing was retaliation for the downing of the Iran Air flight six months earlier. And although it is heresy to say so, when al-Qaeda murdered close to three thousand people in the atrocities of September 11, 2001, I sensed immediately that it was connected to the slaughter of Muslims in Lebanon and Bosnia, to the festering wound of the Israeli-Palestinian conflict.

When I covered the Haitian earthquake in January 2010, I was surprised at the worry expressed by friends and colleagues. They seemed to think I would be traumatised by so much death and destruction. It was far easier than a war, I told them. No one was trying to kidnap or kill me. But most of all, one did not feel the rage that comes from seeing innocents die under bombardment.

In all the wars I covered, the Geneva Conventions were regarded as a quaint museum piece, at best. In 1999, the US and NATO blurred the line between civilian and military targets by bombing a passenger train, power plants, telephone exchanges, the Serb radio-television building – even the Chinese embassy in Belgrade. Time and again, the US military has killed civilians: when they shot down the Iranian Airbus, bombed Albanian refugees in

Kosovo, shelled journalists in the Palestine Hotel in Baghdad, and carried out drone attacks in Afghanistan and Pakistan. As long as it's an 'accident', the Americans seem to think it's okay.

The Israelis learned the lesson well, testing the 'Dahiya doctrine' (named after the Shia Muslim southern suburbs of Beirut) in Lebanon, where they killed 1,287 people in the summer of 2006. Under this doctrine, no distinction is made between civilian and military targets – as demonstrated horrifically in Israel's January 2009 assault on Gaza, in which 1,434 Palestinians were slaughtered.

The words 'international community' make me nauseous, for they have come to embody inaction, indifference and hypocrisy. It was the 'international community' that allowed the siege of Sarajevo to continue for almost four years, during which Serb gunners picked off ten thousand people like ducks. The same 'international community' makes empty promises about lifting the siege of Gaza, about rebuilding Gaza and Haiti. If Barack Obama has a shred of idealism left in him, he must forge an international community that respects the lives of civilians and keeps its word.

I have learned simple things: that governments lie; that, as Benjamin Franklin wrote, 'there never was a good war or a bad peace'. I have learned to appreciate my own good fortune, having seen how little stability, security or well-being exists outside the fortresses of our developed countries.

At the Féile an Phobail in west Belfast the summer of 2010, I was asked if I despaired of what the American poet e. e. cummings called 'manunkind'. I didn't want to sound negative, and strained to find examples of heroism. On occasion, I *have* encountered humour, generosity, altruism, even beauty. But for the most part, I have found the world to be as Matthew Arnold described it: without joy, love, light, certitude, peace, or help for pain. The instruments of suffering are usually remote: fighter bombers at altitudes of tens of thousands of feet; the secret minutes of politicians' meetings. Only occasionally does one glimpse the face of cruelty: in a Serb prison camp commander or, more recently, in an Arizona sheriff who glories in chain gangs of hungry prisoners and the deportation of Mexican migrants.

Despite the sadness and anger, I remain endlessly fascinated by the human condition. I still want to know what will happen. Looking back at this juncture, this *mezzo camino*, I have found something approaching a meaning and a purpose: to be there, to see, and to record.

Howth, County Dublin
August 2010

I
FRANCE

Douce France

City of My Life

I started to love Paris when I was a schoolgirl in California. My widowed mother returned from a tour with her church group carrying a blue plastic Air France shoulder bag, stuffed with film rolls and trinkets. Her souvenirs from Egypt, Rome, London and the New York World's Fair did not interest me. But the silk scarves and perfume, a little brass Eiffel Tower and her snapshots of the Place de la Concorde, the Arc de Triomphe and Notre Dame filled me with premonitory excitement.

In the summer of 1976, I emerged from the Concorde métro station with a rucksack on my back, after flying all night in a charter to Le Bourget. A quarter of a century later, the sense of wonderment is still fresh. There before me were the Obelisk, the Champs-Élysées, the Eiffel Tower, the Seine, the Tuileries Gardens. Growing up, I had almost come to doubt its reality; arriving in Paris as a student was like finding proof that paradise existed.

Four times I packed my belongings and departed, only to return within a few years. Most of my triumphs and disasters, friendships and romances, have taken place in this city. There is scarcely a street or monument that does not hold some personal memory. But Paris also speaks to me of kings and princesses, Jacobins, Communards and characters in novels. Who can pass the Louvre without remembering Louis XIV and François Mitterrand? When I cross a Paris bridge at night, I think of the Camus character throwing herself into the Seine in *The Fall*. The Pont Mirabeau will always remind me of Apollinaire's unrequited love for Marie Laurencin.

Could there be a richer place to live? To hear Parisians say they find Rome or Prague more beautiful always strikes me as betrayal. In its favour, they will tell you that Paris is built on a human scale, and it's true; despite the monuments scattered across the capital, it's never daunting. Unlike most cities, Paris is small enough to be manageable. I've never needed a car here, and allowing for métro changes, you can reach any appointment in forty-five minutes.

It's also possible to enjoy life in Paris without a lot of money, though why a loaf of bread, a flask of wine and a book of verse suffice here but not in London or New York I have never fathomed. My favourite picnic spot is the left bank of the Seine, at the end of the rue des Saints-Pères. The view of the Louvre is free, but take cushions to sit on because the stones are cold and hard.

Every Parisian loves his or her *quartier*. I know a few people who swear by the right bank, but in my opinion there is nothing to compare with the 6th *arrondissement*, where I've lived for the past five years. My best days start with a run through the Luxembourg Gardens. The central vista from Marie de Medici's palace (now the French Senate) and down the avenue de l'Observatoire is as spectacular as anything at Versailles.

But I like the meandering, English-style paths on the western side of the Luxembourg, where you round a corner to find a herd of French firemen stampeding towards you, a woman wearing make-up and jewellery with her designer tracksuit, or lonesome old people walking ridiculous dogs. You hear the 'thunk, thunk' of tennis balls on clay courts, and squeals of joy from children liberated from stuffy apartments to sail toy boats on the ornamental pond. Busts and statues nestle among exotic bushes and flowering trees, and it's fun to see that Baudelaire, Sainte-Beuve or Stendahl look like the Frenchman you've just interviewed. Crowds form around chess matches under the trees on Sundays, when Parisians wearing sunglasses lean their chairs against the arboretum walls to read books and newspapers or snooze.

The cobblestoned rue Ferou is the quickest way from the Luxembourg to the Place Saint-Sulpice. I owe a new appreciation of the church, originally built to keep the peasants out of nearby Saint-Germain, to the former French hostage Jean-Paul Kauffmann. He wrote a best-selling book about Saint-Sulpice, centred on Delacroix's magnificent fresco of *Jacob and the Angel*, just inside the front door to the right. Even if I rarely go in, the painting has lodged in my imagination, like Napoleon's candle-lit banquet for six hundred in the church nave, or the sculptress of angels whom Kauffmann found living under the roof.

A true Parisian has his or her canteen, and I found mine years ago. The Cherche-Midi is an old-fashioned bistro, with naif wall murals of men playing boules, railway carriage benches and bent wood chairs. Hugues Masson, the maître d', knows I like table nine in the corner in winter, and any table on the pavement under the red canvas awning in summer. The olive bread is home-made, like the pasta dishes, which change every day. Carafes of house red are called *fillettes* or 'little girls'. The menu is basic southern French or Italian, the ambiance noisy and cheerful.

Muriel Spark wrote a poem called 'The Dark Music of the Rue du Cherche-Midi', which sums up the charm of my street. The poem begins: 'If you should ask me, is there a street of Europe, and where, and what, is that ultimate street?'

The long, long rue du Cherche-Midi, she answers. In her poetic catalogue, Spark somehow missed number seventeen, where the Duc de Saint-Simon wrote his memoirs. The eighteenth century house at number forty, across the street from my hairdresser, is marked by a plaque as the place where the Comte de Rochambeau planned his 1780 expedition to help American revolutionaries.

Spark's description of my street holds true for all of Paris: 'Suppose that I looked for the street of my life,/ where I always/ could find an analogy. There in the/ shop-front windows and in the courtyards,/ the alleys, the great door-ways, old convents, baronial/ properties:/ those of the past.'

But the rue du Cherche-Midi is also a sad street, haunted by the military prison where Dreyfus stood trial and where Resistance heroes were tortured by the Nazis. Knowing that I'm about to move half a mile away, a friend gave me a recently published book by Catherine Clément, in which the French novelist recounts growing up in the rue du Cherche-Midi during the Second World War.

I hadn't realised that the ugly block between the rue Dupin and the rue Saint-Placide replaced a building that was bombed by the Germans. When the war ended, Clément waited with her mother Rivka outside the Hotel Lutetia every day for her Jewish grandparents, George and Sipa, but they never came back from Auschwitz. What transformations Paris goes through; the Lutetia was a headquarters for the German military intelligence service, the Abwehr, then a reception centre for concentration camp survivors. Now it's a five-star hotel where you sometimes find Isabelle Adjani, Emanuelle Béart or Yasmina Reza giving interviews in the bar.

A few days ago, I was walking with an old friend, the writer Olivier Todd. It was twilight, and Olivier pointed to four windows lit up on the corner of the rue Bonaparte and the rue Apollinaire, opposite the church of Saint-Germain-des-Prés, 'That was Sartre's mother's flat,' he said. 'I used to go there to see him. He slept in that room, which was the library.' Olivier went into La

Hune bookshop to browse. I bought *Le Monde* and headed home, savouring this magic – another Paris treasure to be stashed away in one's mind.

14 July 2001

For two decades French governments have talked about decentralising France. They've passed law after law, poured money into regional councils. To no avail: France will always be Paris.

Balzac understood the irresistible pull of the capital. It is, he wrote, 'a city that swallows up gifted individuals born everywhere in the kingdom, makes them part of its strange population and dries out the intellectual capacities of the nation for its own benefit. The provinces themselves are responsible for the force that plunders them . . . . And as soon as a merchant has amassed a fortune, he thinks only of taking it to Paris, the city that thus comes to epitomise all of France.'

I've already lived three lives here: as a student at the Sorbonne in the late 1970s, as a struggling freelancer in the early 1980s and as an *Irish Times* correspondent since 1996. Over the years, friends and professional contacts from my three epochs have melded.

Though I remain a foreigner, I know this city better than any other: the way it begins to stir, later than other capitals, around 8 AM, the crush of the métro in rush hour, the priceless silence of Sunday. Nothing, in the twenty-eight years since I first set eyes on Paris, has broken its spell over me.

The ponderousness of French bureaucracy can make Paris a frustrating city to work in, but the surroundings make up for it. When I read this quote from Zola in Alistair Horne's wonderful *Seven Ages of Paris: Portrait of a City*, I wished I had written it myself: 'I love the horizons of this big city with all my heart . . . . Depending on whether a ray of sunshine brightens Paris, or a dull sky lets it dream, it resembles a joyful and melancholy poem. This is art, all around us. A living art, an art still unknown.'

To live in Paris is a constant journey between past and present. There are countless personal memories, of a student garret and the flats one has rented, of meals in restaurants and the dresses you fell in love with through shop windows.

Some of the associations are incongruous: the Ranelagh métro station reminds me of the Monets in the Musée Marmottan and the Afghan embassy, where I picked up a visa after the atrocities of September 11, 2001. The Palais de Justice makes me think of Marie Antoinette, awaiting execution in the *Conciergerie*, and the endless hours I spent there during the investigation into the death of Diana, Princess of Wales.

Paris seems to heighten one's moods and intuitions, but it also brings you closer to history. I've liked the somewhat garish Pont Alexandre III even more since Mitterrand had its statues of winged horses covered with gold leaf. When I interviewed the Russian-born writer Andrei Makine, I read his account of the inauguration of the bridge, in 1900, in the presence of the ill-fated Tsar Nicholas. Now I imagine Nicholas spreading mortar with a golden trowel and the poet José Maria de Heredia haranguing the imperial couple with his ode to Franco-Russian friendship.

Most of my mental landmarks in Paris are literary or artistic. There is a building down the street with a plaque saying Proust spent evenings there with his friends the Daudet brothers. When I walk past, if I'm not concentrating on my next newspaper article, I imagine Marcel wearing evening clothes with other young men around a table in a poorly lit, wood-panelled room.

The building I live in was built in 1880. It was a time when the arts flourished, when Monet, Manet and Renoir would meet to discuss painting. Though they tended to live in the 8th and 9th *arrondissements* across the river, I like to think that Impressionist painters – Monet himself? – once sat in my salon.

Baron Haussmann (who called himself a demolition artist) ordained that Paris should be a nineteenth century city. Though many regret the razed, winding streets of earlier centuries, the Haussmannian apartment buildings, with their moulded stucco ceilings, marble fireplaces and modern plumbing, were a revolution in living standards and remain comfortable today. Gustave Caillebotte's painting of workmen scraping a parquet floor captures their grace.

Several times a year, the French festoon all government buildings with red, white and blue tricolours. Though they are celebrating the end of the First World War, or the Second World War, or Bastille Day, you're tempted to take the flags as personal encouragement, the way the poet Apollinaire did on 13 July 1909, when he concluded in a poem: 'They put out the flags in Paris because my friend André Salmon is getting married.' Some of the most moving documentary footage I have ever seen, a surprising amount of it in colour, shows French and US troops arriving in Paris in August 1944.

Apollinaire, the first great French poet of the twentieth century, survived the trenches of the First World War only to be killed by the Spanish flu. There's a plaque on the building where he died on the boulevard St Germain. Apollinaire was not a native Parisian – in fact, neither of his parents was French – but he proved yet again Balzac's maxim that the capital swallows up all that is best in the country.

Apollinaire's 'Zone' is to the French language what T. S. Eliot's 'The Love Song of J. Alfred Prufrock' is to English. On the night before he is to be guillotined, a convict relives his life, walking in his imagination through the streets of Paris. I've long intended to use 'Zone' as a sort of guidebook for an all-night promenade across the city.

'You read the handbills the catalogues the singing posters/ So much for poetry this morning and the prose is in the papers', says Beckett's translation of 'Zone'. At my newspaper kiosk in the morning, I often think of 'the prose in the papers'. I used to watch the old green and white Berliet buses hurtle down the boulevards and recall Apollinaire: 'Now you walk in Paris alone among the crowd/ Herds of bellowing buses hemming you about/ Anguish of love parching you within/ As though you were never to be loved again.'

I recently found a notebook that I had filled with poems and quotations when I went back to UCLA after my year at the Sorbonne. I didn't know then that I would return to Paris, and this text by Camus reflected my nostalgia: 'Paris is far away, Paris is beautiful; I have not forgotten her. I remember her twilights . . . . The evening falls, rustling and dry, over the rooftops blue with smoke; the city rumbles dully, the river seems to reverse its course. I wandered then in the streets.'

Whenever I can, I walk in Paris at sunset. The light, especially on long summer evenings, is incomparable. Paris still seems to rumble, but at its heart the Seine flows silently, the city's soul, splendidly indifferent.

2 August 2004

A Last Farewell

A perceptive Irish friend noticed that this article was more than a tribute to Monsieur Castro. Mingled with my grief at his passing was sadness at having left Paris for Washington. As Gerard Manley Hopkins wrote: 'It is Margaret you mourn for.'

The rue de Bellechasse is sad, because Jose Castro is dead. Monsieur Castro was no relation to the Cuban *lider massimo*, nor was he one of the public figures I wrote about as this newspaper's France correspondent. His widow, Otilia, is the concierge of the building where I lived from 2001 until 2009, and they are like family to me.

Though Madame Castro held the official title of *gardienne*, the couple were a priceless 'twofer', a husband-and-wife team who shared the vacuuming, mopping and polishing. Together they knew every nook and cranny of the 130-year-old apartment building. They were its longest residents, having moved into the shoebox-sized *loge* in the 1970s. Their sons, Bernard and Jose, grew up in the *loge* and attended school nearby in the rue Las Cases.

For eight years, Madame Castro's smile brightened my mornings. Monsieur Castro left early for his job as the head of a maintenance team at Roissy Charles-de-Gaulle Airport. Most days, he took a passenger in his little white lorry, a distinguished lawyer from the first floor of the building, whom he dropped off in the seventeenth *arrondissement*. Working at my desk in the afternoons, I'd hear cheerful chatter as Monsieur Castro's small granddaughters, Luisa and Noémie, followed him around the building.

When public transport strikes sowed traffic chaos and I had a plane to catch, Monsieur Castro drove me to Roissy. Over the years, he fixed my leaking kitchen sink and my oven door, rigged a lamp for my piano music, sawed off the top of a too tall Christmas tree. He took pride in the small thing well done. When I travelled, Madame Castro looked after my cat, who adored her. The Castros were fundamentally good, and I trusted them completely.

On Friday afternoon, as I prepared to head back to Washington at the end of my spring holiday, Monsieur and Madame Castro were watching television when a massive heart attack killed him in seconds. 'He left me,' she repeated to me incredulously. 'He didn't deserve this.' Now, like myself and tens of thousands of would-be travellers, the Castros are stranded in Paris by the Icelandic volcano. Monsieur Castro's casket waits in a funeral home for flights to resume, so he can be buried in his beloved Galicia.

After queuing at Air France for four hours on Saturday to rebook my own flight, I asked if there was anything the airline could do to ensure that Monsieur Castro's remains are repatriated quickly. 'Everybody has problems,' an Air France agent snapped. 'We can't make exceptions.' But this is a bereavement, I protested. 'Not even for bereavements,' she answered.

The Castros were a throwback to another time, when immigrants came from Catholic countries, and no Parisian apartment block survived without a concierge. Young men and women met at dances, courted, married, had children and stayed together.

Jose met Otilia at the Bataclan dance hall in Paris's Oberkampf district on Christmas Eve 1973. She worked as a cleaner in a doctor's clinic. He washed windows for a living. Both hailed from Galicia, north-western Spain; he from the mountain, she from the plain, eighty kilometres apart. At age twenty-five, Otilia was considered an old maid. Jose was three years her senior. It was, she said through her tears, *un vrai coup de foudre*, love at first sight. For more than thirty-six years, they were never apart.

Though their sons have dual nationality, the Castros remained Spanish. 'He said we had to be proud of our origins,' Madame Castro explained. The couple spent every August in Galicia, and refurbished an old stone house there for their retirement. The last time I saw Monsieur Castro alive, twenty-four hours before his heart attack, he grinned when he showed me the leather folder containing his pension papers. 'I am going to retire in June,' he announced.

The day after Monsieur Castro died, Madame Castro put on a clean apron, wheeled the rubbish bins in through the cobblestone entry, hung laundry in the back courtyard. 'If I don't work, I'll go crazy,' she said. 'The children want me to sleep at their house, but I want to stay here, with our good memories

. . . . A few minutes before my husband died, we were laughing. I said, "Papie, we're getting old now; two granddaughters and a third on the way." He said, "Yes, Mamie, we must start thinking of ourselves soon."'

19 April 2010

La France de Sarkozy

Nicolas Sarkozy's
Victoire Extraordinaire

'*C'est extraordinaire!*' is Nicolas Sarkozy's favourite expression. He uses it most often to describe real or imagined criticism of himself, as in: 'When I talk about the nation, I'm accused of being a nationalist. When I talk about immigration, I'm accused of being a racist. When I talk about patriotism, I'm accused of being a fascist. *C'est quand-même extraordinaire!*'

Whatever one thinks of Sarkozy, you've got to hand it to him: his victory in the French presidential election may not have been a surprise, but it was nothing short of *extraordinaire*: the real-life culmination of a Hollywood screenplay entitled *The Fabulous Destiny of Nicolas Sarkozy*.

Roll the clocks back a few years. Bernadette Chirac, the outgoing first lady who was allegedly gifted with infallible political judgment, told her entourage that Sarkozy would never become president of France. He was too short, too foreign-looking and had no provincial roots – hitherto a requirement for every French leader.

Nothing predisposed Sarkozy to becoming the sixth president of the Fifth Republic. As the extreme right-wing leader Jean-Marie Le Pen ungraciously reminded France during the campaign, three out of four of Sarkozy's grandparents were foreign.

On his father's side, he is descended from minor Hungarian aristocracy; his father, Pal Nagy Bosca y Sarkozy, used to tell him: 'With a name like yours, you'll never get anywhere in France.' His maternal grandfather, who raised him, was Benedict Mallah, a wealthy Jew from Salonica.

Sarkozy failed the entrance exam to 'Sciences Po' because his English wasn't up to scratch. Unlike the failed socialist candidate Ségolène Royal – and most of the country's political elite – he did not attend the École Nationale d'Administration. That was probably a blessing.

Taunting the socialist benches of the National Assembly, Sarkozy once said: 'You don't talk like the people do; that is why you lost them.' Sarkozy's directness may be his greatest advantage. Time and again, voters have told me they liked him 'because they understand what he says'.

The French are also fascinated by Sarkozy's thirst for power; if he wants it so badly, he must deserve it. There's a good dose of revenge in Sarkozy's ambition.

'*Je vais les niquer tous*' ('I'm going to screw them all'), a fellow journalist once heard Sarkozy mutter repeatedly during a helicopter journey.

Despite Sarkozy's outsider status, there now seems to have been a certain inevitability to his rise. Within months of joining the Raffarin government as interior minister in 2002, he became the most popular member of the cabinet.

Action – or at least the media semblance thereof – was the secret to his success. Tony Blair's government was furious with France for allowing thousands of Kurds and Afghans to pour across the English Channel? Sarkozy closed the camp at Sangatte. French lorry drivers threatened an umpteenth strike? Sarkozy broke the strike in one day, by threatening to confiscate their licences.

When the former prime minister Alain Juppé founded the Union for a Popular Movement (UMP) in November 2002, Sarkozy insisted that Juppé be given a two- rather than three-year mandate as leader. Was he already plotting his own takeover of the party?

He and his wife Cecilia refused the seats reserved for them in the second row at the launch, ostentatiously placing themselves front and centre. A year later, Sarkozy announced that he intended to succeed President Jacques Chirac.

There followed a battle of Shakespearean, or perhaps Oedipal, proportions, with Sarkozy constantly vaunting his superiority over Chirac. The president's rule was 'a house of cards' on the verge of collapse, Sarkozy told the 237 right-wing deputies he invited to dinner shortly before Bastille Day 2004.

Chirac made a last attempt to call the unwanted upstart heir to order. 'I take decisions; he executes them,' Chirac told the nation in his annual televised interview.

Having provoked Chirac, Sarkozy then adopted the same strategy he would use during the campaign against Royal: he played the poised statesman who refuses to respond to aggression. Against the better judgment of his closest advisers, including his wife, Sarkozy resigned from his post as finance minister to stand for president of the UMP.

Commentators widely compared his 28 November 2004 'coronation' as head of the party to Napoleon Bonaparte's lavish consecration almost exactly two hundred years earlier. Napoleon-like, Sarkozy spoke of his 'grand design'. Unlike Royal, who asked voters what they wanted, Sarkozy told them what they needed.

The losing socialist candidate accused Sarkozy of 'brutalising' France. She failed to understand that the country may be at a stage where it *wants* to be 'brutalised'. Sarkozy promises to share his energy, determination and confidence with the country, as if by transfusion.

The outline of Sarkozy's presidential programme was already present in his November 2004 acceptance speech: the rehabilitation of work, revision of the thirty-five-hour week and the welfare system, and the abolition of death duties, so the French can pass on 'an inheritance built by the sweat of the brow'.

When Sarkozy finds himself out of sync with the French mood, he never publicly changes policy. He opposed the law banning the wearing of Islamic headscarves in French schools, but shut up when he saw how popular it was. He proposed US-style affirmative action to integrate French minorities, but stopped talking about it when it raised hackles. His condemnation of French 'arrogance' in opposing the invasion of Iraq went down badly, so during the campaign he repeated that the US had made a grave error.

France's new president is a man of paradoxes. The son and grandson of immigrants, he takes pride in having expelled a record numbers of would-be immigrants from France. He is a tough crime-buster who yearns to be loved; a short man who once scratched out his height on his driver's licence, and mysteriously appeared to be the same height as George W. Bush (who is some fifteen centimetres taller) on the retouched photograph of their meeting. The self-styled 'spokesman of the people' is fascinated by pop stars, celebrities and millionaires.

The reactions of two acquaintances this weekend seemed to summarise national schizophrenia about Sarkozy. An elderly woman who holds dual French and Irish nationality told me: 'I can't help liking that young fellow – he's so un-French!' She even romanticised the 'look of sadness' she always detects in his eyes.

A neighbour in central Paris, a businessman whose company trades in Asia, told me he'd go early to the polls, then leave the country until the celebrations blow over. 'I can't stand the thought of France being in Sarkozy's hands for the next five years,' he said. 'He and his gang are mafiosi. I don't want to hear and see the *sarkozystes* gloating.'

The country that Nicolas Sarkozy is about to take over is a land of hope and fear. Will he teach the French the merits of hard work, and usher in prosperity and full employment by the end of his five-year term, as promised? Or will he cow the press – a process that has already started – inflame race relations, pit rich against poor, and preside over war on the immigrant *banlieues*? These possible outcomes, positive and negative, are part of the Sarkozy paradox. And they are not mutually exclusive.

7 May 2007

Europe Gets Set for the Sarkozy Treatment

President Nicolas Sarkozy's armchair was strategically placed in the door of the Élysée Palace, so the air conditioning from the *Petit Salon* wafted over him. It was the hottest day of summer so far, and the French leader pulled his jacket off while two of his top advisers, jackets on, sweated in the scorching sun beside him.

A servant brought the president's mirror shades, the ones that accentuate his resemblance to a mafia don. Sarkozy was receiving several dozen European correspondents for a background briefing on France's EU presidency on his terrace.

He pulled an ankle over one knee, and the raised leg jerked with nervous energy. His Highness asked for more umbrellas to shade the journalists. The other leg too started jiggling. Microphone in hand, like a pop star, Sarkozy jumped up and launched into the Sarko show.

For an hour and a half, in the noon sun, Sarkozy cajoled, seduced and belittled his interlocutors. The short sentences were direct, unambiguous and frequently punctuated by '*hein,*' an inelegant interjection signifying something approximating '*N'est-ce pas?*'

'I do the questions *and* the answers,' Sarkozy boasted at one point in the monologue. He does not tolerate criticism, and those of us who dared ask impertinent questions bore the full brunt of his sarcasm.

My colleagues from Brussels were fascinated and repelled by the Sarko show. 'I kept thinking about the dinosaurs on the European stage,' one said. 'No other European leader has Sarko's energy or ability to hold people's attention. The thing that struck me most was the naked aggression of it; the way he stood and leaned over us . . . .'

Aggression is a word one hears often in connection with Sarkozy. In the past week alone, the chief of staff of the French army, a journalist and a technician at France 3 television, the head of France Télévisions, the president of the European Central Bank, the EU trade commissioner and French trade unions have all been victims of presidential wrath or sarcasm.

These incidents bring to mind earlier presidential *faux pas* – like the hostile bystander to whom Sarkozy said 'Get lost, asshole' at the agriculture fair last winter. He's widely accused of 'desecrating' the presidential office, though others say he's dusted off a fossilised institution.

As Sarkozy's confidence rating again descended to an abysmal 33 percent last week (it was 63 percent when he was elected in May 2007), it was obvious that the president's attitude is irritating his compatriots. 'I've rarely seen anyone who shows such disdain for his fellow human beings,' says Alain Genestar, the former editor of *Paris Match*, who was sacked for publishing a cover showing Sarkozy's second wife, Cecilia, in New York with the man whom she would later marry.

Immediately after his divorce, Sarkozy's courtship and remarriage, to the top model-turned-singer Carla Bruni, shocked conservative voters and precipitated his plunge in opinion polls last winter. Though Bruni was initially a handicap, the couple's state visit to London in late March changed that. Carla's class seems to compensate for Nicolas's rough edges. 'She calms the president down,' aides at the Élysée keep insisting.

Sarkozy seems as agitated as ever, but Bruni took credit for attenuating his 'bling-bling' reputation. Her new album has received rave reviews despite lyrics comparing the 'high' she gets from Sarkozy to drugs, and an admission that she has had 'thirty lovers in forty years'. A poll in *L'Express* magazine shows that 51 percent of the French think Bruni is a good First Lady. When a correspondent asked whether she would accompany the president to Dublin on 21 July, a French diplomat joked: 'You voted No [to the Lisbon Treaty]. If you vote Yes next time, then you get Carla.' In the wake of Ireland's rejection of the treaty, Sarkozy announced that he would travel to Dublin in an effort to understand the No vote. He has already postponed the trip once, and will spend half a day in Ireland. 'What do you expect?' an official said. 'He's a man in a hurry. It has to fit into his schedule.' With French newspapers translating the Fine Gael MEP Gay Mitchell's comment that 'the last thing' Ireland needs is for Sarkozy to come 'riding into town', the French president might even cancel his visit.

Though Sarkozy has long abandoned his advocacy of a *directoire* of the six most populous countries (France, Germany, Britain, Spain, Italy and Poland) to run Europe, it's hard to shake the impression that he respects only the powerful, in particular *les Anglo-Saxons*. In a telling detail at his reception for foreign ambassadors last August, there was free seating for all, *except* the US and British ambassadors, whose front row, centre seats were reserved.

'France is back in Europe,' Sarkozy announced on the night of his election. Within weeks, he had unilaterally vetoed negotiations on questions pertaining to full Turkish EU membership, resumed his crusade against the European Central Bank and announced that France would not respect the Eurogroup's stability pact (on reducing deficits) before 2012. As black sheep of the fifteen-strong Eurogroup, France is second only to Greece. Yet on the eve of the EU presidency, the French president promised lower taxes on 'ecological' cars and houses, restaurants, CDs and DVDs.

Diplomats and officials describe Sarkozy as impatient and incapable of listening – characteristics that will not help him resolve Ireland's rejection of the treaty. In an e-mail leaked in April, an Irish official wrote that the referendum was being held *before* the French presidency because of 'the risk of unhelpful developments during the French presidency, particularly related to EU defence' and called Sarkozy 'completely unpredictable'.

On Saturday night, I attended a dinner party in the 16th *arrondissement*, a few blocks from Carla Bruni's house. All the guests had voted for Sarkozy. They were delighted when he became the first president to put women and minorities in positions of power. But now they're disappointed; all criticised his 'aggressiveness' and 'vulgarity' but said they saw no alternative to him.

Though there were disappointing aspects to his reform of the *régimes spéciaux* (public-sector pensions), the university system and thirty-five-hour working week, the dinner guests credited Sarkozy with being the first French president to 'take on' such special interest groups as transport workers. His law on economic modernization will free up competition and raise the retirement age to sixty-one.

A former left-wing cabinet minister later told me that the socialists want Sarkozy to stay in power long enough to 'do the dirty work' of economic reform, which they dare not undertake themselves, so they can breeze back into power when the pain is over.

With the EU presidency, Sarkozy's image as a personally unpleasant but extremely energetic, if sometimes arbitrary, reformer has been projected on to the European scene. 'I am president of France. I am president of Europe,' he boasted at the weekend.

France has developed a love-hate relationship with 'Sarko', in which belief in the necessity of economic reform mingles with fear of the president's erratic, autocratic ways. Sarkozy doesn't like sharing the limelight, but there are steady hands – French Prime Minister François Fillon, German chancellor Angela Merkel – to reassure us.

For at least four more years, Sarkozy is the only show in France. In Europe, there are only five and three-quarter months left to go.

8 July 2008

Why Obama and Sarkozy
Can Never Truly Be Friends

The presidents stood at twin lecterns in the East Room of the White House. They could not have looked more mismatched, but they professed near-identical views. Both want the UN Security Council to pass tough sanctions against Iran, quickly. Both want Israel to stop colonising the West Bank. And both say that winning in Afghanistan is crucial to the security of the West.

'Rarely in the history of our two countries has the community of views been so identical between the United States of America and France,' President Nicolas Sarkozy crowed.

How could two men espousing the same policies convey such different impressions? The healthcare victory has put a new spring into Barack Obama's step, even if his opinion poll results lack bounce. Sarkozy's party has just lost regional elections, and his approval rating is at an all time low of 30 percent.

Sarkozy appeared tense and distracted throughout their twenty-two-minute press conference. While Obama spoke, Sarkozy's eyes darted about the reception room, as if he expected someone to lob a grenade at him. When Sarkozy spoke, Obama turned politely towards him and listened.

Sarkozy related the most telling anecdote. In what looked like another act of Obama-mimicry, Sarkozy had taken his wife, Carla Bruni, to Ben's Chili Bowl for lunch. (In January 2009, Obama lunched at the U Street diner with Washington mayor Adrian Fenty.) 'When I walked in, I saw a huge photograph of President Obama,' Sarkozy said. 'And I'm afraid that when you go back to that restaurant, you may see a smaller photograph of the French president.'

Sarkozy was vain enough to bestow his picture upon a Washington restaurant, in the hope that it would hang beside Obama's.

No other head of state has been invited, with his wife, to dine *à quatre* with Barack and Michelle in their private dining room, the Élysée kept saying. Sarkozy needed Obama to burnish his image.

And strange as it may seem, the world's most popular politician, the star whom other heads of state and government vie to befriend – indeed serve – has been faulted for having no buddies among world leaders. Obama has tried to circumvent governments, to reach out directly to world populations. But his domestic critics say that his global populism is hurting US interests.

At the White House press briefing on the day of Sarkozy's visit, the questions were more informative than the answers. Was the White House trying to 'make up with the French president', a correspondent asked. Robert Gibbs, the press secretary, feigned ignorance. 'There have been perceptions that there was a snub, that [Sarkozy] didn't get quite the treatment that he thought he should get in their prior visits together,' the journalist explained.

Sarkozy is often his own worst enemy. At Columbia University, he commented on the healthcare bill, saying: '*We* solved the problem fifty years ago . . . . Welcome to the club of states that don't dump sick people.'

'He said it in French, but you could hear the smirk,' commented Chris Matthews of MSNBC television.

Sarkozy also told the US that it needed to 'reflect on what it means to be the world's number one power' and to be a country 'that listens'. The *New York Times* told him to stop lecturing, and to send more troops to Afghanistan.

Despite the intimate dinner, you couldn't help but notice that the White House did the bare minimum. Dinner started at 6.30 and lasted less than two hours. There were no photographers allowed in the Oval Office during the bilateral meeting – a courtesy accorded to more honoured guests.

Obama *has* befriended leaders, just not the Europeans traditionally cosseted by US presidents. He's reserved his warmest hospitality for the Indian prime minister Manmohan Singh, who enjoyed the first state dinner of the Obama presidency, and Taoiseach Brian Cowen, guest of honour at the White House St Patrick's Day reception for five hundred guests. On these occasions, Obama mentioned the 'oppression' endured by the US, India and Ireland. The adjective 'British' was understood.

Therein, I suspect, lies the biggest difference between Sarkozy's and Obama's world views. Before Sarkozy became president, his UMP party attempted to pass a law requiring French schools to teach 'the positive role' of French colonialism.

Three times in twenty-two minutes, Sarkozy mentioned the transatlantic directorate formed by himself, Angela Merkel, Gordon Brown and Barack Obama. Obama looked uneasy.

Each time Obama is perceived to snub a former colonial power, I recall the passage in *Dreams from my Father* where the future US president imagined the experiences of his grandfather, Hussein Onyango, who worked as a servant to British officers in Kenya. 'He still hears the clipped voice of a British captain, explaining for the third and last time the correct proportion of tonic to gin.'

Sarkozy hero-worships *les Anglo-Saxons*. One of Obama's first acts as president was to send a bronze bust of Winston Churchill (which George W. Bush had borrowed for the Oval Office) back to the British ambassador.

3 April 2010

Mes Français

Isabelle Adjani

Isabelle Adjani walks into the bar of the Hotel Lutetia, her long black tresses trailing from under a floppy fake leopard fur hat. She dumps her dark overcoat and Sonia Rykiel shoulder bag unceremoniously on a chair. She is wearing a loose white linen jacket over black trousers, but keeps the hat on. In the dimly lit room, frequented by film stars, publishers and writers, it is her only disguise.

At first it is disconcerting to have those sapphire-blue eyes fixed on you, as if one were afraid of receiving the full force of what she calls her 'charge of emotion', the intensity of Adèle H., Camille Claudel, La Reine Margot and now Marguerite Gautier. They call her mysterious, secretive.

The writer Stéphane Denis says Adjani 'is the actress who cries better than any other', that 'she'll have a red nose for eternity'. Does she mind being type-cast, so often playing hysterical, even mad, women? 'It doesn't bother me – as long as people don't confuse me with the characters,' she says.

There is not a trace of make-up on the translucent white face. Most of the men I know talk of her as a sex goddess, but today, with her graceful hands weaving like butterflies and the famous eyes darting about as if to pick words from the walls, Isabelle Adjani is Alice in Wonderland. Then she admits it. 'There is always an overlap between life and the character I'm playing. I think I have a charge of human emotion to communicate, and that people want to receive it. There are actresses who are gifted for frivolity – that's wonderful too, and it makes people happy. But for me, the goal will always be to go to the heart of things. If I give nothing to the audience, it's not worthwhile.'

Adjani is playing the lead in *La Dame aux Camélias*, written for her by the novelist René de Ceccaty from the classic 1848 novel by Alexandre Dumas *fils*. The Théâtre Marigny is sold out, and every night a teary-eyed, red-nosed

Adjani is pelted with flowers during her standing ovation.

She savours the triumph all the more because it marks her first stage appearance in seventeen years. The last one, Strindberg's *Miss Julie* in 1983, was disastrous. Adjani felt attacked by the male lead and dropped out after thirty-eight of ninety scheduled performances. There were a half-dozen screen roles in the meantime but, apart from *Miss Julie*, Adjani had not acted on stage for twenty-four years. When I mention this, she makes a clownish grimace and dives for her handbag. Twenty-four years? What was she doing?

'I was trying to live,' she explains. 'I always thought the saddest thing at the end of my life would be for someone to ask me, "What did you do?" and I'd say, "I was an actress". So I was trying to live my life, my loves, my children, and more or less managing to do so. I don't see time pass. Every once in a while I say to myself: "Ah, it's been four years, five years, six years, and I haven't worked."' Adjani had her first son, Barnabé, now twenty, with the film director Bruno Nuytten, with whom she made *Camille Claudel* in 1988. She describes her eldest son as 'rather literary, very interested in music, healthy, balanced, someone who loves happiness – really, I have no worries about him'.

She has never spent a day apart from five-year-old Gabriel Kane, the son of the actor Daniel Day-Lewis – not even when she presided over the jury at the Cannes Film Festival in 1997. 'He has a contagious energy,' she says of Gabriel Kane. 'He's passionate, curious, wonderful. He's physically strong and he's bilingual.'

Adjani lived for an aggregate of several months with Day-Lewis in his Wicklow home. 'I still have furniture there. I spent Christmases there. You could see forever. One day we went hiking in the hills and there was a snowstorm – I didn't know nature could be so violent. We used to pile peat logs on the fire. I found myself in his world. It's a magical memory, but with painful moments.' Their son has not yet visited Ireland. 'But it's a country he resembles,' she says. 'In the way he runs wild out of doors, you sense where he comes from.'

Her visits to Wicklow 'could have been happy', Adjani says. But there is always a tinge of bitterness when she alludes, never by name, to 'the father of my son'. Gossip magazines referred to her relationship with Day-Lewis, which started in 1989, as 'on and off'. She laughs an excessive laugh, even for such an accomplished actress. Yes, it was 'on and off', she says. As for the fax he allegedly sent her in the final break-up, she hoots a musical, almost hysterical laugh filled with pain and derision. The blue saucer eyes dart around faster than ever.

Isabelle Adjani is often described as a jet-setting nomad with no fixed address. At the moment, mother and son live in an apartment near the Théâtre Marigny. 'My whole life's plans were with the father of my child,' she says. 'And they were stopped all of a sudden. I didn't know where to settle.' Soon after Gabriel Kane was born, she took him to live in Switzerland, because Swiss laws were more favourable to mothers in child custody cases. 'There was a bad atmosphere between us. I needed all my strength to keep going, to be positive. I didn't want to give in to demands that I found unfair. I arranged everything so mother and child could be in peace until harmony was restored.'

So is harmony restored now? Are she and Day-Lewis on good terms? 'We aren't on any kind of terms at all,' Adjani says sadly. 'He can see his son when he wants to.' She doesn't even know where Day-Lewis lives, she adds.

The sagas in which Adjani acts invariably end in tragedy, but she says she still believes in love. 'This story [with Day-Lewis], I wanted it to exist. But to be together, it takes so much understanding. When you start a love story, you have to chase away the ghosts of suffering.' And now? 'I have too much to do,' she says, 'between the theatre and my little boy. It seems to surprise people, a woman alone – and yet it's not a lonely solitude. I wonder if the thing I'm sorriest to lose isn't Ireland. When the wounds are healed I'll return there. My happiness in Ireland may come later.'

Perhaps on tour with *La Dame aux Camélias*. The Paris run has been so successful that there is talk of taking it abroad, and Adjani would like to go to the 'Anglo-Saxon countries'. The role of Marguerite Gautier is said to bring luck to actresses who play her. Sarah Bernhardt, Greta Garbo and Vivien Leigh were among the most famous stage and screen Marguerites. The great divas, Renata Tebaldi, Montserrat Caballe, Maria Callas, have all sung the lead in Verdi's 1853 operatic version, *La Traviata*. 'I think it's true,' Adjani says. 'It's brought me happiness. I'm as happy working now as I've ever been not working. Each evening seems to pull the day towards it.'

Adjani worked hard to perfect the role she seems to play so effortlessly. No other *tragédienne* could get away with talking with her back to the audience, clutching the bedsheets and writhing on the floor as she's dying. 'I put a lot of life into dying,' she laughs. She doesn't want Gabriel Kane to see her as Marguerite. 'If he were in the theatre, he'd run through the rows, climb onto the stage and stop me from dying!'

Celebrity came too early to Adjani, when she joined the Comédie-Française at seventeen, and it is something she wants to spare her own sons. Gabriel Kane knows his father is an actor. The little boy 'talks like Tweety-pie'

– with a lisp. 'If it doesn't go away, at least he'll be safe from becoming an actor!'

The real Marguerite Gautier was Alphonsine Plessis, better known as Marie Duplessis. A country girl from Normandy, she became a courtesan or *demi-mondaine* who, had her clients not been dukes and counts, would have been called a prostitute. Marie Duplessis was considered the most elegant woman of 1840s Paris. She was the first love of Franz Liszt, and Alexandre Dumas *père* introduced her to his son, who joined the ranks of her lovers, in 1844. Dumas *fils* wrote his classic novel after her death from tuberculosis in 1847. Tourists still make the pilgrimage to her grave in Montmartre.

The courtesan holds a special place in French culture. Balzac, Zola and Maupassant also wrote about them, but Dumas *fils* claimed his Marguerite/Marie was particularly noble. Adjani insists she is not Marguerite. Yet Micheline Boudet's description of *La Dame aux Camélias* in a 1993 book seems written for the star: 'She seems to give herself, then pulls back, in a game of seduction all the more clever for seeming spontaneous. Woman of snow then suddenly woman of fire, how could she not be desired, adulated, adored?'

Nervous about her return to the theatre, Adjani insisted on three months of rehearsals before *La Dame aux Camélias* opened. It must be exhausting to juggle admirers, find true love, fight creditors and tuberculosis and die in just three hours every night – twice on Sundays. But she thrives on it. The French literary critic Hector Bianciotti has built a sort of altar to Adjani as Marguerite – alongside his memorial to Maria Callas. 'I've been admitted to the vault of stars,' she laughs.

In 1973, Adjani became the youngest actress to enter the Comédie-Française. Her German-born mother, Augusta, is thrilled to see her back on stage in *La Dame aux Camélias*. 'For her, that's my true vocation, the origin of my desire to be an actress – and she's right. I didn't become an actress to be on television every Sunday or to be in cinema.'

But the play was also emotionally wrenching for mother and daughter because it reminds them of Isabelle's father, Mohamed Cherif, an Algerian-immigrant garage mechanic who died of emphysema and heart disease in 1983 at the age of fifty-eight. The heroine's financial difficulties, her fatal illness and refusal to accept death are 'things we lived with at home', Adjani says. 'To have my mother in the theatre intensified it so much; it's as if your umbilical cord was swinging back and forth through the audience.'

Mohamed Cherif Adjani joined the French army during the Second World War and fought in the Italian campaign. He met Augusta in Bavaria at the end of the war and took her home to Algeria. 'But it was too hard for my mother. They went to Marseilles, Strasbourg, then [the north western Paris suburb of] Gennevilliers. They were two uprooted people. They settled in France at a time when immigrants were badly treated, badly integrated. You never get over the suffering of your parents.'

Her father had a long, noble, sad face, and spoke beautiful French, Adjani recalls. To Annick Cojean of *Le Monde*, she recounted the condescension of the French aristocrats who employed him. The countess would pat little Isabelle on the head because she was pretty. 'I often think of these people whom I saw behaving so badly to him,' Adjani told Cojean. 'I say to myself, it must have been strange for them to see this name, Adjani, that they shouted the way you call a dog, become much better known than their little title.'

As a child, looking out the window of the council estate where she grew up, Isabelle promised herself she would escape from Gennevilliers. 'My father's proudest moment was when I was accepted at the Comédie-Française,' she says. 'Because it was an institution in his mind, it replaced the university where he wanted me to study. The cinema was something else – an unknown, something dangerous.'

Before her father died, Adjani had planned to travel with him to Algeria. But in the end, he wanted to go alone – the journey was a pilgrimage for him. 'Algeria was a source of pride and of pain for my father,' she says. 'When we were children, we would go to Bavaria, to my mother's family, in the summer. It was open, easy. But Algeria was a wounded, separate world. There was no access to my father's past. There was a secret in my father's life which I don't know. I began to realise it only after his death.'

In the mid-1980s, as the racist National Front gained strength in France, Adjani joined SOS Racisme, the group fighting Jean-Marie Le Pen. 'All of a sudden, people discovered that Isabelle Adjani, who was considered a French star, wasn't French at all,' she laughs.

It was only after her father's death that Adjani felt free to explore her Algerian origins. 'All these taboos between my father and me were like an enormous boulder,' she says, shaping a stone in the air with her hands. 'It was like a stone that broke apart, and I went there under the impact of that emotion.'

In 1988, during rioting in Algiers, Adjani saw a television interview with a young Algerian who had been tortured by police. 'I collapsed in tears,' she says. 'I talked to [the philosopher] André Glucksmann about it and he said, "We can't go because we're Jewish. Why don't *you* go?"' She found herself at a students' meeting at Algiers University, appealing for democracy and free elections.

A decade later, when thousands of Algerians were dying in massacres which the military-led government attributed to Muslim fundamentalists, Adjani met the human rights campaigner Salima Ghezali, and their four-page dialogue, as critical of the regime as it was of the Islamists, was published in *Paris Match*. The star was fast becoming the Algerian generals' *bête noire*.

Last June, Adjani struck again. The Algerian president Abdelaziz Bouteflika made a state visit to Paris. Not only did Adjani decline the Élysée's invitation to dinner, she gave an interview to *Libération* newspaper in which she condemned 'the horror of the exactions of the Islamists' and 'these other crimes committed by the army in the most organised darkness and secrecy'. Adjani joined forces with the International Federation of Human Rights to draw attention to the 'disappearance' of ten thousand Algerians.

In response, President Bouteflika said he 'adored' Adjani and her beauty. 'So condescending,' she says, shaking her head in the bar of the Lutetia. 'Politicians' lies. I was shocked by the reception at the Élysée. It was racist. They invited everyone in France who had anything to do with Algeria. Bring all the *bougnoules* [a derogatory term for Arabs] together in the phoney Casbah to eat Parisian couscous.'

The killing continues in Algeria, and Adjani feels at a loss to know what to do. She is haunted by the idea that 'we', the French, somehow poisoned Algeria through 132 years of colonisation. She supports the campaign launched last autumn to force the French government to apologise for the atrocities French troops committed during the 1954–62 independence war. 'It would be liberating, healing,' she says. 'Even if it's only symbolic, symbolism is all that is left to those poor people.'

As a schoolgirl, Adjani collected money for Biafra. Had she not become an actress, she says she would have been a humanitarian worker. 'Maybe I'd have gone to the Third World; maybe I'd have worked in an office. But I need to care for others.' Saint Isabelle? Perhaps the most surprising role of all for a woman we've so often seen in diamonds and haute couture, and yet she is convincing. 'When you're an actress, attention focuses on you,' she says. 'But you must deflect it back on others.'

That, she says, is why she is so happy to be back on stage. 'There's nothing between people and you – no safety net. It's old-fashioned, pure, a closed place where the vibrations pass – through words, gestures. There is something magical, fabulous at stake. Like a moment of communion with the audience:

the confidence with which people sit there waiting, their wish for a meeting point between their lives, their humanity and you.'

Adjani wanted her stage comeback to be 'as discreet as possible – so that people would know I was working in the theatre for the sake of doing theatre'.

She waited until the production was well under way to talk to journalists, and then gave very few interviews. 'What people say about what they are doing has become more important than what they actually *do*,' she jokes. 'Theatre should be a means to do things at a truer, more human pace, to take time to say things. The audience are there and they can't talk on their mobile phones. They can't go to the fridge for a cola; they can't go to the toilet. I needed to stop the fast-forward, the technology. Maybe that's what it means to grow older.'

Every night when the performance is over, the fans line up at the artists' entrance. Adjani is usually the last to leave the theatre. 'I ask myself, "If I was moved by a play and went backstage and the actress spoke to me, would it matter?" and the answer is "yes". What touches me is the people who say, "I came four hundred kilometres to see you", or the old ladies who say, "I have to catch my train. I wanted to bring my daughter but two tickets were too expensive". Every day I receive affectionate threats – people who write to say, "You won't leave us again, will you?" And it's like a contract. It's overwhelming for me. It's proof that it all has a meaning.'

13 January 2001

Marcel Marceau

Marcel Marceau chats with students at the end of the day at his École de Mimodrame in Paris. I hang back in the rear of the theatre to watch the world's greatest mime, the inventor of the art in its modern form. Marceau's face looks bleached, as if a half-century of paint had dyed his animated features white. In his bright jumper, baggy trousers and white shoes, he moves with the grace of a ballet dancer.

He looks as if the craggy head of Methuselah has been attached to a twenty-year-old's lithe body. In speech and gesture, a child's exuberance alternates with sad wisdom. This is as it should be, for Marceau defines everything through contrast: 'Comedy and tragedy, life and death, reality and dreams, shadow and light,' he tells me. 'Every world has its contrary. Good and evil. This is what I try to show in my art.'

We could sit in the theatre armchairs to talk, but no, Marceau wants to be where he has spent his life: centre-stage, beneath the blinding spotlights. The shadow my hand casts on my notebook is so dark that I cannot see what I am writing. Marceau talks as if the audience were there before him, accompanying each story with mime-like gestures.

His chance meeting with Charlie Chaplin was the high point of his life, Marceau says. 'I saw *The Little Tramp* as a child, and that's when I knew I wanted to be a mime. . . . A mime shows the soul inside man; that's why Chaplin was so important to me. When he did films like *The Little Tramp*, he was all mankind.'

In 1967, Marceau was waiting for a plane at Orly Airport, en route for Rome, where he was to play Professor Ping in Roger Vadim's film *Barbarella*. Chaplin, his wife Oona and several of their nine children were in the airport café. Marceau's cousin said, 'Chaplin is looking at you'. Marceau told the *Paris Match* reporter and photographer who were travelling with him to stay behind, not to spoil the meeting with his hero.

'Chaplin said, "Hello, Marcel Marceau. I have seen all your posters in Paris. Children, come and meet Marcel Marceau."' Marceau has recounted the meeting hundreds of times, but he still relishes the telling. 'I said, "You know, Mr Chaplin, you are a god to me." I started walking like *The Little Tramp* and he mimicked me mimicking him. I was forty-four then; he was seventy-eight, but still good-looking, with his white hair. Oona said, "Charlie, we have to go to Vevey". I felt I would never see him again, and I took his hand and kissed it and wouldn't let go of it. He had tears in his eyes.'

When Marceau told his old friend Vadim (who studied theatre with him in the 1940s) what had happened, Vadim compared the moment to the Renaissance encounter of Michelangelo and Raphael. 'When Michelangelo was sixty-four, people said he was old-hat,' Marceau explains. 'Raphael was nineteen and he was already considered a genius. He went into a church where Michelangelo was sculpting, and Raphael fell on his knees and kissed the feet of Michelangelo, and Michelangelo wept.

'It is possible that I represented something similar for Charlie Chaplin. When he went to London in the 1920s, hundreds of thousands of people would go into the streets to see him, like for the Beatles, like for a king. And then nobody recognised him. He had not made films in years, and I was not only Marcel Marceau the mime, but a new generation. When I kissed his hand, he thought about time, that he had no more life before him.'

It cannot have escaped Marceau's attention that on 18 March he will turn seventy-eight – Chaplin's age when they met. Today, mime students from twenty countries represent a continuation of the art form to which he has devoted his life, yet the fear that mime could be lost, that he could be forgotten, constantly recurs. 'Fortunately I have made films of my work,' he says three times during our two-hour conversation. 'Films deal with reality. You can go back to them. The theatre always runs away; who remembers the great stage actors of the past?'

Nothing enrages Marceau more than to hear it said that mime is old-fashioned. 'Nothing is old-fashioned, but many things pass because the tradition is not kept,' he says. 'Kabuki and Noh, and the Indian Mahabharata, are many hundreds of years old, and nobody says it's old-fashioned. An art form is not a fad. But we have to be very careful to keep the power of the classical form, which is beyond time.'

Will he ever retire? 'I will die,' he announces, as if his mortality were in doubt. 'Maybe, one day *debout* like a tree.' His arm slams onto the table with

49

the dead weight of a body falling onto the stage.

The producers of Marceau's world tour wanted to call it a 'Farewell Tour'. Marceau screws up his nose in disgust. 'Producers are always frightened,' he explains. 'The only one who is not frightened is the actor on stage. I told them, "No farewell tour". The younger generation will think it's "Bye-bye, adieu" and they don't want that – they want a star. This is not a farewell tour – it's "Marcel Marceau is back in Dublin!"'

Forty years have passed since Marceau first performed at the Gaiety, nearly twenty years since he was last in Dublin. Although he still works 250 days a year, he seems never to have forgotten an engagement. 'Irish theatre audiences are wonderful,' he says. 'At the end of my first show at the Gaiety, someone shouted "Can you speak?" and I said, "Thank you very much, ladies and gentlemen. It touches my heart."' When he opened his Paris mime school in 1978, the first wave of students were mostly Irish – Vincent O'Neill, Jonathan Lambert, someone called Carney. Jonathan Lambert, the son of Ireland's most famous puppeteer, Eugene, helped Marceau create the *Soliloquy of Three Lost Souls*, which was performed in Dublin.

Marcel Mangel was born in Strasbourg in 1923. His father was a singer who earned a living as a butcher, but took his son to the opera and cinema – to see Charlie Chaplin. Marcel's mother loved books, and although the family was not wealthy, he has happy memories of cathedral bells at night, of the cooing pigeons that his father raised. 'My family gave me love, the best education. I was fifteen when the war started. It broke my family.'

As an art student in Limoges, Marcel forged new identity papers for himself during the Nazi occupation, changing the Jewish name Mangel to Marceau, after a revolutionary general mentioned in a poem by Victor Hugo. A cousin arranged for him to be hidden in a Catholic boarding school – just like Louis Malle's film *Au Revoir les Enfants*.

Marcel counterfeited documents and helped transport Jews to Switzerland for the Resistance. Had it not been for the Second World War, he says, he might never have become a mime. 'We lived in silence. Everything was compartmentalised. Speaking was dangerous. It was like the Foreign Legion, where no one knows your true identity.' Even Etienne Decroux, who began to teach him the art of mime in 1944, did not learn of Marcel's Jewish origins until after the war.

Does being Jewish matter to him? 'You know who the greatest Jew was?'

Marceau responds elliptically. 'Jesus Christ. The tragedy of the world is this obsession with race. I respect the cult of religion, but not orthodoxy . . . . I believe that man transmits life to others, through a book, a painting, even a theatre performance. Deity is in man.'

Marceau's father died at Auschwitz, but he seems reluctant to talk about him. 'Of course my father was my father, but you have to cry about humanity. Hitler was responsible for the deaths of 60 million people, and wars continue. If I go back to my father, I am a selfish man, and I'm saying that he was more important than the others.'

Nor does he wish to discuss his two ex-wives and four children. 'I like to keep a certain mystery about me,' he says. 'The relationship between art and life is that I was underground and after the war I kept butterflies because I said, "No more war. Freedom."' His fingers flutter away as they do in a famous sketch where Bip, the white-faced alter ego he invented after the war, chases a butterfly. 'The butterfly dies in my hand, but you don't weep,' Marceau says. 'You're touched to see his heart stop beating.' Years after he invented the sketch, Marceau realised that he had been inspired by a scene in *All Quiet on the Western Front* where German and French soldiers face each other in the trenches. One tries to catch a butterfly that lands on his rifle, and is shot dead.

When pressed, Marceau says he is pleased that all his children are artistic. His sons, from his first marriage, Baptiste and Michel, are a yoga professor and a musician. His daughters, from his second marriage, are Camille and Aurelia. Camille is a painter, and Aurelia is an actress who works with his ex-wife in a mime centre in southern France. 'Family is not important to me,' he says. 'I had no time to be a family father. If I had, I would have stayed in the same town. I would never have toured the world. We are all like gypsies; I have spent more time in the sky than on the ground. I am like Ulysses.'

If he had it to do over again, Marceau would change nothing. 'My art would not have been known throughout the world. What would make me sad? If in my lifetime I was forgotten.'

After the war, Marceau joined Jean-Louis Barrault's company where he played Harlequin to Barrault's Pierrot. But Barrault, his friend and rival, enjoyed a long career as a speaking actor and director. Marceau chose to maintain silence. 'To be the mime who inspired the world is better than being one of two hundred well known actors,' he says. 'I wanted to make it an art form on the level of theatre or opera.'

Although he has a dedicated following in France, where he is an *Officier de la Légion d'Honneur*, the US has given Marceau his greatest triumphs. His first tour there in 1955 was scheduled to last two weeks, but was sold out for six months. Later, Japan would declare him 'a living national treasure'. Two years ago, the mayor of New York declared his birthday, 18 March, to be Marcel Marceau Day. 'I have three generations of fans in America,' he explains. 'The people who came to see me in 1955 now return with their grandchildren.'

In the US, Marceau made what he calls 'the most extraordinary meetings', Charles Laughton, the Marx Brothers, Stan Laurel, Marlon Brando, Ginger Rogers, Yehudi Menuhin. Michael Jackson, who learned his 'moon walk' from Marceau, went on stage with him in New York. So did David Bowie. The magician David Copperfield has become a friend. 'He came to see me in the 1970s,' Marceau recalls. 'He said, "You make the invisible appear; I make the visible invisible." Once we were sitting together on a plane and I asked him, "David, can you make this plane disappear?" He said, "Yes, but I'd better not."'

For all his charm, Marceau can turn irritable in a second: when he's annoyed by a question, when he remembers the French critic who said that mimes should not philosophise. Philosophising is something he loves to do: about the shortness of life, good and evil, war, humanity, the sum of gestures which he calls 'the grammar of mime', the need for perfection in art, and that impalpable ingredient without which there can be no art – depth of soul. Yes, he says, depth of soul is equivalent to suffering.

When it comes to his own creations, Marceau's enthusiasm is boundless. He invented Bip, a character with a white Pierrot face, bell-bottom tights, a striped shirt and felt hat with a flower, in 1947. Bip's walking in the wind and stair-climbing pantomimes are classics. 'Bip is a Don Quixote fighting wind-mills,' Marceau says. 'The twentieth century was the most cruel . . . . You live in the middle of this and you have to create your character.'

Marceau's repertoire includes fifty Bip pantomimes, and between eighty and a hundred style pantomimes. His show in Dublin will be divided between the two, but he laments the impossibility of performing all of them in one evening. 'I will do some classics, like *The Trial, Youth, Maturity, Old Age and Death* and *The Creation of the World*. And I will do new ones, including *The Bird-keeper* and *Soliloquy of Three Lost Souls*'. In the latter, a tramp tells two others his sob story on a park bench.

Although Marceau never speaks on stage, he sometimes uses music. 'When I do *The Creation of the World*, I play the second movement of the 21st sym-phony. I have the impression that Mozart wrote it for me.' In the US, he recalls, a group of priests once attended his performance. 'Afterwards they asked me if I was religious. I told them I don't practise, but when I do *The Creation of the World* and *The Trial, Youth, Maturity, Old Age and Death*, God enters me. They approved.'

Marcel Marceau walks me to the theatre door.

For two hours he has been a living poem, a bubbling compendium of aphorisms on art, life, the soul, creation. He's extremely talkative for a man sworn to silence, I say. 'You see,' he jumps back, with a twinkle in his eye, 'I could have been a speaking actor.'

27 January 2001

Jeanne Moreau

At the beginning of Marguerite Duras' autobiographical novel, *The Lover*, the ageing writer told how a man approached her in public and said: 'I find you more beautiful now than when you were young. I liked your young woman's face less than the ravaged one you have now.' Duras wrote that, of all her self-images: 'This is the one that pleases me, the one where I recognise myself, which enchants me.'

Duras wrote these words; the narrator of the film version of *The Lover*, Jeanne Moreau, gave a voice to them. The two are arguably the finest French woman writer and actress of the past half-century, and they are inextricably linked in the minds of millions of French people. Duras died in 1996, but two months before her seventy-fifth birthday, Moreau is at ease with herself and the world, organising gala charity dinners, running a foundation to promote young screenwriters, and directing theatre and film productions.

Most people fear death and time, Moreau says. Not her. 'I'm living proof of the passage of time,' she laughs. 'Look at me! And after all, death is the most mysterious adventure.' Duras and she were friends from 1959 until 1974, Moreau says. Their friendship did not end. 'We just stopped seeing each other. She was surrounded by militant feminists, and male admirers too. Marguerite was fascinating, and they wanted to keep her to themselves. They pushed away other people.' By that time, Moreau had starred in two films based on Duras novels, Peter Brook's *Moderato Cantabile*, for which she won the best-actress award at Cannes, and Tony Richardson's *Sailor from Gibraltar*. Duras directed Moreau in *Nathalie Granger*. Moreau first assumed Duras' persona when she narrated *The Lover* in 1991. Then, in 2001, Moreau played Duras in Josée Dayan's wonderful film about the last sixteen years of Duras' life, *Cet Amour-là*.

It's a strange experience to meet Moreau after seeing *Cet Amour-là*, because it's impossible to shake off the conviction you are meeting Duras. Though Moreau maintains her performance was 'neither her nor me; not an imitation but a creation', she is conscious of her power to appropriate a character for all time. 'If I had played a cleaning lady, no one could imagine a cleaning lady different from me.'

Then there is that voice, like no other, with a magic approaching witchcraft. It is the voice of more than 120 films, hard as flint, with the denseness of fog and the crackle of flames, nurtured on countless cigarettes. 'One's aim in life should be to die in good health,' Moreau often says. So why does she chain-smoke? 'That has nothing to do with it,' she snaps. Surely she is denying all the evidence. 'What evidence?' I change the subject.

Louis Malle, the director who in 1958 plucked Moreau from mainstream French theatre and cinema to make her the New Woman of the New Wave, recognised her contradictions. Before the New Wave, Malle once said, 'Cameramen would force her to wear a lot of make-up, and they would put a lot of light on her, because, supposedly, her face was not photogenic.'

In *Lift to the Scaffold*, Florence/Moreau wanders moodily through Paris to Miles Davis's jazz score, not knowing that her paratrooper lover became trapped in a lift after murdering her husband. Malle showed Moreau's face only by the light of windows on the Champs Élysées. 'She could be almost ugly, and then ten seconds later she would turn her face and would be incredibly attractive,' he said. 'But she would be herself.'

The years have deepened Moreau's contrasts. The glamorous star, so often seen at Cannes and Hollywood, in diamonds and Saint-Laurent, answers the door wearing jeans, fringed black suede boots and a red jumper. For such a powerful personality, she is surprisingly short, and the array of stuffed animals in her buttercup-yellow sitting room strengthens the illusion of vulnerability. Like the characters she plays, Moreau is capricious and determined, impulsive and controlled, irritating and endearing, bloody-minded and full of wisdom. She is capable of prima donna tantrums, one suspects, and extravagant generosity. They don't make actresses like this any more.

Moreau's interview manner is combative; she has a disconcerting habit of remaining silent after a question, luring the journalist into useless peroration. Just when her clipped answers and resistance to perceived intrusions on her privacy – 'We're not going to talk about *me*' – become exasperating, she delivers an eloquent soliloquy or looks into your eyes and smiles, and sunshine breaks over Paris. You forgive her. Like two generations of directors and cinema-goers, you've been conquered.

Moreau's father, Anatole Desire, ran a café in Montmartre and wanted her to be a boy called Pierre. To the embarrassment of the family, her English mother, Kathleen Sarah, née Buckley, had been a dancing girl. Anatole was determined that his daughter should be an English teacher, and kicked her out of the house when he learned she was secretly studying drama.

Kathleen Sarah's family were from the south west of Ireland, and Moreau feels more Irish than English. 'Being Irish gives me melancholy, and that is very, very precious.' One of her many projects is a French adaptation of the last chapter of Joyce's *Ulysses*.

At the age of twenty, Moreau joined the Comédie-Française, where she worked with Jean-Louis Barrault. At twenty-six, she co-starred with Jean Gabin in *Touchez Pas au Grisbi*. When Malle, a then twenty-four-year-old whose only professional experience was filming underwater with Jacques Cousteau, asked her to play Florence in *Lift to the Scaffold*, Moreau's agent advised against it. She fired the agent. The role made Moreau famous the world over.

But she took a risk working with an unknown director. 'My whole life I took risks,' she says dismissively, as if the decision were self-evident. 'What is it we call "taking risks"? Life is given to us to do things, not to keep repeating ourselves.' As Jackie, the compulsive gambler in Jacques Demy's *Bay of Angels*; as the heartless, manipulative woman who drives a Welsh schoolteacher to distraction in Joseph Losey's *Eve*; as the utterly charming Catherine, who dooms the friendship between two writers, one French, one German, in François Truffaut's *Jules and Jim*, Moreau has always played strong-willed women who defy convention. I cannot imagine her playing a shrinking violet.

'Certainly not!' she exclaims. 'I didn't want to give that sort of image to other women; I have far too much respect for women.' Yet she does not consider herself a feminist. 'It means belonging to a group. I'm too attached to my solitude.'

When Yann Andrea, a homosexual less than half her age, shows up on Duras/Moreau's doorstep in *Cet Amour-là*, she tells him she has lived for ten years 'in happy solitude'. 'People who live together are often alone,' Moreau says. 'And they suffer from this solitude within a couple. There is no deep relationship – just sex.' But human beings sometimes surpass their own solitude, achieve a kind of fusion. 'That is what lasts. Passion never does. That kind of love approaches divine love; there is no end to it.'

In Moreau's words, *Cet Amour-là* is about 'a boy who's in love with a woman because of her books and a woman who lets him in and won't let him leave, who plunges into alcohol and writing to produce her most flamboyant works, which bring her international fame and fortune'. It is the true story of Duras' affair, for the last sixteen years of her life, with Andréa.

The film makes an unlikely tale convincing, I comment. 'Why is it unlikely?' Moreau asks. It's not the sort of love story that happens every day, I explain. 'Among exceptional people, these things happen,' Moreau continues. 'I'm not talking about myself. We must not talk about me. [The American painter] Georgia O'Keeffe lived the last twenty years of her life with a man much younger than her. [The French artist] Louise Bourgeois has a man living with her who is very, very young.' I must have 'an absolutely conventional image of the relationship between men and women,' Moreau scolds. 'People who fall in love, who fuck, who marry or don't marry, and who split up. Whereas in their case [Duras and Andréa], it was a spiritual relationship, from soul to soul.' Moreau was married twice: when she was twenty-one, to the film director Jean-Louis Richard, with whom she had a son, and at forty-nine, to William Friedkin, the director of *The French Connection*. She confirms a list of her famous lovers: Lee Marvin, Louis Malle, Pierre Cardin. 'That's correct,' she says. But before I can ask about the others, she adds: 'That's sufficient.' Vanessa Redgrave named Moreau as correspondent in her 1967 divorce from the director Tony Richardson on gounds of adultery. Moreau doesn't think much of marriage. 'It it not really necessary,' she sniffs.

But has she ever known the spiritual, soul-to-soul love she attributes to Duras and Andréa? 'We're not talking about me, Madame,' she says. 'I am the vehicle, the actress. Whether it happens to me or not doesn't matter. You're younger than me, but you've had enough experience to know that people fall hopelessly in love and separate, and at the end, there is often bitterness. An experience like Marguerite and Yann's is *the* experience – that's why it is called *Cet Amour-là*.

'Homosexuality or not, there is sex – whether it's homo or hetero,' Moreau continues. 'We have to stop this racism. When you say, "an older man with a young man" or "a woman with a homosexual man", it's racism. So what? I lived for four years with Pierre Cardin, who is homosexual. I am the woman of his life – the only one.' In January 2001, when Moreau became the first woman to be admitted to the French Académie des Beaux Arts, she was introduced by her former lover, Cardin. After listing her leading roles, Cardin publicly violated Moreau's legendary discretion. 'In Venice, in the Hotel Danieli, in that large room where Musset and George Sand lived, we made love, our bodies wrapped around each other,' he said. 'Is there any more beautiful way to live?' Moreau rose to the occasion, thanking Cardin for his excellent memory.

'It made me laugh,' she says now. 'I wasn't about to interrupt him. If it made him happy, then it made me happy.' The actress who was synonymous with French licentiousness says she's troubled by the way sex is shown in contemporary cinema. 'The sexual act is treated as something banal. It has become a consumer product,' she says.

'It's a pity, because it sows despair. It's de-humanising.' Moreau links the portrayal of casual sex with our lack of concern for the deaths of hundreds or thousands of people. 'It's rooted in the same phenomenon. If you consider sex like a glass of water when you're thirsty, the human body is no longer something precious.'

In *The Lovers*, her second film with Malle, Moreau played the bored wife of a newspaper director in provincial France who leaves her family for a student she's just met. The film created a scandal when it was released in 1958, because it showed oral sex.

'People talked about it because of the sex,' Moreau recalls. 'For Louis Malle and me, it was about love. We were deeply disturbed by the reaction.' Moreau's conversation is dotted with allusions to 'Orson' [Welles], 'François' [Truffaut], 'Luis' [Buñuel] and 'Jo' [Losey]. Welles called her 'the greatest actress in the world'. She remembers the director, who died in 1985, as 'vibrant, strong and fragile . . . so involved with his own fight with the outside and the inside of himself that he didn't have time to see other people's films.' When Moreau directed her first film, *Lumière*, about the relationship between four actresses, Welles was the only male director who encouraged her.

Moreau says she loved all the directors she worked with, 'though not in the same way'. Her relationship with Malle 'was emotional, an affair that I didn't have with the others'. Truffaut ran out of money when he was making *Jules and Jim*, so Moreau bailed out the production with earnings from her previous film. They still couldn't afford a sound man, and the entire film had to be post-synced.

Before playing Duras in *Cet Amour-là*, Moreau reread all Duras' books, as well as Andréa's account of their affair. 'It was like reading a novel of which Marguerite was the heroine,' Moreau says. 'She ended up the sum of all the women who inhabited her – and who must have been her.'

So is Jeanne Moreau the sum of all the characters she's played? 'I'm beyond that . . . I don't know . . . I'm the interpreter. That means whatever it means.

I am the intermediary with the public, who brings a work to life. It goes through me, to become tangible.'

She claims to be 'a woman before I'm an actress,' but I wonder. For cinema is Jeanne Moreau's greatest love, the one passion that endures, 'because it's the reflection of the world, the mirror'.

30 November 2002

Michel Déon

Michel Déon has lived quietly in the west of Ireland for thirty years. Though he writes every day in the Old Rectory in County Galway that his wife, Chantal, transformed into a stud farm, the French writer has always taken time to watch and listen to the Irish people around him.

As Déon writes in *Cavalier . . . Passe Ton Chemin!* (Horseman . . . Pass By!), published in French by Gallimard, Greece, the family's previous home, obsessed him, but Ireland kept him. His two best-known novels, *Les Poneys Sauvages* and *Un Taxi Mauve*, were partially and wholly set in Ireland. But they were published in the early 1970s, before the Déon family settled permanently in County Galway.

In the intervening decades, Déon has written prodigiously, producing more than fifty novels, essays and plays. But he has largely ignored his adopted homeland. Now *Cavalier* has righted that oversight. Déon has produced a poignant, often funny two-hundred-page description of Ireland and its inhabitants, as seen by one of France's greatest living writers.

Chantal's fox-hunting introduced Déon to the 'horsy set', some of whose Anglo-Irish members had seen better days. In wanderings through the countryside, he met a white-haired postman who warned him that retirement was a death sentence, and a woman of the roads known as Tall Sarah, haunted by the loss of her six children.

Patrick Joseph Smith, a labourer, arrived at the Old Rectory driving a tractor, followed by his collie. 'A man who is loved by his dog cannot be completely bad,' Déon thought.

In a suspense-filled chapter, Déon is stunned to see the village priest conducting his own funeral service. Unknown to Déon, he had a twin brother, also a priest.

A strangely attired would-be poet asks the French *académicien* for literary advice. As part of his Irish education, Déon follows in the footsteps of William Butler Yeats, and establishes friendships with John McGahern and Ulick O'Connor.

Under the pen of a less skilled wordsmith, a ruined aristocrat whom Déon met on a fox hunt might have become a cliché. But we watch with the writer, horrified, as the man pours himself glass after glass of wine, port and spirits, falls asleep in the dog kennel and eventually commits suicide. Every time he recalls the wasted life, 'The same sad diagnosis comes to me: *fin de race*'. The end of a bloodline, the dead man 'symbolised perfectly the middle English aristocracy that came centuries before, following in Cromwell's wake, to establish themselves as conquerors. Ireland had slowly engulfed him, sapping his virtues and instilling the slow poison of its sluggishness in a curious movement of the pendulum'.

Déon captures perfectly the eccentricity of Ulick O'Connor, 'elegant navy-blue blazer sprinkled with a layer of dandruff on the shoulders, grey trousers sagging above his runners'. At their first encounter, at a publisher's cocktail party in the Shelbourne Hotel, O'Connor objects to an English writer, recounts his eviction from Gay Byrne's *The Late Late Show*, and tells Déon that he has been a lawyer, ventriloquist, magician, Irish pole-vaulting champion and boxer, as well as a writer.

'There's a risk Ulick will be angry, but I also said kind things about him,' Déon shrugs. 'He doesn't mind being sniped at.'

The book alludes to O'Connor's visits to the Déon home, but leaves out my favourite anecdote: Chantal Déon's dismay at finding that O'Connor's fountain pen has leaked on the sheets.

'If Chantal read about it, it would make her furious all over again; I didn't want to remind her,' Déon explains.

Déon's friendship with John McGahern grew out of a meeting at the Étonnants Voyageurs literary festival in Saint-Mâlo. Déon noticed the Irish novelist when an audience member reproached McGahern for not taking a stand on Northern Ireland. Anger transformed McGahern's tranquil face, Déon writes: 'He reminded the audience that a writer is free to think what he wants to, and that what he thought of . . . this interminable civil war was nobody's business, especially not a fool who knew nothing about the problem.'

Déon admires 'this mixture of pity and cruelty with which [McGahern] delves into the heart and soul of his characters'. At the end of Déon's visit to

McGahern's farmhouse in County Leitrim, McGahern tells the Frenchman he has just completed an autobiographical book about his father and mother.

Déon was born in 1918, fifteen years before McGahern. But they shared the revisiting of their childhoods. At the end of the chapter on McGahern, Déon writes: 'Is there a time in the life of a writer when, having masked or distorted what was most dear to him . . . the need to speak openly about it imposes itself irresistibly?'

Just as *Cavalier* is Déon's summing up of his decades in Ireland, *La Chambre de Ton Père* (Your Father's Bedroom) was the story of his childhood in Paris and Monaco, where his father was a high-ranking official. The autobiographical novel subtly recounts the boy's discovery of his mother's infidelity and the heart-rending moment when she tells him: 'I never loved anyone but your father.'

'McGahern's childhood was less happy than mine,' Déon says. 'He lost his mother, who was marvellous, and his father was very strict. I lost my father, and though my mother was wonderful, she had great faults. These things mark you terribly. At first you want to hide them, even to yourself. And then one day you want to talk about them.'

At his age, Déon says he thinks often about death, but insists it is without sadness. He quotes an autobiographical title used by his friend and fellow *académicien* Jean d'Ormesson: '*C'était bien*' – it was fine. Nor are the deaths of the characters in his book tragic. George S., an Englishman stricken with terminal cancer, invites the Déons to dinner in his mobile home and savours his Château-Beychevelle wine. In an attempt to console the mother of Richie K., killed by a kick from a horse in County Wicklow, Déon tells her that 'Richie has certainly found horses to brush down and ride, up there'. Mrs K's face lights up, and she replies: 'Oh yes . . . Otherwise he'd already be back among us.'

One of the people who most marked Déon was Patrick Joseph Smith, 'Old Pat-Jo', the labourer who virtually became part of the family. 'Born elsewhere, he would have become an architect, engineer or entrepreneur, probably without being more happy,' Déon writes. He fondly recalls Pat-Jo's 'natural nobility, his reserve, the mischievous sparkle in his eyes'.

When Déon's son, Alexandre, restores a home in Paris, he brings Pat-Jo over to help. Alexandre takes Pat-Jo to the Louvre, the Eiffel Tower and the Champs-Élysées 'without managing to impress him'.

Later, Déon visits Pat-Jo when he is dying in hospital. The Irishman tells the French writer that he is about to be reunited with his mother ('healed, without her wheelchair'), his brothers and sisters. 'They'll be very happy to see me, to touch me to be sure it's true, that I really am the survivor of the family, thanks to the Virgin and little Bernadette,' he says. 'When you're certain of that, all that is left is impatience.'

Déon called the workman 'Old Pat-Jo', though he was ten years younger than Déon. 'Everyone is younger than me now, even the popes!' Déon laughs. There is a touch of longing for lost faith, even envy, in his description of Pat-Jo's death.

'What good fortune to believe in that!' Déon says. Though he and Chantal were raised as Catholics, they no longer practise. 'Something remains though. The imprint of a childhood around priests . . . . When churches are very beautiful, when there is beautiful music and paintings, I wonder if I don't have faith.'

Déon rages against tourism ('almost worse than war') and the destruction of the Irish countryside by developers. Bits of his beloved Portumna forest disappear every year, and the bungalows move ever closer to the Old Rectory.

'Livestock no longer cross national roads to change pasture, and it seems to me the weather is less damp and windy,' he writes. 'New roads pass through countryside from which the carcasses of cars and old tubs used as drinking troughs have been removed, but which are more and more fenced in by barbed wire hung on cement posts. What became of our hawthorn barriers, of thorn hedges and wild fuchsia? . . . Oh my children, what are you doing to one of the most poetic countries of Europe? Prosperity has fallen upon Ireland like paedophilia upon the low-ranking clergy.'

Farmers' sons in County Galway drive Jaguars to the pubs, Déon tells me. 'People drink more than ever. The girls sleep with everybody. It wasn't like this thirty years ago. I am happy for the Irish, if they are happy like this.'

Whatever about Ireland's shortcomings, the overwhelming tone of Déon's book is one of affection. The Irish may often blight their rural landscape, he says, but they are talented musicians and superlative writers. Ultimately it is their power of speech that most impresses him. 'Even deprived of their essential rights,' he writes, 'a people still have speech to defy their oppressor. And if they are gagged, they retain the remedy for all misery: the interior language that enables you to be yourself and to be all others.'

This book is Déon's tribute, his way of thanking Ireland. His joy in writing becomes the reader's delight.

21 May 2005

Carla Bruni

It's best to walk the last fifty metres up the steep, cobblestoned lane to Carla Bruni's house, because it's difficult for a taxi to turn around in the narrow cul-de-sac. This hidden corner of Paris' sixteenth *arrondissement*, with its villas and walled gardens, reminds you of Montmartre painted by Maurice Utrillo, or Paris of a century ago, as photographed by Eugène Atget.

It's like entering a time warp, where the only things that move are falling leaves. I ask myself which Carla Bruni I'm about to meet: the glamorous high-fashion model, the *ingénue*, the *femme fatale* or the regal consort? For, as she'll tell me when we part an hour and a half later: 'There are probably several women inside me.' Together, they comprise a unique twenty-first-century First Lady.

Beneath the white portico, along the stepping stones through the garden, the smiling, middle-aged Italian housekeeper ushers me into a high-ceilinged room where a slender woman is curled up in an armchair by the fire. Carla Bruni rises slowly, stretches one arm, then the other, blinking, exactly like my cat when he leaves the fireside. She wears a plain, tight-fitting blue pullover and blue trousers. She addresses me formally – *'Bonjour, Madame'* – and shakes my hand. She returned from New York the previous evening and half stumbles out of the room saying, 'I'm so jet-lagged!'

Bruni's brief absence gives me a chance to study the room where the president of France takes refuge most weekday evenings. Two walls of floor-to-ceiling French doors open to the garden. A bicycle belonging to Bruni's seven-year-old son Aurélien is propped against the window. In the corner, two guitar cases sit on armchairs, facing each other, as if in conversation. The fireplace is surrounded by bookshelves containing the complete works of Shakespeare, Victor Hugo, Lamartine, Verlaine, Jules Vernes, Saint-Simon . . . .

Bruni's long-haired pet Chihuahua, Tumi, snuggles up to me on the sofa. Even the dog seems feline. Clara, the yellow Labrador puppy who was a gift from the Canadian Prime Minister Stephen Harper, had to be entrusted to a trainer. 'She went *pipi* on the bed, kept us awake all night!' Bruni laughs. '*Mon mari* has to sleep!'

Beneath the coffee table there's more contemporary fare: books by Rama Yade, France's junior minister for human rights, and the philosopher Raphael Enthoven, Bruni's previous partner and Aurélien's father. MAC cosmetics spill out of a make-up bag on the large, square coffee table, next to a can of Diet Coke, a pack of Vogue cigarettes and a pair of reading glasses.

This is the house of Carla Bruni, songwriter, poetess and singer. When she lives in the Élysée Palace, she becomes Carla Bruni Sarkozy, presidential spouse. And when she travels abroad, her passport indicates that France's newly naturalised First Lady is simply Carla Sarkozy, trophy bride and photo opportunity. The three share the same playful and amused personality. With carefully preserved distance, Bruni analyses her own and others' behaviour, never taking herself too seriously. If there's one completely subjective blind spot, it's for the man she proudly calls *mon mari*.

Don't expect any daring quotes about the boredom of monogamy, about being a tamer of men, or how ill-humoured the French are. To use the title of a Yeats poem which Bruni turned into a song, 'Those Dancing Days Are Gone'. Despite Bruni's protestations that there is absolutely no self-censorship, the public figure of Carla Bruni Sarkozy has seeped into the private Carla Bruni. And if, as one strongly suspects, she tells little white lies about past lovers or having smoked marijuana, well it's all in the national interest, *raison d'état*.

'I care a lot about my profession as a singer. It's the meaning of my life,' Bruni told *Le Parisien* newspaper when her third album, *Comme Si de Rien N'était* (As If Nothing Had Happened) was released in the summer of 2008.

Today, Bruni tells me she wants it all: to be a great songwriter, First Lady and devoted wife. 'First Lady is not a profession,' she notes. 'I'd like to become a better singer, because I can't go where I want to with my voice yet.' Bruni has taken voice lessons twice-weekly for the past ten years. 'I'm more a songwriter than a singer, because I wouldn't have sung if I hadn't written my songs,' she says. 'It's not easy for me to sing in front of people. As soon as I have an audience, the emotion goes out of my voice. I am very shy.'

Several times during the interview, Bruni illustrates a point by breaking into song. The two people she quotes most often are the French singers Serge Gainsbourg and Barbara, both deceased. 'Music has always been very present in my life,' she says. 'I don't know if it was in my blood or in the air – probably both.'

The black lacquered baby grand piano which she brought from her child-hood home stands in a corner. Bruni's father, the engineer and industrialist Alberto Bruni Tedeschi, composed operas in his spare time. Her mother, Marisa Borini, was a concert pianist who met Bruni's genetic father, Maurizio Remmert, a classical guitarist twelve years her junior, when they played music together. Herbert von Karajan, Maria Callas, Renata Tebaldi and Rudolf Nureyev were guests in her parents' home when Bruni was growing up.

'L'amoureuse' (Woman in love) is the title of the single on Bruni's latest album. 'Love is the only thing worth having', she sings. The song is about being in love with life and with Sarkozy, 'but it's about all women in love,' Bruni explains. 'We're all the same, at the beginning, when we're in love. You have an impression of drunkenness, of exaltation. I wanted to describe this sensation at the moment when it crystallises. Obviously, the song was triggered by the love I feel for *mon mari*. But it's neither him nor me precisely. It's about that feeling of walking on clouds.'

Bruni met Nicolas Sarkozy at a dinner party in the home of the retired advertising executive Jacques Seguela in November 2007. 'With *mon mari*, it's a blessed love because he was ready to fall in love. I was ready to fall in love. Both of us were free. We were ready. We wanted it.' Sarkozy had divorced his second wife the previous month, and Bruni had recently separated from Enthoven, after seven years together.

'I want to find my double,' Bruni sings on her new album. Bruni and Sarkozy 'are hunters who met – predators,' the fashion designer Karl Lagerfeld told *Vanity Fair*. 'It's a good thing. He had seduced many women, and she was a kind of seductress. When two like this meet, it can be good.'

'He's so clever, Karl!' Bruni laughs. She says she can't judge her relationship from the outside, but speaks of Freud's theory of transference, an identification with the loved one. 'When you fall in love, you start talking like the other person. You steal his expressions. You're under the influence.' Sceptics claim that Bruni loves Sarkozy for his power, for the finger on the nuclear button. Is power the ultimate aphrodisiac, I ask her. 'It's more a source of worry or fatigue,' she says. 'But he's been a professional for more than twenty years; it's an integral part of his personality. So obviously that is part of his charm. I don't find power particularly aphrodisiac, but I find Nicolas particularly attractive.'

Carla Bruni Sarkozy is a one-woman fan club, her husband's most effective propagandist. Each time he wraps up a summit early, the presidential press corps assume he's eager to rush home to Bruni. 'I hope so,' she laughs. 'But the truth is that he's quick. He's a fast man, who gives the impression of a locomotive. He tries to fold things to fit his time. He comes to conclusions very, very quickly. And he is hypernesic – the opposite of amnesic. He remembers everything, even things that don't interest him.'

Her husband is impatient, Bruni admits. 'But especially, there is very little time between the moment when he decides something and the moment he does it – contrary to most people. When there's a problem, Nicolas starts to resolve it immediately. He grabs the bull by the horns . . . I thought I was quick, but when I met him I realised he was quicker than me, much quicker.'

Sarkozy's detractors find him aggressive. 'He's not very aggressive. He's impulsive,' Bruni corrects them. 'So, for example, he responds to provocation. It's difficult to tell someone, "Be impulsive only for positive things". Speed and impulsiveness are important engines, especially for the life he leads, which is heavy with responsibility. If he were slow and apathetic, I assure you that during the European presidency . . . [Bruni alludes to praise for her husband's handling of France's presidency of the EU when the global financial crisis started.] Fortunately there was this energy, this impulse. He never hesitates to dive in, to set an example, which brings the others on board.'

Bruni watches all her husband's press conferences on television. 'He jokes a lot,' she says with relish, and I realise this is another thing they have in common. I imagine Bruni writing puns on the chalkboard as a schoolgirl, leaving fake spiders on other girls' chairs, then sitting primly in the front row, secret prankster and teacher's pet.

Sarkozy 'could have had a great career as a performer, because he's very, very good at it,' Bruni continues. 'He's a great orator. He improvises a lot in his speeches. I read them beforehand, and I see the difference between the song and the interpretation, so to speak. He's artistic, the way he places his voice; it's a natural talent, which he has had for a long time.'

When he was younger, Sarkozy told Bruni, 'he didn't find himself particularly interesting or intelligent. He didn't find himself seductive, but when he talked, he felt people listening, that he could change something in their minds or hearts or the way they were thinking. He felt he had that. I think that's why he went into politics.'

So was it through his command of language that Nicolas Sarkozy seduced Carla Bruni? 'He still seduces me,' she says. 'We talk a huge amount. All the time. All the time.'

When Bruni's last album was released, a British newspaper labelled it 'Sex and Drugs'. There are a few racy verses. In '*Ta tienne*' (Yours), the song most evocative of Sarkozy, Bruni sings: 'I give you my body, my soul and my chrysanthemum . . . you are my lord, my darling, my orgy . . . I burn for you like a pagan . . . .' The song was half-written before she met Sarkozy, she insists. And she composed it with a sense of fun. 'What I write is not the way you read it. You read it thinking it's me.'

The verse that attracted most attention comes from another song, '*Je suis une enfant*': 'I am a child/ Despite my forty years/ Despite my thirty lovers/ A child.' Bruni never tried to hide her affairs with rock stars, intellectuals and politicians. Only thirty lovers? I ask her. She pleads artistic licence. 'There were probably fewer, but it didn't work for the rhyme. When I write a song, I think about the song, not what people will say . . . I didn't write it as First Lady of France! There are mischievous things in my songs, and it amuses me a lot that people take them literally. They're really missing the point . . . I'm happy that people read my texts, even if they do it only because I'm First Lady. It gives me satisfaction as a songwriter.'

Another song, '*Tu es ma came*' (You're my drug), also raised a few eyebrows. The Colombian government objected to the verse 'more deadly than Afghan heroin/ More dangerous than Colombian white'. In another line, Bruni sings: 'I breathe you in, I breathe you out and I swoon.'

She feigns disbelief that the French might wonder if their First Lady tried drugs. 'Never!' says Bruni. 'I always hated people getting high. Not only I do I not like these things, I condemn them, because you can't get rid of them once you're hooked!' The only addictions she admits to are exercise, Diet Coke, cigarettes, and Sarkozy.

In the song '*Notre grand amour est mort*' (Our great love is dead), Bruni recounts the end of her relationship with Enthoven. 'We separated because we'd become very good friends,' she says. 'If we didn't separate, maybe we would have started falling in love with other people, lying to each other.' In the song, Bruni turns their break-up into a source of melodramatic derision: 'Our great love is dead, we must wrap it in white/ Perfume its body, watch over it three nights . . . .'

'You take a sad, shabby feeling, and when it's a little tragic, you digest it for a while, then you make something almost happy of it,' Bruni explains. 'It renders something that was negative, a failure, positive. It enables you to move on . . . .'

Only once, in '*Salut marin*' (Bye sailor), the song she wrote for her brother Virginio, who died of AIDS and lymphoma in 2006, does Bruni's grief come through, subtly, in one line. Virginio's death was the worst thing that has happened to her, she admits. He took with him 'our crystal childhood, and our youth of honey', she sings.

Bruni's mother sold her husband's antique collection, raising €18.7 million for a foundation named after Virginio. In '*It's easier for a camel . . .*', Bruni's older sister, the film-maker Valeria Bruni Tedeschi, shows the three children playing in the magnificient interiors of Castagneto Po castle. 'This is all I've kept,' says Bruni, pointing out the mirror above the fireplace, an ornately painted *sécretaire* and a statue of an African slave behind the piano. 'It reminds me of my childhood, of the insouciance of my childhood.'

So what is it like to be Carla Bruni Sarkozy, the woman who has every-thing? Though she has never known 'the terrible suffering of poverty or illness,' Bruni assures me that 'I have all the others. You lose many things in the course of a life. You're not spared . . . I am a human being, with the same problems as everyone else, even if I am very privileged.'

Bruni has spent years in psychoanalysis, and writes down her dreams every morning. Analysis teaches one 'absolute responsibility for all feelings,' she says. 'It is not romantic, not erotic . . . . The only place where artistic creation and psychoanalysis meet is in dreams, because there's such mad creativity in the subconscious.'

Bruni shows me a large orange book on the piano, facsimiles of the film-maker Federico Fellini's diary of his dreams, complete with his watercolours. 'Analysis serves one purpose,' she says. 'It gives you a little suitcase that you carry around, so you don't make others carry your life, your decisions, your history. It helps you mature in the sense that you've understood your own his-tory, and especially, you take responsibility for it. It gives you a great deal of wisdom.'

Bruni says she maintains a distance from her public image, though 'there's little difference between me and my image'. That image is 'a different place, something else. I don't fall into it. I never say to myself "I am Carla Bruni. I'm a model" or "I am a singer. Henceforward I am First Lady of France". I never say that to myself. Sometimes I say, "Hey, I'm a singer. I've been invited to sing, so I must sing better." Or "Hey, I'm First Lady of France. I must be a credit to this country."'

What we see of Carla Bruni is only her reflection in the mirror, she says. 'The heart of hearts, the deep-down-inside that everyone has, well I have it too. And that's where I live.'

It must be a happy place, because she laughs when she says it.

29 November 2008

Sophie Toscan du Plantier

Anyone who read a newspaper in Ireland or France at the end of 1996 learned that Sophie Toscan du Plantier, the wife of a French film producer, travelled alone to her isolated, two-storey white house at Dunmanus West outside Schull, County Cork in the week before Christmas. On the morning of 23 December, her lifeless body was found on the frozen path below her house, her head smashed by a stone.

Nearly three years have passed, and Sophie's killer is still at large. Her husband's frustrated outbursts against the Garda Síochána have made headlines. So have interviews with the self-proclaimed 'prime suspect'. Yet for all the attention devoted to the crime, the public knows little of what mattered to the victim and to those she loved: that she looked like her great aunt Alice, the one who married a marquis; that she was deeply attached to her parents' native Lozère region in south-central France; that she was confirmed in Notre Dame cathedral; that she passed her *Baccalauréat* at a Dominican convent in Rome, where she started a lasting friendship with a Mexican girl named Gina.

Sophie remained natural in the artificial world of cinema, refusing to wear make-up, choosing the simplest clothes and decoration for the homes she lived in. Her family compare her west Cork home, where she had her bed raised on a platform so she could see the lighthouse at night, to a monastery. Sophie attended art exhibitions almost religiously, forcing her adolescent son and stepson to go with her. Will any book record that she charmed two French presidents? Or that on her way to Ireland on that fatal trip, she stopped at the maternity clinic to hold her newborn nephew, Baptiste? She repeated then that she wanted to have a baby girl. Whatever the difficulties of her marriage with Daniel Toscan du Plantier, one of her last telephone calls from Ireland was to their gardener at Ambax, near Toulouse, ordering a linden tree as a Christmas gift for her husband, to be planted outside their bedroom window.

It would take volumes of such details to portray a life brutally interrupted, and even then, as her father Georges Bouniol was quick to tell me, it would be only an outline, an empty silhouette of his daughter. Yet somehow, one feels, people ought to know that she read Rimbaud, Proust and Brendan Behan, that she wrote constantly, compulsively, that her killer also robbed the world of a promising woman of letters. Those who knew her best describe a woman of rare physical and spiritual beauty, self-assured, but privately doubting her own talent, generous and loyal in friendship, demanding and often unhappy in love.

On 5 December 1999, her father Georges and her mother Marguerite Bouniol, Marie-Madeleine Opalka, the aunt who was her confidante and close friend, and her uncle Michel and aunt Marie-France attended a memorial Mass in Goleen to mark the third anniversary of Sophie's death. 'Every year, we feel torn apart when we arrive and see Sophie's house from a distance, over-looking the valley, waiting for us,' Marguerite Bouniol told me. 'Every year, our hope of seeing justice done decreases.'

'We were her parents,' Georges Bouniol, a retired dentist, said, his voice breaking with emotion when we met in the bourgeois Paris apartment where Sophie grew up. 'We made her. We could not follow her, we could not protect her . . . .' He is reluctant to speak of his grief, loath to see his only daughter reduced to a news story.

Sophie's mother, a small, energetic woman as brave as she is wounded, has a different philosophy. 'I want to talk about her, because I don't want us to for-get her,' she says as we watch a video taken on 28 July 1985, Sophie's twenty-eighth birthday. The tower of St Eustache Church, where Sophie was baptised and where her family held a memorial service after her death, looms behind her. Sophie looks at the camera, her long, naturally blonde hair blowing in the wind, one moment smiling joyously, the next sad as a madonna. 'Later, her face was thinner,' her mother says. 'I found her more beautiful at thirty-nine, when she had little wrinkles, when her face had more character.'

Marie-Madeleine Opalka says that Sophie was 'the most beautiful baby I have ever seen – absolutely ravishing. From the moment she was born, I admired her. I was fascinated by her.' Those who knew Sophie often use the adjectives 'luminous' and 'weightless'. 'She was light – she walked on the tip of her feet, as if she were dancing,' Opalka continues. The niece she remembers was spirited and passionate, aware of her powers of seduction, but playfully detached. 'When she arrived somewhere, the air vibrated in a special way: there are few people who have such an aura,' Opalka says, adding that Sophie had several *amitiés amoureuses* – romantic but platonic friendships – with men who admired her. Her second husband, Daniel Toscan du Plantier, says Sophie was fiercely independent and had 'an obsessive sense of mystery. She liked to have lots of secret gardens – even after we married, I'm not sure I knew everything about her.'

Through Daniel, Sophie met some of the world's most famous film directors – Satyajit Ray, Constantin Costa-Gavras, and Andrzej Wajda. She had a nonchalant way of throwing together a salad late in the evening and making anyone feel at home. Before meeting Sophie, Daniel had been married to the actresses Marie-Christine Barrault and Francesca Comencini. He lived for ten years with Isabelle Huppert. But Sophie, the only one who was not an actress, was the greatest star, he says now. Opalka recalls how Sophie caught the eye of the late François Mitterrand at a reception. She and Daniel were invited to a private dinner at the Hôtel de Ville when Jacques Chirac was still mayor of Paris, Marguerite Bouniol says. Sophie told Chirac about the documentary she was making on African art; he asked when it would be broadcast. A few months later, Chirac, by then French president, sent her a fax to say how much he enjoyed her programme.

Yet despite their celebrity friends and the many glossy photographs of Sophie on Daniel's arm at film festivals and awards ceremonies, she hated media attention. 'I had a friend who wanted to do a story on us for *Paris Match*,' Daniel Toscan du Plantier told me in an interview in his office near the Eiffel Tower. 'She fled the house, saying, "You'll pay for this some day". She was right, because when she died, the photos were everywhere – without her.'

In two of the family's favourite photos of her, Sophie turned her back to the camera. Daniel prefers one taken in the garden at Ambax in the summer of 1996. Sophie reaches into a wall of ivy (in fact the kitchen window), her blonde hair in an Alice in Wonderland plait down her back. In a heart-breaking, handwritten little book she wrote for Sophie, Marguerite Bouniol describes a photo taken at her sister Marie-Madeleine's sixtieth birthday party, two months before Sophie was killed. 'One can see only your hair, which lights up the scene all by itself,' she wrote. 'The Eiffel Tower, a few forms, are in the background . . . only your hair is there, magnificent, luminous. Your face is turned towards the night, your eyes towards the heavens, towards the stars where you would soon be lost!'

Bouniol says that Sophie had 'a certain reserve' when talking to her mother, but that she told everything to her aunt Marie-Madeleine Opalka, an exuberant woman with a taste for showy hats and jewellery, who is married to the Polish painter Roman Opalka. Snobbery is the least of the faults that Opalka attributes to Daniel, whom she reproaches for letting Sophie travel to Ireland alone when she was exhausted after completing a television documentary called *Le Pli* for Arte television. The family also found it difficult to understand why Daniel did not travel to Ireland after Sophie's death, and how he could bring a young eastern European secretary home a few months later. He married the secretary on the very day the family dedicated a cross to Sophie in Ireland. In the meantime, the young woman had given birth to a baby daughter named Tosca, a name Sophie had wanted for the child she hoped to have.

In the book Marguerite Bouniol wrote in tribute to her daughter, she comments on the tact, kindness and attentiveness shown by local Gardaí each time the family travels to west Cork. Opalka tells me: 'We, Sophie's family, cannot accept that Daniel, who couldn't even be bothered to go there, speaks ill of the Irish police.' It was the coroner's late arrival which made it impossible to establish the hour of Sophie's death or conduct DNA tests that might have identified her killer; the police could do nothing until he arrived. 'We, the family of Sophie, who truly loved her, are grateful to the Irish police,' Opalka adds.

But although they dislike each other, Opalka and Daniel Toscan du Plantier use many of the same words about Sophie. Both say they recognised prodigious, untapped talent in her; that she was completely fearless but remained strangely innocent. 'Even in her thirties, eternally a young girl,' Toscan du Plantier describes her. 'Alice in Wonderland . . . she lacked the protective shell the rest of us develop,' Opalka says.

Sophie Bouniol was divorced and raising her young son alone when Daniel Toscan du Plantier first met her in 1988. She had handled public relations for the French film promotion board Unifrance since 1983, but did not get along with the manager. She intended to resign, according to her mother, but when Daniel Toscan du Plantier became chairman of the board, he urged her to stay until she found a new job. The woman he met was 'very beautiful, very difficult', he said. 'She looked like an angel, but she had a volcanic character, and became aggressive easily.' Opalka disputes this. In the thirty-nine years she knew Sophie, she says, she never saw her angry. If she lost her temper with Daniel, there were good reasons.

'Sophie was impulsive. She had an incredible capacity to break off relationships suddenly,' Toscan du Plantier says, citing the way she left her first husband after their son was born. 'If she wasn't happy with the way things were, she left. She did it to me often. She just disappeared – I don't know where she went. After a while it became a joke between us. She had an almost mystical ideal of love – extremely demanding. She wasn't someone who had casual affairs. She was very easily disappointed. She wanted a sort of spiritual absolute.' Opalka cleared up the mystery of Sophie's disappearances: when she was angry with Daniel, her niece used to come to her home in Geneva.

During the 1989 Cannes Film Festival, Daniel Toscan du Plantier invited Sophie Bouniol to a dinner hosted in a château by *Le Monde* newspaper. She refused initially, saying she didn't want to mix her work and social life. But since she was responsible for relations with the press, he insisted. When they arrived, the first thing she did was to tear up the place card saying 'Toscan du Plantier, Escort'. The French cabinet minister seated next to Sophie mistook her for Daniel's former companion, Isabelle Huppert. 'He started complimenting her on her performance in [the film] *Violette Nozière*. She turned bright red and left the table,' he recalls. 'When she didn't return, I went out to the courtyard and found her, furious. I can still hear her saying, "I am not the clone of your mistresses". She wanted to walk back to Cannes, but I persuaded her to finish dinner. Later, she insisted that I drop her on the outskirts of Cannes so I wouldn't know where she was staying.'

That was how their courtship started. Back in Paris, Toscan du Plantier went to the building where Sophie worked on the Champs-Élysées and telephoned from the café downstairs. 'She said she didn't have time to see me. I insisted and she said, "All right, but only three minutes". She remained standing. I said, "What can I do to see you?" I was getting divorced from Francesca Comencini. Sophie said she wouldn't go out with a married man and asked me to send proof to her mother that I was no longer married. I photocopied the lawyer's file. Her mother wrote back saying I had a bad reputation, but that her daughter was old enough to make her own decisions. Then I received a telegram. It said "Sophie B.", and her phone number.'

As the deputy mayor of Paris's 2nd *arrondissement*, Marguerite Bouniol married her daughter, then thirty-three, to Daniel, then fifty, in June 1990. 'Later I was sorry I had performed this marriage,' she says now. 'Maybe it brought them bad luck.' Sophie stopped working at Unifrance and gradually established herself as an independent film producer. There were difficult years, Daniel admits, during which they were briefly separated. Opalka says her niece was disappointed by both her husbands – that, sadly, she never found the man who would have made her happy.

As a teenager, Sophie spent two summer holidays with a family called MacKiernan in Dublin. 'They had ten children, and at first the children ate in the kitchen and Sophie in the dining room – until she insisted that they all eat together,' Bouniol recalls. The MacKiernans took Sophie around Ireland in a caravan. 'She always said, "I love this country",' Bouniol adds. In the early 1990s, Sophie decided to buy a house in Ireland. 'Find myself another country, why?' she wrote in her diary. 'I already have one; but another, so it will be mine, so that I will conquer it, so that we will deserve one another.' Sophie and her cousin Alexandra, Opalka's daughter, spent weeks sleeping in cold bed and breakfasts, while they house-hunted. At one point, she hesitated between two homes. 'What is my preference?' she wrote prophetically, describing two contrasting landscapes. 'It is difficult to choose between gentleness and violence'.

After Sophie's death, her mother found dozens of notebooks and manuscripts among her belongings. 'I had underestimated her,' she says. 'I didn't take her seriously enough. I am trying to make up for it now, by typing all the texts that I find.' Among those she lent me were Sophie's diaries from trips to Rome and India, a novella about a peasant spinster in her parents' home village of Combret in Lozère and a fairy tale about a flower and a sea urchin. But the most striking is entitled *L'A de la T*, an abbreviation for '*L'Amour de la Terre*', or 'Love of the Land', as if Sophie dared not openly declare her affection for the wilds of west Cork.

L'A de la T is a beautiful and sometimes funny description of Irish fog and damp, shades of grey and light, sheep and cattle grazing, of a city woman striving to recover her dulled senses of hearing, sight and smell. 'The surroundings are varied and unchanging at the same time,' she wrote. 'I must find my place, like all living creatures here.' The most haunting image is that of a fox stalking the lambs. 'This animal that pulls me unwittingly into his clandestinity, forcing me (but you also) to remain silent, to become his companion in hunting.' Much later, Sophie finds a dead sheep by the path. 'A devoured cadaver with his skeleton and skin spread out a little further away. Raw wool, white and animal, dirty and smelling; in fact the whole scalp of a body . . . an empty envelope mixed with dirt and blood. What remains of the jawbone is still flexed, almost open. You die in the wind, in the sea, on the land here; the rottenness is spread out in daylight, perfectly naturally.'

Did Sophie Toscan du Plantier have a premonition of her own death? Two months earlier, when she and Daniel arrived at their country home at Ambax, Sophie stopped a woodcutter trimming trees in the cemetery where she would be buried. In her book for Sophie, Marguerite Bouniol recalls how Sophie feared reaching the age of forty. She once compared the palm of her hand with those of her aunt and mother and commented that her lifeline was only half as long as theirs. There was the way she said '*Adieu, maman*' – 'Farewell' – instead of '*Au revoir*' the last time they spoke on the telephone, the way she kept saying she missed her dead grandmothers.

Later, Sophie's mother, father and aunt would meet the Alsatian artist and his wife who had been among the last to see her. On the afternoon of 22 December, Sophie was walking on Mizen Head when she was suddenly seized with panic and ran to her friends' house. They gave her tea and begged her to spend the night, but she refused: she had chores to do the next day before returning to France for Christmas with Daniel and his children. Among the belongings that Gardaí returned to Sophie's family was a bilingual edition of Yeats they found on Sophie's bed, open to a poem called 'Death' which begins: 'Nor dread nor hope attend/ A dying animal . . .'

Sophie's writings show that she wanted to be remembered, at least by those who knew her. Her son Pierre-Louis is a tall, gangly maths and science student of eighteen. He did not talk during the evening I spent at Sophie's parents' home. He listened and looked through the pile of his mother's books which Marguerite Bouniol had stacked on the table. When he and I walked to the métro station later, he said he had remained silent out of respect for his mother – that he has in any case blocked out many memories of her. But he does not want to sell her house in Ireland. 'It's my house now, and I want it to be open to all my mother's friends and family, as it was when she was living. I go there and people are kind to me. Each time, I return to find her belongings, her smell. I sleep in her bed, and I feel she is with me – I am happy.'

11 December 1999

An unpublished report on the death of Sophie Toscan du Plantier conveys the savagery of the French woman's killing in west Cork in December 1996, and has provided her family with details on her death.

'It is hard to read, but it gives a far more clear and precise picture than newspaper reports, which were all we had to go on,' says Jean-Pierre Gazeau, the dead woman's uncle and the president of the Association for the Truth about the Death of Sophie Toscan du Plantier. Gazeau, a professor of astrophysics, provided a copy of the report to *The Irish Times*. He does not want his ageing sister, Marguerite Bouniol, Toscan du Plantier's mother, to read it.

In a landmark defamation trial, Judge Patrick Moran ruled in January 2004 that six newspapers had been entitled to identify the English journalist Ian Bailey as the chief suspect in Toscan du Plantier's killing. Bailey said scratches on his face, hands and forearms, first noticed the day Toscan du Plantier's body was found, were caused by his killing three turkeys and chopping down a Christmas tree.

Newspapers reported that the dead woman had organic matter from her assailant under her fingernails and a clump of hair in her hand. The then state pathologist, Dr John Harbison, recorded: 'I took scrapings from the fingernails of both hands and placed them in plastic bags . . . . A number of hairs, almost a dozen, were adherent to an even wound around fingers of the right hand. Because of dried blood these were removed with difficulty and some of them parted. I found one long and one very short hair adherent to the back of the left hand.' Bailey gave Gardaí a sample of his DNA in January 1997.

Liam Horgan, the Garda superintendent in charge of the investigation, confirmed in a telephone interview that three sets of DNA tests have been conducted 'over time, as the technology improved'. The tests have been inconclusive so far, but Superintendent Horgan said the samples, held in a secure place in Dublin, could still yield the identity of Toscan du Plantier's killer. Several years have passed since the tests were last conducted. 'Some blood samples are so minuscule that they could not be analysed. As technology advances, we can go back to it,' Superintendent Horgan said.

The thirteen-page post-mortem report by Dr Harbison makes up most of the twenty pages that the coroner sent to Marguerite Bouniol. The document also includes a cover note to Mrs Bouniol, dated 8 April, from the coroner for south and west Cork, a summary signed by Dr Harbison three months after the killing, a two-page report by the Garda Síochána to the coroner, and results of toxicology and chemical pathology tests on the dead woman's body – all of which were negative.

The Garda report notes that Toscan du Plantier's body was found 'in suspicious circumstances' – surely one of the great understatements in the annals of crime. In clinical language, Dr Harbison describes the scene at Dunmanus West on 24 December 1996: 'In the approach to these cottages, I observed the dead body of a female lying on the grass verge on the roadway. The principal feature of the body was that the head, shoulders and both arms were heavily blood-stained.'

Dr Harbison describes the body in terms of a multitude of wounds, bruises, lacerations and haemorrhages. Her mother had told me that her beautiful daughter's face was 'a pulp'. Dr Harbison lists 'laceration and swelling of the brain, fracture of the skull, and multiple blunt head injuries' as the cause of death.

The dead woman wore a short cotton top, a pair of cotton 'long johns'-style underpants and boot-like shoes with socks sewn into the top. The underpants had caught on barbed wire as she fled and were stretched for about three feet between the wire and the body.

'The dead woman had long hair which had become entangled in vegetation,' Dr Harbison wrote. I couldn't help recalling the Yeats poem found beside Toscan du Plantier's bed. It began: 'Nor dread nor hope attend/ A dying animal . . .'

'It was obvious that she had severe head injuries because there were gaping wounds on the right side of the forehead and the right ear was severely lacerated at its lower edge,' Dr Harbison continued. He identified two possible weapons near the body: 'Beside the deceased's left shoulder and head was a flat slate like a stone which was heavily blood-stained . . . . Between the deceased's body and the wire fence and within nine inches of her left hand was a nine-inch cavity block.'

The block rested on the dead woman's blue dressing gown, and appeared to have been taken from a hut built around an electric water pump, twenty to thirty feet farther up the hill. Dr Harbison mentions two blows on the dead woman's shoulder blades. 'These could have been the imprints of that block, administering a glancing blow,' he wrote. The body did not appear to have been dragged over the ground. Toscan du Plantier's killer must have pursued her as she ran down the hill, towards a neighbour's house.

Ian Bailey covered the killing for several newspapers. He denied allegations that he reported things only the killer would have known. In the *Sunday Tribune*, dated 29 December 1996, Bailey wrote: 'The evidence indicates that she was pursued down the rocky track from her home and killed by repeated blows to the back of the head.'

Rumours initially oriented the investigation towards France. In the same article, Bailey falsely reported that 'Ms du Plantier . . . had recently informed [her husband Daniel] she intended to remarry her first husband,' adding: 'on several occasions she had visited west Cork with different companions'.

Sophie Toscan du Plantier was not raped or sexually assaulted, Dr Harbison wrote. When I interviewed Daniel Toscan du Plantier in 1999 (he died in 2003 at the age of sixty-one), he speculated on the motive of his wife's killer. 'I can imagine it well,' he said. 'She could be extremely cutting. She faced someone who was probably drunk, and he made a pass at her and she rejected him in an insulting way and he went crazy. It was like her to go outside to talk to him; she wasn't afraid of anything.'

In December 2003, when Bailey sued newspapers for libel, a landscape gardener, Bill Fuller, testified that Bailey, speaking of himself in the second person, told him: 'You did it. You saw her in Spar on Saturday. You saw her walking up the aisle with her tight arse. You fancied her. You went up there to see what you could get. She ran off screaming. You chased her to calm her down. You stirred something in the back of your head. You went too far. You had to finish her off.'

In addition to Fuller, Bailey is reported to have told or strongly implied to at least seven other people (Helen Callanan, Yvonne Ungerer, the wife of the French author and illustrator Tomi Ungerer, Malachi Reed, Richard and Rosie Shelley, Diane Martin and Marie Farrell) that he killed Toscan du Plantier. Farrell, who had earlier said she was threatened by Bailey, retracted her testimony in 2005. Bailey has claimed the 'confessions' were misunderstood, that he was either joking or recounting what other people said about him.

The *coup de grâce* was apparently administered once Toscan du Plantier was already prostrate. 'I was able to look at the ground when the body had been moved to note that there was a slight depression with blood on it where the head had lain,' Dr Harbison wrote. 'This indicated to me that the body had been in that position when the blows were struck.'

The state pathologist's report raises two mysteries: what caused 'the curious situation that the drops of blood on the clothing were for the most part quite circular, a few with slight "blobs" on the edges, as if they had fallen vertically on to the long johns rather than dribbled downwards from the deceased's head onto her legs'? The folded part of the cloth was not stained, creating 'the impression that this blood therefore fell on these trousers while in that infolded state'. Could the drops on the dead woman's pyjamas be the blood of her killer? Future DNA tests may tell.

And what caused the 'fine parallel abrasions' that Dr Harbison said resembled 'the imprint of a Doc Marten boot' on the dead woman's neck, face and right forearm? Did her killer stomp on her body?

No one told Toscan du Plantier's family they had a right to receive the post-mortem report. 'When I was in Dublin in February, the sister of a murdered man told me we could ask for it,' Gazeau explains. 'I asked Marguerite to write to the coroner, which she did.' The coroner, Frank O'Connell, promptly forwarded the report to Bouniol when he obtained it from his predecessor, who retired in December 2006. Under normal circumstances, a coroner's inquest is held when a murder investigation is concluded. The family is entitled to be invited. But no inquest has been held in this case, because the Garda investigation continues.

'The coroner's inquiry was opened by my predecessor solely to take formal evidence of identity, to determine the cause of death and release the body,' O'Connell explained. 'The inquiry was opened and adjourned until after the police inquiry, as required by section twenty-five of the Coroner's Act of 1962 . . . . I gave Mrs Bouniol everything I have. As long as the police are conducting an investigation, particularly one as difficult as this, they keep the evidence to themselves. This is one of the saddest cases I have come across. My heart goes out to Mrs Bouniol.'

Superintendent Horgan regrets that the case has not come to trial. 'Somebody killed Sophie Toscan du Plantier in December 1996,' he says. 'My responsibility is to bring that person to justice. I am hopeful that we will.' There is always the possibility of new DNA results, a confession, or that 'other witnesses come forward with evidence not offered until now,' he continues.

'People are still very interested and anxious to help; I still think we are gaining a bit of ground. It's a priority here and will remain so.'

10 May 2008

History Is Ever With Us

Has the French Revolution Ever Ended?

The city bristled with rumours that morning, 220 years ago today. It was a time of economic crisis, even hunger, and the spring had been taken up with the election of deputies to the Estates General (a consultative body that had not convened for 175 years) and the drafting of lists of grievances.

The king's soldiers had carried out manoeuvres around Paris for several days, strengthening fears of a plot by the aristocracy to end growing demands by the Third Estate, as the commoners were known. 'What is the Third Estate?' the revolutionary Abbé Sieyes wrote in January 1789. 'Everything. What has it been until now in the political order? Nothing. What does it want to be? Something.'

The word went out: the people needed arms to defend themselves, and there were weapons in the old Bastille fortress, which was used as a prison. Thousands of Parisians flocked there. The governor, the Marquis de Launay, attempted to negotiate with the mob.

At about 5 PM, the mob lost patience, stormed the fortress and freed its seven prisoners. De Launay was executed and decapitated, along with Flesselles, the provost of merchants. Their heads were stuck on pikes and paraded through the streets of the city. The French Revolution had claimed its first victims.

Some thirty thousand people would die in political violence before Napoleon seized power, ending the revolution, a decade later.

Or perhaps it wasn't over.

President Nicolas Sarkozy speaks of the difficulty of governing a country that has committed regicide. The late-twentieth century French historian François Furet argued that the French Revolution never ended – an idea that has become widespread.

Former Prime Minister Dominique de Villepin, an amateur historian, adopted a similar theme in a text he wrote for a ninty-eight-page magazine published by *Le Monde* newspaper to commemorate the 220th anniversary of the taking of the Bastille.

'There is a predisposition to revolutions that has always been specific to France,' Villepin wrote. 'Did the French Revolution ever end? The debate is more relevant than ever . . . . France is quick to flare up because she has not managed, in two centuries, to build a lasting political and social consensus, constantly replaying the confrontations of her past.'

Furet defined the Jacobins (members of the Society of Friends of the Constitution, who multiplied across France in 1789) as 'the civilian army of the Revolution . . . its tribunal, the guardians of orthodoxy that excommunicated and in turn founded the Terror'. Although the word 'Jacobinism' often holds a negative connotation, it has become synonymous with strong central government and national independence, two hallmarks of the modern French state.

French people seem surprised to learn that foreigners regard their revolution as unnecessarily bloody. Although the American Revolution predated theirs by thirteen years, there's a certain pride in the fact that the more violent French experience became the yardstick by which other revolutions were measured. The 1979 Iranian revolution and its subsequent terror were compared many times to the French Revolution.

The revolution imbued France with a certain romanticism about rebellion. Camus wrote lyrically of his love for *l'homme révolté*. Acts that would be considered antisocial in any other society – farmers burning food, lorry drivers blocking highways – were for decades tolerated here on the grounds that everyone has a right to be dissatisfied. Sarkozy has only begun to dent the practice.

Public protest is a ritualised, theatrical tradition in France. Riot police have a legal adviser behind their helmeted ranks, and protesters organise their own *services d'ordre*. I live in a neighbourhood of government ministries, and scarcely a week passes without riot police facing bellowing demonstrators beneath my windows.

I'll never forget the middle-aged, middle class woman lawyer whom I met in a protest march by lycée students about ten years ago. She had no personal interest in the issue, but regarded protest as sport: '*J'adore manifester!*' ('I *love* protesting'), she told me.

Then there was the young man from the immigrant suburbs I met at one of the marches that brought down Villepin's First Job Contract (CPE) in 2005. He was perfectly polite while we chatted, but as the confrontation with the cops heated up, he pulled on his hoodie, said 'Excuse me, but I have to go to work' and bounded off across the Place d'Italie to throw stones at policemen.

Protesters are the modern-day descendants of the *sans-culottes*, the vigilantes who patrolled the streets during the Terror. The aristocrats too have their twenty first century equivalent. In *Farewell to the Queen*, an award-winning novel about the last days of Maire-Antoinette in the Palace of Versailles, Chantal Thomas described how, after the servants had fled, members of the court would stand before a door, waiting in vain for it to open, because they didn't know how to turn a doorknob. I couldn't help thinking of an *énarque* (a graduate of a prestigious *grande école*) and former minister who had boasted to me he did not know how to use a computer or drive a car.

Left-wing twentieth century French historians tended to see the revolution as a proto-communist precursor of modern rebellions. More recently, the interpretation has shifted back to something resembling Alexis de Tocqueville's assessment in *The Ancien Régime and the French Revolution*, which the French nobleman, historian and politician published in 1856.

Tocqueville believed the revolution was more conservative than it appeared and that it was the result of long term trends, not a brief explosion. And although France's revolutionary tradition survived, he noted, it inevitably ended with the rule of a strong man.

France beheaded Louis XVI, then Robespierre, and was then governed by the Emperor Napoleon, the Bourbon restoration, a second republic, a bourgeois monarchy, the third and fourth republics, and finally the monarchial presidents of the fifth republic.

With the possible exception of the third and fourth republics, criticised as weak and unstable, the search for a providential leader – a king by any other name – has survived repeated revolutions; as enduring a legacy as revolt and the simulacra of political violence. The king is dead. Long live the king.

14 July 2009

II
LEBANON
&
ALGERIA

I moved to Lebanon in 1989, as a contract stringer for the Financial Times *and* TIME Magazine. *I began covering Algeria for* TIME *two years later. For much of the 1990s I went back and forth between these two Arab countries, which had both been profoundly marked by France. Their civil wars had different causes, but there were similarities in their turmoil.*

Lebanon

Going West in Beirut

I wrote this article, my first for The Irish Times, *a few days after returning from my maiden voyage to Lebanon, at Christmas 1987.*

The Greek Cypriot official in Larnaca had only to glance at my American passport. 'Go and see him,' he said, referring not to a representative of the Lebanese government but to a Phalange militiaman in civilian clothes.

After numerous questions regarding our religion, destination and contacts in Lebanon, we were allowed to board the *Empress*, sailing to Beirut. Upstairs in the combination bar, lounge and casino, several hundred Lebanese had gathered to begin the overnight journey. Most were Christians, returning to East Beirut for the holidays. Because they feared kidnapping, robbery or murder on the road from the airport through the Hizballah-controlled southern suburbs, they preferred to endure an uncomfortable eleven-hour boat ride across the Mediterranean.

In the lounge, well dressed men and women sat in armchairs around low coffee tables, consuming great quantities of spirits and cigarettes. But the real action was at the roulette and blackjack tables, where even the playing cards and poker chips bore the symbol of the Phalange: a triangle, like a cedar tree, inside a circle.

From time to time, a gambler wandered over to the bar, pulling out wads of hundred dollar bills to pay for a drink. Where did all this money come from? From the sale of weapons?

The barman, a thin, middle-aged individual with a kind face, asked if we would be going to his village in southern Lebanon. The Druze had destroyed most of the houses there, but his was still standing. He had let it to a Muslim woman called Aisha. Could we check up on it for him?

We woke early and went on deck to see the coastline. From this distance, with snow-shrouded Mount Sannine rising behind it, Beirut was as beautiful a city as I had seen. My companion, a long-time European resident of West Beirut, pointed out the Holiday Inn, on the green line, and the building where he lived, just to the right on the horizon. As we approached the port, it became apparent that the high rise hotel was gutted, as were the buildings around it. The glass had been blown out of all the windows and the walls were spotted with shell holes.

A friendly United Nations official was on the quayside. Between the demands of the Amal militia, the presence of a majority of guerillas in the Chatila camp, and general chaos and disorder, he said, it was now nearly impossible to help the twenty thousand Palestinian refugees in Beirut. Were we going to the west? 'It's very bad now,' he said. 'We've had to double our body-guards. Be very careful. You see, the French are buying hostages, and the kid-nappers need replenishment'.

There was no mistaking that this was East Beirut, and Christian territory. Posters of Bachir Gemayel, killed by a bomb in September 1982, were much in evidence. We saw only one likeness of his younger brother, Amin, who never inspired the same degree of Christian adoration as Bachir. Impeccably coif-fured and dressed in a three-piece, European-cut white suit, the full-length fig-ure of Lebanon's president seemed to stride down the central reservation.

That morning's French-language paper, *L'Orient-Le Jour*, carried advertise-ments for readily available French luxury items alongside appeals for news of kidnap victims. The property column offered a 'ruined house' for sale in the mountains.

We finally got through on the telephone to a friend in West Beirut who agreed to pick us up. The 'weather' was fair, he said; it should be safe to come over. The sooner we started, the better. He would meet us at the museum crossing.

A Phalange militiaman in plain clothes offered us a lift there in his shiny black BMW. A photograph of Bachir Gemayel dangled from the rear view mirror, and an effigy of the driver's name-saint was perched on the dashboard. My companion pointed to the razed ground of Tal Zaatar camp, where two thousand Palestinians had been massacred by the Phalange in 1976. Our driver listened stony-faced to the explanation. It was, after all, his people who did the killing.

The boulevard we drove down suddenly ended in a sort of parking lot. We had reached the green line, a strip of destroyed buildings approximately three-quarters of a mile wide by six miles long that effectively divided the city into Christian and Muslim sectors. Two units of the Lebanese Armed Forces – the Muslim 6th Brigade in the west and the Christian 8th Brigade to the east – patrol their respective sides and often confront each other. Add to this the occupying Syrians and Hizballah, who use abandoned buildings for offices or as way stations for hostages, and it is not a place to linger.

The gutted national museum (hence 'museum crossing') stands next to more ancient, Roman ruins. We walked quickly past the first checkpoint and the Barbir Hospital, much shelled by the Israelis during the siege of 1982 but still functioning. The avenue, interrupted by giant earthworks overgrown with plants, was once a principal thoroughfare lined with embassies and government offices. Now many Lebanese commute daily to homes, schools or jobs on the opposite side. They stop at checkpoints and, like us, scurry silently across.

Races are still held every Saturday afternoon at the nearby hippodrome, the only place where Beirut Muslims and Christians still mingle in large numbers. Just past the racetrack, a forlorn sign says: 'Property of the French Embassy, Entry Forbidden'. Although the embassy residence, at the western end of the line, is abandoned, the tricolour still flies above it, a ghost of the mandate authority which created modern Lebanon forty-four years ago.

Over the next two days, in our drives around West Beirut, I would see how the city's iconography alters with its politics. In the mostly Druze area of Ein el Mraisse, the face of the murdered leader, Kamal Jumblatt – looking for all the world like Salvador Dali – stared at us. Since the Syrians returned in February 1987, drawings of a benevolent-looking President Assad have appeared throughout West Beirut. The Druze, Sunnis and Shia all post photographs of their martyrs. Ayatollah Khomeini's face parallels Bachir Gemayel's counte-nance on the other side of the 'line'.

Could this really be the most dangerous city in the world? There were hilly streets and old buildings with brightly painted balconies and shutters, walled gardens, fruit stands, flower shops and chickens stacked in cages on the sidewalks. To a newcomer, East Beirut seemed too French, a kind of cheap imitation of Europe. By contrast, West Beirut had a character all its own.

Here was the Movenpick restaurant, where the first occupying Israeli soldier was killed by the resistance in West Beirut in 1982. The bullet holes are still visible in the shiny, silver wall. No, don't point! my friend said. Don't *ever* point from a car in West Beirut. We turned sharply to avoid a traffic jam. A car coming from the right collided with us. They weren't kidnappers, just careless drivers, but we ignored the damage and drove on quickly.

The presence of Syrian soldiers is considered slightly reassuring: kidnappers are not likely to nab you within shouting distance of them, But several Syrian soldiers have been found shot this past month, and they are keeping a low profile.

West Beirut is a place of both life and abandonment. Along the seafront lies the former British embassy, now a school, and the American university: three of its teachers, including Brian Keenan, from Belfast, have been kidnapped. Here was the spot where they picked up the American journalist Terry Anderson, I was told: a mean pavement beside a mosque. Over the next two days, our drives were punctuated by kidnap sites: innocuous-looking restaurants and street corners.

At the Spaghetteria restaurant, the conversation was enjoyable, the view superb, and the white wine well chilled. But the restaurant held its own reminders of the war: the Mediterranean reflected in a bullet-shattered mirror; shell casings used as candleholders.

The American embassy stood around the corner from the Spaghetteria. 'There were bodies hanging there and there,' my friends said, nodding towards the jagged protrusions of steel and cement that are still suspended over the wreckage. The centre of the embassy collapsed, but the outer parts are standing – inhabited, ironically, by Palestinian refugees.

It is a whole world transformed. The Holiday Inn, the gutted building I had seen from the sea, from the other side, that same morning, is a monolith that marks the green line. For a quarter of an hour we drove very fast, on and on, through the bumpy streets of what manifestly had been a thriving urban centre. There was not a soul to be seen. Most of the abandoned buildings, despite visible damage, retained the colour, shape and details of their original design. Many bore names of familiar banks, or airlines, so that one had an eerie feeling of travelling through a ghost city, or perhaps a testing ground for neutron bombs that left buildings but no people. The destruction was all the sadder, one's sense of waste more overwhelming, because the area provided such a clear image of its former grandeur.

West Beirut is also a place of sudden contrasts. A turn to the right and there were the shop window displays of busy Hamra Street. Every time I stepped out of the car I was conscious of people staring at me and my blue-eyed companion: Americans and Europeans are a rare sight in West Beirut.

At Smith's grocery store in Sadat Street the shelves were well stocked with Danish caviar, French cheese, English biscuits. The problem in Lebanon these days is being able to afford them. At the cash register we put down dozens of Lebanese 250-pound notes, the highest currency denomination but now worth about thirty-five Irish pence. Ten years ago, each was worth fifty Irish pounds. Our plane tickets out of Beirut were to cost hundreds of thousands of Lebanese pounds. For people who still have money – and there are many who do – there is the inconvenience of twelve-hour-a-day electricity cuts; I grew accustomed to seeing generators on balconies. Telephones work only sporadically because the PTT headquarters was devastated in repeated fighting.

For a foreigner, there are other concerns. We watched the cars on the Corniche, not out of idleness but anxiety. They drove slowly back and forth, shark-like, sometimes parking across the street from the flat in which we stayed. The archetypal kidnap car, I was told, was a BMW or Mercedes sedan without numberplates, with smoked glass and a curtain in the rear window.

It was an image we carried with us as we left for the airport. We had taken precautions: only trusted friends knew our travel plans. We did not put our names on our flight reservations and we removed from our belongings anything that might be misunderstood by a Hizballah gunman.

The road to the airport was a series of grim historical reminders. There were the Palestinian squatters at Mar Elias, refugees from refugee camps. Near the sandy, weed-infested roundabout my friends dubbed 'kidnap corner' lay the great crater where fifty-eight French paratroopers died in a suicide bombing on 23 October 1983.

From here the foreigners enter the poor, fervently Islamic and extremely dangerous world of the southern suburbs. Unlike the rest of West Beirut, there is nothing colourful or charming to be found here. The land is flat and sandy. Many of the buildings, like those in the Fakhani district, where Palestinian leaders once lived, were bombed beyond recognition. The Palestinians used the sports stadium next to Fakhani as an arms dump, so the Israelis bombed that as well.

From the roadway it is still possible to see a large dirt pit where the highway turns southeast around Chatila, a mass grave from the 1982 massacre. The camp, up a slow incline to our left, looked empty except for one old man shuffling through the front gate. There are more mass graves inside the camp, among a clump of green trees.

Mohammed, our driver, took a circuitous route through the flooded roads down to the last, most dangerous stretch of highway. We were now in the heart of the southern suburbs, probably just a few blocks away from the basements in which Western hostages are held. We passed the shattered camp of Burj al Barajneh, where Shiite gunmen were searching Palestinian women at the entrance.

There, in front of us, was a monument to the Lebanese guerillas who died fighting the Israeli army in southern Lebanon, and behind it, a huge, larger-than-life wooden effigy of the vanished Imam Musa Sadr. Like the Amin Gemayel I had seen in East Beirut, the imam smiled down at us. Unlike Amin, he wore a turban, beard and flowing robes. He 'disappeared' in Libya in 1978, the hero of every Lebanese Shia Muslim. How much further apart than the few miles separating these two likenesses are the lives of their respective adherents.

There were two more landmarks: the large, ugly, unfinished mosque that is the spiritual home of Hizballah gunmen and suicide bombers, and the flattened ruins of the US Marine headquarters where 241 servicemen died just seconds before their French colleagues in the twin suicide attacks of 23 October 1983. The bomb blast that killed them gouged a twenty-foot crater that is still there.

There were Syrian soldiers at the airport. They opened the boot of our car and searched through our luggage. The damage from the bomb that killed five people at the airport terminal in November was still evident. At least a hundred people queued in the cold outside the building while Syrian soldiers searched for weapons or explosives.

Our jet home was almost thirty years old, with 'NEW' painted on the fuselage in large red letters; it had just been repainted in California. Over half of Middle Eastern Airline's flight crew are Christian. So many were kidnapped or attacked on their way to work at the airport that they are now bussed from East Beirut with armed guards. Knowing this, I asked our flight attendant where he was from. 'From Beirut,' he said. Yes, but which part? 'There is only one Beirut,' he insisted, knowing we knew he was lying.

9 January 1988

A Civilisation in Ruins

The residents of the Christian port town of Byblos have dragged their mattresses up the long stone ramp, across the moat and into the town's twelfth-century Crusader castle to sleep behind its battlements. The walls are up to eighteen feet thick – adequate shelter from even the most deadly 240mm artillery shells.

In an earlier Islamo-Christian conflict, the Lebanese Maronites took the side of the Crusaders against their own Muslim neighbours, even as the Frankish invaders raped, pillaged and murdered their way to Jerusalem. So it seems only fitting that the Christian inhabitants of today's Byblos should again seek refuge in the Crusaders' shadow.

By day, the mattresses lie on the ground inside the roofless castle, their striped cotton covers a thoroughfare for lizards. The keeper of the fortress, with its massive ramparts and arrow slits and adjoining Phoenician, Egyptian and Roman ruins, seventy-three-year-old Artine Chichmanian, is himself something of a monument.

A diminutive, chain-smoking hunchback with one blind eye – an Armenian survivor of the Turkish massacres – he refuses to leave the site of his life's work. He spouts French poetry as he scurries through waist-high weeds, down into the tunnels of a necropolis where Phoenician royalty were buried. 'This is the tomb of Prince Abi Shemu. He lived almost two thousand years before Christ,' Chichmanian says. 'I was with Pierre Montet when it was uncovered in 1932. I told him to dig here.'

The grounds are an overgrown bric-à-brac of abandoned archaeological excavations, foundations of ancient cities built one on top of another, pagan temples, obelisks and colonnades, tombs, and a small, exquisite Roman amphitheatre perched on the promontory above the Mediterranean. To the outside world, Lebanon has become synonymous with misery and devastation.

But the country is still capable of ambushing you with its beauty. The Lebanese Tourist Board has stopped paying Chichmanian's pension, and few visitors come to witness the present, sad interlude in the history of what many archaeologists believe to be the world's oldest city, more than seven thousand years continuously inhabited. Shells are bursting in the sea a couple of miles down the coast. With their artillery, the Syrians are still trying to blockade the Christian ports, but old Chichmanian ignores the explosions, which have become routine.

He is eager to prolong our conversation. He extracts photographs of his four sons from a shirt pocket. 'I was only a child when I left Turkey, during the Armenian massacres. But I love this country and I have become a true Lebanese. That is why I did not want my sons to carry guns, to help destroy it. I sent them away, to live in Europe.'

Twenty miles south of Byblos, Lieutenant Elias Achou presides over more recent ruins. He is one of those young men, a gunman, whose occupation Chichmanian so deplores. The twenty-five-year-old Phalangist lacks the old man's pedantic flair, but he takes his job as seriously.

The Christian Phalangist militia holds most of the hundreds of miles of front line encircling the Christian enclave which is under Syrian siege. Lieutenant Achou commands the unit billeted in the empty buildings around Martyrs' Square, in what was, before the civil war started fourteen years ago, the very centre of Beirut. A bullet-shattered bronze Statue of Liberty, a woman holding a torch leading the Lebanese people to independence, still stands there. Martyrs' Square is now at the heart of Beirut's mile-wide dividing 'green line'.

Achou leads me through passageways that have been smashed through the walls of buildings along the west side of the square. Sniper fire patters a few blocks away, a mere irritation after the deafening, cataclysmic blast of artillery shelling we have experienced in previous weeks.

'Keep your head low, stay close to the wall,' Achou cautions, as we emerge into the open and cross clanging metal planks next to red earth embankments. The scrap metal has been laid on the ground to warn us of surprise attackers.

We climb crumbling stairwells in the half-light, to a third floor that is sandbagged on the west side, open onto the expanse of the square on the east. A foolhardy militiaman has ventured out into the open to plant a Phalangist – not a Lebanese – flag in front of the statue to Lebanese liberty.

It is almost as if Trafalgar Square in London had been emptied of buses, cars and pedestrians, the roads torn up and trenches dug there.

Wind whistles through the skeletons of buildings, some with signs that still proclaim their former purpose: Rivoli Cinema, Khoury Taxis, Najjar Emporium. Trees and grass have broken through those paving stones left undisturbed by the fighting. The place smells faintly of sewage.

On the third floor, from which I survey the square, there is a row of gymnasium-style lockers and rusting metal camp beds lined up as if in a dormitory. M-16 rifles hang by their shoulder straps from the hooks in the lockers. Only a few of the beds have sheets or mosquito netting. A militiaman sleeps on a bed with flies swarming over him. One of his comrades sits on a mattress nearby, reading through a pile of Phalange party magazines. Near the open façade, several militiamen have gathered around a game of tric-trac – backgammon – played on an inlaid Damascene folding box. These people understand the monotony of war.

Back down the stairs, through another passage, five Phalangists wait as a sixth stirs a pot of Turkish coffee next to two Russian heavy machine guns on tractors. Ten feet away, the militiamen have erected a shrine holding candles, statues of Maronite saints and the Virgin Mary.

We have reached the farthest Christian-held point of the green line. Up more dark, disintegrating stairs there is a sort of shooting gallery, its floor carpeted in spent bullet cartridges. The wedge-shaped gun slits in the wall are just like those the Crusaders used to fire arrows from the castle at Byblos.

Christian politicians insist that this war is between Lebanese and foreigners, not between Christians and Muslims. But is that really true? Achou points at the nearest building, scarcely fifteen yards away. 'They are there,' he whispers, although this seems to be more for dramatic effect than out of fear. Who are 'they' – The Druze, the Amal, the Syrians? He waves his arm in an all-encompassing gesture and then states with more finality: 'The Muslims.'

Moving in a semicircle six feet back from a gun slit, Achou gives a tour guide's description of the landmarks we can glimpse on the other side of the invisible line. 'There on the left is our parliament building, on the Place de l'Étoile. And that is the Great Mosque, towards the sea. The building with the arches was city hall.'

These structures have a grace never equalled by Beirut's property developers, who continue, despite the war, to put up ugly, modern concrete and glass high rises on both sides of the green line. The thirteenth century mosque and the Ottoman Seraglio, like all the buildings on the green line, are worm-eaten by bullets. But here, in the Byzantine domes of the mosque and the harmony of blue sky, peach-coloured stone and the brilliant green foliage that has overgrown the streets, Beirut's beauty is shocking.

What does Achou want to do when the war is over? He stops and turns around to consider the source of the question, as if he had never before given it thought. His intelligent brown eyes are blank, confused. 'I was nine years old when the war started,' Achou finally says. 'I don't know what I will do.'

His enemies are so close, does he ever want to talk to them? 'We shout at one another. "You son of a bitch, your mother is a whore." Things like that. It always makes them start shooting.'

It is a game, here on the front line. The last casualty in Achou's unit was killed almost one year ago, while more than 350 civilians have died in the inhabited areas on either side of this no man's land since March. Because artillery has a longer range, because there is too great a risk of shelling your own men if you aim for forward positions, because bombarding civilians is a more effective way to draw attention to grievances and terrorise the population, the war goes on literally over the heads of the men who are meant to be fighting.

In Lebanon, the front line is one of the safer places to be.

Financial Times, *24 June 1989*

'Normal Life' in Beirut

Nineteen-year-old Private Yahia Saloum sat on the bottom step of our apartment building's stairs, dazed and frightened, and stared out into the street where the shells were falling.

Blood was beginning to seep through the gauze wrapped around his chest, and he kept looking down to measure its progress. Just a few millimetres to the side, and the shell fragment might have hit his heart.

When the Syrian artillery battery down the road began firing on ships breaking the Syrian blockade of Christian ports around 10.30 PM, Saloum and his friends in the Syrian army were unprepared for the retaliation that followed.

Nor had they expected to be targeted. Since the almost-daily artillery battles started in March, Christian gunners across the bay in East Beirut had aimed at the Syrian howitzers positioned 500 yards from the soldiers' barracks.

Saloum and his colleagues did not think the Christians would ever concentrate so much firepower on their barracks, located in the ruins of the unfinished Sheraton Hotel on West Beirut's seafront.

The Sheraton is only a few hundred yards from our apartment building. Minutes before the explosions started, we realised that this was more than the nightly ritual exchange of shellfire.

As the bombardment crept closer and closer, we deserted our apartment and ran two floors downstairs to where the landlord, his sister and her two daughters crouched on cushions against the thickest wall of the building.

Amid the continuing explosions, we barely heard the Syrian soldiers rattling the wrought iron gate to the apartment building. They were even more frightened than we were. The Syrian battery near the barracks had been hit, one said. In the faint light of the candle melting onto the marble floor, it was a few minutes before we saw the bandages under Saloum's shirt.

There was a barrage of what sounded like hundreds of machine guns firing. We thought for a moment that General Michel Aoun's Christian Lebanese army might be landing on the beach, and that the Syrian soldiers billeted in the ruined hotel were fighting a landing party. But there was a simpler explanation. The Christians had hit an ammunition truck at the barracks. The rumble of exploding shells and bullets went on for five minutes.

One of the soldiers chain-smoked as he tried to justify their predicament. 'We are strong,' he said. 'We could overthrow Aoun in twenty-four hours, if they would let us go into East Beirut. But they won't let us.'

He picked up his gun, asked us to take care of his wounded friend and left with the other soldier. When they came back a few hours later, the landlord insisted that they take Saloum to the hospital.

As they left, the shells were bursting just outside the house. One exploded in the field across the street. From the balcony we could see the front of the barracks burning bright orange against the palm trees. The full moon lit up the smoke. The bombardments continued until 4 AM.

At daybreak, eight trucks hit by the Christian artillery still smouldered near the blackened façade of the old Sheraton. There was a new crater in the road, fifteen feet from our building. Tiles had fallen off the wall in our kitchen.

Ten people were killed and sixty-one wounded in the overnight bombardments, which spread to all areas of the ciy. The casualty figures did not include Saloum, for the Syrian army never reveals the numbers of its wounded or dead.

Despite the daily bombardments, anything is possible in Beirut after fourteen years of civil war and invasions. Middle class Lebanese women still look forward to weekly visits from their 'beauty technicians', who for 1,000 Lebanese pounds (€1.50) make house calls to give manicures, pedicures and facials. For a few dollars more, professional plant watchers care for the indoor gardens that flourish in Lebanon's semi-tropical climate.

If the ladies tire of their wardrobes, the boutiques in West Beirut's Verdun district still sell Saint Laurent, Dior, Fendi and Ungaro designer fashions.

When shipments of new swimsuits were held up by Syria's blockade of Lebanon's Christian enclave, many Muslim women who spend their days around the pools at the Gulf Club and the Summerland and Coral Beach hotels in West Beirut refused to appear in public in last year's designs.

Now they order their swimsuits from catalogues, and each time the shellfire stops and Beirut's dividing green line is opened, the swimsuit couriers take their merchandise from east to west, along with sellers of bread, vegetables and five-gallon gasoline cans.

But window shopping in Beirut is not what it used to be. Storefronts are sandbagged, and people feel vulnerable on open sidewalks that are exposed to the artillery fire. Last week, four pedestrians were killed when a shell coming from the Christian sector of the city hit Hamra Street, West Beirut's main shopping district, at 9.30 AM.

When I told a Lebanese friend that I wanted a kitten, she drove me to a pet store just a few hundred yards from the Syrian artillery batteries on the tip of West Beirut's peninsula. There were canaries, parakeets and cockatoos.

In a cramped cage at the back of the shop, an immaculate white Persian stared out with eyes, one topaz-orange, the other sapphire-blue, that begged for liberation. The Persian cost $200, so the thousands of alley cats that live in West Beirut's piles of uncollected garbage seemed better candidates for adoption.

In only two weeks, my friend and I were able to rent an apartment on the seafront and furnish it with a refrigerator, washing machine, radio-cassette player and colour television. The Hitachi store delivered our appliances the day after the purchase – not bad, even by American standards.

But if anything is possible here, appearances are also deceiving. The batteries for the radio-cassette deck expired after one day. A Lebanese-made pirated recording of the Berlin Philharmonic playing Beethoven symphonies turned out to contain only pop music after the first movement.

'Don't worry,' Mustafa, our landlord, told us. 'When there is city power, you can run the washer and the water heater.'

Beirut's power plants often run out of fuel oil with which to generate electricity, so we do not know yet if the washing machine functions. Mustafa temporarily dissuaded us from buying an expensive, noisy generator for $2,000, promising that his stolen power line would run the refrigerator.

Overconfident, we stocked the refrigerator with wine and soft drinks in preparation for a combination house-warming and birthday party. The red alarm light on the refrigerator flickered next to the green 'functional' indicator. The drinks stayed warm, and an electrician warned us that Mustafa's magic wire would burn out the brand new Italian refrigerator motor.

Since our seafront neighbourhood of Ein Mreisseh often vibrates to the sound of explosions, several people declined our party invitation. 'How can you have a party in these conditions?' a friend's mother asked, scandalised.

But for thirty or so brave souls who ventured out for our luncheon,

Goodies Delicatessen delivered pasta and fruit salads, and a delicious chocolate fudge cake. Juan Carlos Gumucio, the only Bolivian correspondent in the city, made home-made *ceviche*. White-haired Farouk Nassar, the dean of the Lebanese Press Corps, smoked cigars on the balcony and let it be known he was hungry.

After our guests departed, we were about to start eating the leftovers when the shelling started again. We dragged the mattress into the corridor, where two walls protect us from the incoming shells. We sat down to enjoy our wine and *ceviche* by candlelight as the floor shook and two more window-panes shattered.

San Francisco Chronicle, *5 August 1989*

Juan-Carlos Gumucio committed suicide in February 2002, at the age of 52. Farouk Nassar died of natural causes in December 2005, age 79.

Poems for Lara:
One of Beirut's Innocents

At eight o'clock on the morning of 8 November 1989, Ghassan Matar drove his daughter, Lara, his only child, to school.

'I noticed that she was wearing make-up and I asked her why,' Ghassan says. 'She said: "Daddy, have you forgotten that today is my seventeenth birthday?"'

Just seven hours later, Ghassan was woken from his afternoon sleep by the blast which, unknown to him, killed Lara, just two blocks away from the family's apartment in West Beirut. Her birthday cake was still in the cardboard box from the pastry shop and the groceries had been bought for that evening's celebration.

Ghassan turned on the radio to learn about the explosion that had shaken the walls of his apartment building. Could his daughter have been hurt? He was reassured by a note he found next to the telephone; the last words his daughter wrote. 'Daddy,' it said, 'I have gone to the club to play squash.'

Ghassan remembers the next hours with painful clarity. 'At four o'clock, a friend of ours telephoned. She asked me: "Where is your daughter?" When I said she was playing squash at the sports club, the woman demanded: "Are you sure? Try to be certain." I called my wife at work and we drove to the club, but she wasn't there. Someone said Lara's best friends, the Itani children, had been wounded. We went to the hospital emergency room. When we walked in, her friends threw their arms around us. That was when I knew what had happened.'

Ghassan and Maggie Matar, now aged forty-eight and forty, say neither time nor sympathy has done anything to diminish their grief for their daughter.

Since Lara's death, Maggie has given up her job as a fashion designer and spends her days at home, dressed in black, surrounded by photographs of Lara and by her daughter's piano, books and clothing. Ghassan continues to work as the deputy editor of a weekly news magazine, but without his former enthusiasm.

'When Lara was killed there was a voice inside me which told me: "It's over. Life isn't worth living",' Ghassan says. 'Another voice said: "You can do something for her." I felt my only salvation was to write to Lara. I made a promise to write to Lara each day, to publish my poems when there were enough for a book, and to live to keep this promise. It is the only way to give her a kind of immortality; to make her unique among the 150,000 people who have died in this war.'

Ghassan Matar's first collection of poems to his dead daughter was published in Arabic last month. It has been widely acclaimed by Lebanese and Syrian literary critics. It is a popular little book because it is about the tragedy of Lebanon's children: not just their loss of life – an estimated forty thousand children have been killed in the war, according to the United Nations – but their loss of innocence.

Lara Matar could scarcely have remembered her two and a half peaceful years before Lebanon's civil war started in 1975. Like her, nearly a million children in Lebanon have now experienced a childhood marred by shelling, car bombs, assassinations, gun battles and the desperate anxiety of their parents. They have spent hundreds of hours sheltering in basements and stairwells. They have witnessed relatives and friends die or flee the country and have frequently been forced to move to safer locations.

'I ought to have enjoyed my youth and adolescence,' says twenty-five-year-old Amal Mesh, who was ten when the war started. 'But it was occupied by the war.'

A Muslim, Amal Mesh had to flee with her family from the Christian quarter of Ashrafieh. In 1982 she spent the three months of the Israeli siege of West Beirut in an underground shelter. Her worst memory is of seeing three small children and their mother killed by a shell in her street during the 1986 militia war.

'The mother was holding one of the children,' she says. 'The father had two legs amputated. I see him every day, sitting on a wheelchair and selling vegetables. These experiences are in me. I can never wipe them out – the experience of cheap death.'

The war has endowed Lebanese children with early maturity. Maya Dagher is only nine years old. 'Why are [the Christians in East Beirut] shelling each other every day?' she asks. 'When nothing is left there, they'll ask for a lot of money for reconstruction. It's not logical.'

On 29 June, Maya and her two sisters were woken at 5.45 in the morning by the sound of a car bomb which wounded six people. 'Our parents were still sleeping,' Maya says. 'But I couldn't go back to sleep. I wonder why they continue this war. We children never knew the pretty time before. I wish I could have lived in those days, when there weren't any checkpoints. I have food and clothes and friends; I don't need anything, except not to be afraid.'

Randa Khoury, a professor of child development at Beirut University College (BUC), has three children born in the war and she has observed Lebanese children at the college's nursery school. 'We cheat in a sense, by trying to create a normal situation where there is no normality,' she says. 'My oldest child vomits when she sees destroyed buildings, and my youngest will not be separated from her father and me for even a few hours.'

At the BUC nursery school, children are terrified by loud noises or bright lights. Most of the children bite their nails, suck their thumbs or stutter.

Perhaps more damaging is the apprenticeship of violence. 'These children learn from what they have seen on the streets or from their parents,' Khoury says. 'There are no government schools any more and at least half the children in Beirut get no education. They become juvenile delinquents before they reach adolescence. I think a lot of them will become militiamen or prostitutes.'

Yet the pages of Lara Matar's photo albums show a life apparently untouched by the war until the moment of her death.

There are no pictures of tanks or guns. But there are snapshots of birthday parties, a holiday in Egypt, Lara as a chubby adolescent, Lara with braces on her teeth. Then there is the child, almost a woman, who played Chopin on the piano, read French and English novels and classical Arabic poetry.

'She wanted to do everything at once – ballet, sports, horse-riding,' her father says. 'It was as if she had a premonition that she would not be able to do anything.'

The car bomb that killed Lara Matar and three other people exploded at the moment the plane of the Lebanese president, René Moawad, touched down at Beirut Airport. No one was ever sure if it was meant as a warning to the newly elected leader, or if it had been intended to kill him on his route from the airport. Nine days later, President Moawad and twenty-three others were killed by a more powerful explosion.

Ghassan Matar holds no one, only the war, responsible for Lara's death. But his refusal to apportion blame does not lessen his bitterness and sense of loss. 'It is the innocents who die here,' he says. 'The death of an adult is bearable. But I am overwhelmed by the death of children.'

Financial Times, *21 July 1990*

The Qana Massacre

The Lebanese village of Qana is supposed to be the place where Christ changed water into wine. Since 18 April 1996, however, Qana has been remembered not only for a miracle, but for a massacre. I was travelling in the area with a convoy from the Irish battalion of UNIFIL when Israeli artillery opened fire on a compound where hundreds of Lebanese were known to be sheltering. This was my eyewitness report.

At 2.10 PM we had just left the village of Hinniyeh when we heard what sounded like outgoing Katyusha rockets from the wadi beyond the next ridge. Minutes later we heard incoming artillery. As we continued down the road, a plea for help came over the military radio network from Qana, where the UN's Fijian Battalion has its headquarters. 'This is Fiji Batt,' the radio crackled. 'We have taken six rounds.' The soldier was asking UN commanders to make the Israelis stop shelling.

Minutes passed, during which the air pressure fluctuated each time another shell exploded. Then the voice returned. 'They have hit Fiji Batt headquarters . . . the rounds are coming in here now . . . we have been fired upon. We *are being* fired upon . . . we have casualties . . . one of our main buildings in Fiji Batt has been demolished.' That was followed by a long silence as more minutes ticked by. Finally, the voice of a Lebanese army liaison officer came clearly over the radio: 'The people are dying here!' he shouted. 'We hear the voice of death. Do you understand?'

We soon did, all too well. As dozens of ambulances raced past us back toward Tyre, we reached Fiji Batt's compound and saw bodies of Lebanese refugees lying in heaps two or three deep, burned hands and feet protruding from under blankets that dazed UN soldiers had tossed over them. Soldiers sprayed water on the smoking ruins of a conference hall where corpses were indistinguishable among the charcoal and ashes. In what was left of the officers' mess only the lower walls and part of the roof had survived. Most of the men, women and children who had been huddled in this room did not. Their blood was everywhere. It splattered the edges of the ceiling. It dripped down the steps, gathering in puddles. It coated the boots of the peacekeepers who were attempting to sort through bodies in the hope that someone might still be alive. 'Look at my shoes!' exclaimed a horrified Lebanese UNIFIL official who was sobbing on the shoulder of a Swedish colleague. 'I am standing in meat.'

It was impossible to tell how many had died, though they were thought to number at least a hundred. Wearing rubber gloves, Fijian soldiers methodically scooped up body parts in large piles. Meanwhile, UN soldiers paced the parking lot collecting scraps of flesh in black plastic trash bags. In disbelief, one stunned peacekeeper hoisted the body of an infant; the child's head had been blown off. Nearby, a Lebanese woman embraced an old man whose shoulder had been almost completely torn from his lifeless body. 'My father, my father!' she wailed. At the top of his lungs, a Lebanese man cursed America for giving Israel the money and weapons to attack his country. And along the white tiles of the walkway where rescue workers were carrying out the bodies, there was a trail of scarlet footprints. A new memorial for Qana – no longer inscribed with water and wine but stained instead with blood.

TIME Magazine, *29 April 1996*

Algeria

Dying to Go to School

At 8.15 AM, six men holding hatchets, sawn-off shotguns and knives burst into the classroom at Oued Djer, a small village fifty kilometres south west of Algiers. They seized fourteen-year-old Fatima Ghodbane and tore from her head the Islamic scarf she had only recently started wearing. As Fatima's classmates watched, the men dragged her outside and bound her hands with wire. One of the guerillas pulled her head back by the hair and stabbed her several times in the face. Then he slit her throat.

'This is what happens to girls who go to university,' the murderer then told Fatima's classmates and teachers, shaking the knife, which was still covered with Fatima's blood. 'This is what happens to girls who talk to policemen. This is what happens to girls who don't wear the *hidjab* [Islamic covering].'

Before dumping Fatima's body in front of the school gates, the killers carved the symbol of the Armed Islamic Group (GIA) on her hand. Fatima's death, in March 1995, is not an isolated case. According to the last recorded government figures, 101 teachers and 41 students of both sexes were killed in 1994 by Islamic extremists who attack schools because they are a symbol of the government.

No one is sure why the GIA, which was formed in 1993, singled out Fatima Ghodbane for this butchery. Until her death, she and her eight brothers and sisters had lived peacefully with their widowed father, a retired builder. 'No one ever threatened us – neither me nor my children,' Fatima's grieving father later told journalists.

So why was Fatima murdered? 'She was very beautiful,' says Mouloud Benmohamed, a reporter on *El Moudjahid*, the Algerian government newspaper. 'Her friends believe she may have refused to have a "pleasure marriage" with the leader of the group, the *Emir*.'

The GIA apparently believes that the 'holy warriors' of Islam have a right to claim sexual pleasure before they sacrifice their own lives in the name of Allah. The 'pleasure marriage' is, in effect, a licence to rape.

Since the civil war between Islamic fundamentalists and the military-backed regime broke out four and a half years ago, more than fifty thousand Algerians have been killed. Of this figure, some five hundred women – 1 percent of the total war casualties – have been murdered by rebels. But feminist groups and the government have given wide publicity to the kidnappings, assassinations and rapes that have taken place. A television series made by *El Moudjahid*'s Mouloud Benmohamed this spring attained the highest ratings of any Algerian-made programme. Viewers were shown the corpses of mutilated and decapitated women, and heard lurid accounts from several young women who had escaped captivity.

Nawel, a twenty-eight-year-old divorcée, admits to being 'completely hooked' on the macabre documentaries. 'One girl told how she and her mother had been kidnapped and taken to the mountains by her own brother,' she relates. 'He married them off to his friends in the GIA. The girl managed to get away, but the mother didn't. It scared me, but I watched the next Friday night because I wanted to know how these women were kidnapped, how they'd escaped . . . I don't want it to happen to me.'

Common criminals have been quick to take advantage of the anarchy to rape and pillage. No one can ever be sure whether envy, a recent snub or an old property dispute lies behind the killings. 'We've got to the point where people are assassinated for the sake of assassination, because they're easy victims,' says Zohra Flici, president of the government-backed Association of Families Victimised by Terrorism, whose own husband, a doctor, was murdered in 1993. 'Some women are killed because they are related to members of the security forces, some because they refuse pleasure marriages, and some because they are journalists, teachers or students.'

The sad distinction of being the first woman 'martyr' of Algeria's terrible war fell to twenty-year-old Karima Belhadj. Unknown outside her native country, her pretty face and long hair are now a familiar image throughout Algeria, printed as they are on posters which are carried in protest marches against the war.

Until her death in 1993, Karima lived in Les Eucalyptus, a dusty, sinister slum on the eastern outskirts of Algiers. As a secretary at the Police Welfare and

Sports Association, she was among the 8 percent of Algerian women to hold a paid job. With a salary of €150 a month, she supported her parents, three brothers and two sisters.

Karima wanted to continue her studies, but was forced to find a job when her father lost his with a water-bottling company and her brothers were unable to find work. She fell in love with the bus driver who used to take her to college, and they were engaged. Every night when she came home from work, she would embroider clothes for her wedding trousseau. 'She loved life,' says Karima's mother, Hassina. 'She liked to sew and cook. She liked hairdressing for her friends and her sisters. We told each other everything. She was my best friend.'

On 6 April 1993, Hassina was making preparations for Karima's wedding when she heard shots. Her son, Rida, ran out into the street. 'Karima was lying on the ground,' he explains. 'Her eyes were open and there was a big hole between them, and blood flowing out of her head. I see that image of her all the time, and I ask myself 'Why? Why? Why?' For just €12, the boy across the street had pointed Karima out to the gunmen as she got off the evening bus.

A Koran lies under the TV set in her family's home, and a picture of Mecca hangs on the wall above the sofa. But the Belhadj family's version of Islam is unacceptable to fundamentalists, who want the Koran to rule every aspect of life. 'For them, it's inconceivable that a girl goes to college or works,' says journalist Mouloud Benmohamed. 'They started attacking women because they're a symbol. Women are the backbone of the family in Algeria; if you terrorise women, you terrorise the whole society.'

The seeds of Islamist oppression of women were sown by Algeria's post-independence rulers. Women fought alongside men in the 1954–62 war of liberation against France. But during three decades of eastern bloc-style socialist government, they were given only a few token cabinet positions. Algeria's 1984 Family Code is considered one of the most backward in the Arab world, for it makes women lifelong wards of their fathers, brothers, and husbands.

Fundamentalist scorn for women's rights is bound up with their hatred of the West, but it is also rooted in an Algerian tradition of misogyny. 'No society that entrusts its affairs to a woman ever knows prosperity' is a common adage in Algeria. When Sheikh Ali Belhadj, an imprisoned Islamic leader, said he would abolish unemployment by forcing women to stay at home, he was applauded. Yet the Algerian government itself is accused of abusing women in this war. Torture is routine in Algerian prisons.

A young man, who gives his name only as Mohamed, was accused of making inflammatory sermons against the government. The nineteen-year-old, bearing visible marks of torture on his legs a few days after his release from Algiers' Serkadji Prison, provided shocking evidence of what can happen to a woman in police custody. Under interrogation at the Chateauneuf police station, he caught sight of the mother of a man he knew. 'They tortured and raped her in front of her son,' says Mohamed. 'I saw her when she came out. She was naked and covered in blood. We heard other women screaming, but we didn't know where they were.'

Only days before they murdered fourteen-year-old Fatima Ghodbane, the GIA threatened to kill the wives of policemen, gendarmes and soldiers unless the government agreed to free all the Islamist women it held. Both the government and exiled Algerian fundamentalists have included women victims in the horrific photograph albums they publish of each other's atrocities.

Little wonder then that Algerian women are increasingly resentful of men. 'The girls end up hating anything that has to do with men or religion,' says fifty-five-year-old Ourida, an Algerian schoolmistress. Divorcée Nawel is more blunt. 'I wept for joy when my daughter was born,' she said. 'If it had been a boy, I'd have thrown him away because he would have grown up to be like all Algerian men.'

Women have most to lose from the GIA's campaign against education. Although Algerian schools are mixed, the GIA has insisted that girls and boys be separated, and that music and gym classes for girls be shut down. In the countryside, where government control is tenuous, most schools have dropped French classes and sports for girls, in an attempt to placate the militants.

Schoolmistress Ourida works in one of the more prosperous quarters of Algiers, but fundamentalists who pray at the mosque across the street keep a close eye on her school. 'It's a sneaky, subtle pressure,' she says. 'We find tracts glued to the walls. Since 1993 we've stopped singing, dancing and sports. We still raise the flag at the beginning of the week, but I tell the children to sing the national anthem very softly.'

Ourida has sent her own two adult children abroad. She no longer travels within Algeria, and car bombs have made her afraid to go shopping. 'Algeria is one big prison,' she says. Even teaching, her lifelong passion, gives her little satisfaction.

'Children aren't the same any more. They're sad. I think often of Fatima, whose throat was slashed in front of her school last year. I think of the car bomb off the Place du Premier Mai; they set it off just as the kids were coming out of school. After the explosion, they found little hands stuck on the walls, heads without bodies. I think of the girls who have been raped: some of them have committed suicide. These are the things that have marked us. We all feel raped in our souls, if not in our bodies.'

28 June 1997

Massacre at Bentalha

The villa on the dusty, empty street is one of many houses of horror in the ghost town of Bentalha. Some member of the urban working class, perhaps a taxi driver or a factory worker, put his life's savings into this unfinished house with its kitsch Moorish arcade on the roof terrace, where a dried-up river of blood clogs the drainage pipe.

The owners probably abandoned this villa years ago, when the eastern sub-urbs of Algiers became a rear base for Islamist guerrillas. Refugees from worse areas moved into abandoned homes, and on the terrible night of 22 September, the residents of Bentalha sought safety in the houses with armoured doors and walled gardens.

Now the wooden shutters hang charred on their hinges, and black soot climbs the walls like silent screams. The steel gate is twisted and gaping where it was blown open by the killers who invaded Bentalha. The front door stands ajar, and wine-coloured stains flown down the stairs. 'More than forty people had their throats slashed here,' says the gendarme who follows me as I try not to step in the blood. Mattresses lie like burned logs amid the pools of black-ened, coagulated liquid.

Elsewhere it is redder, swirled and smeared, where the bodies were dragged out. Ordinary objects are scattered over this scene of carnage: women's hair curlers, plastic slippers, a Dali-esque melted clock. On the top floor, in the laundry room, blood is splattered over the wall.

In a nearby unfinished house made of red brick and cinder blocks, Boubker Hansali, an unemployed mason, drags his limp leg up the steel ladder to the neighbouring rooftop where he cowered with his wife and two children through the night of 22 September, listening to the screams of his dying neigh-bours, watching their slaughter by the flames of burning houses. 'Thirty-six people died in that house,' he says, pointing to a grey façade across the square.

'I saw one of my daughter's girlfriends, a girl of twelve, thrown from that balcony, there on the third floor.'

Hansali starts crying. He is one of the few survivors to have stayed in Bentalha, because he has nowhere to go. 'A psychiatrist came here once, for two minutes,' he says. 'No one from the government has helped us.'

Beyond Hansali's street lies the front line: miles of fields and forests leading up to the Atlas Mountains. The army has cut down all the nearby trees and burned them to deprive the guerrillas of cover. Army helicopters hover like gnats above Ouled Allel, to the southeast, and we hear the explosions of the rockets they fire.

'The people who massacred are being massacred too, by the state,' Hansali says. After the disgrace of recent atrocities, the army initiated what it bills as a major offensive against the Armed Islamic Group (GIA), which it blames for the killings. Three days ago, another operation was started in the forests of Bainem, west of Algiers.

One month has passed since nearly three hundred people were slaughtered in Bentalha. The basic facts of the massacre – who committed it, and why – are still disputed. Most of the killers wore Islamic Afghan costumes. But some wore army uniforms. And why did the Algerian army, which has several positions nearby, ignore pleas for help? It seems that guerrillas who earlier enjoyed support here turned on those who no longer wanted to help them. 'They fed the terrorists,' a policeman posted in Bentalha said. 'So why should we save them?'

In a recent televised confession, a woman named Zohra Quid Hamrane claimed she was forced to accompany the killers to steal the jewels of the women they massacred at Bentalha. Another woman, Nacera Zouabri, the sister of the GIA leader, Antar Zouabri, has also been captured. She allegedly made bets with male killers on the sex of unborn infants, then slit the bellies of their mothers. The Algerian public became so obsessed with the story of Nacera Zouabri that a general warned them not to 'turn a cockroach into the Algerian Diana'.

Rais, a few miles from Bentalha, holds the grim record for the biggest massacre of the war. A security source says 390 people were killed here on 29 August. At the community school, surrounded by gutted cars and houses, I met Omar, a teacher who is the sole survivor of his family. His father, mother and nine brothers and sisters all died with their throats slashed, and his three nieces were kidnapped by the guerrillas. He trembles and his voice quavers. 'I want an international commission to investigate the massacres,' he says. 'Why

113

didn't the army intervene? Why didn't they come out of their barracks?'

The Sidi Rezzine cemetery, where the victims of Bentalha and Rais were buried, lies next to the busy national highway into Algiers. The high buildings of the capital can be clearly seen in the distance. More than five hundred mounds of red earth are lined up in rows, with bricks to mark the heads and feet of the dead. Their names and ages have been hastily painted on plywood markers: Mehri Samagh, 8, Hossein Mejrab, 7, Walid Ghala, 4, Sihab Frahi, 3, and Hayat Kalam, 7. The majority of the dead are women and children. Why, I ask the gendarmes who escort us. 'Because the men ran away,' they answer.

21 October 1997

Killed for a Column

Two years before he was murdered, Saïd Mekbel told his eldest son, Hafid: 'If anything happens to me, promise me you'll drink a beer in my honour.' It was 1992 and the civil war was only starting, but Algeria's most famous newspaper editor and columnist had a premonition. 'He received so many death threats that we kept them in a folder at home and laughed about them,' Hafid, now aged thirty-three, recalls in the small, three-room apartment he shares with his French mother, Marie-Laure.

Hafid Mekbel fled Algiers in 1993, after witnessing the killing of a policeman by other policemen. 'My father said I should go, that the war was his generation's problem, that it was created by those who gained independence from France in 1962, and that my generation shouldn't be involved.' For three decades, the Mekbels and their two sons had formed an inseparable foursome, but the war began to chip away at their close-knit family.

Like the *pieds-noirs* of colonial days, the Mekbels were forced to choose between '*la valise ou le cercueil*' – the suitcase or the coffin. Following Hafid, Marie-Laure returned to France in January 1994. She is fifty-five years old now, and works as a secretary in a law firm. Saïd Mekbel knew he would be killed if he stayed. He survived two assassination attempts, but still refused to abandon his country.

On Saturday 3 December 1994, Hafid Mekbel slept late. The telephone call from a family friend woke him. Only later would the family learn the details. Saïd Mekbel was eating lunch with a colleague in the Marhaba pizzeria, less than forty metres from his newspaper, *Le Matin*. 'He was careful, he never sat with his back to the door,' Hafid says. But the well dressed young assassin was a regular customer of the restaurant. No one tried to stop him as he approached Mekbel, took out a pistol and shot him twice in the head.

Mekbel's staff raced across the street from the newspaper office. One of them described what he saw: 'In the back of the restaurant, sitting behind the table, still holding a knife and fork in his hands, his head leaning slightly forward, as if he were looking at the food on his plate, Saïd was still breathing. I told him, "Saïd, hold on. We're taking you to the hospital." I reached out to caress his hair but pulled my hand back, covered with blood.'

In their Paris suburb, Marie-Laure and Hafid Mekbel were not surprised by the news. 'We had been expecting it. Even so, I didn't really believe he was dead until I saw his picture on the television.' Hafid's eyes fill with tears. 'I went to the café at the Liberté métro station and drank a beer, as I had promised.'

His father had founded a football team at Sonelgaz, the state-owned gas company where he also worked as a mechanical engineer. Every weekend, Saïd Mekbel was the team's goalkeeper.

'I had a football game scheduled [in Paris] that afternoon. So I drank my beer alone, then went to the match, and I played well and we won.' That was Hafid's tribute to his father.

Saïd Mekbel's newspaper column was called 'Mesmar J'ha' – 'J'ha's Nail', after a North African folklore figure named J'ha, who sold a house but insisted on keeping one nail stuck over the front door. Mekbel used the same title for more than five hundred articles written between 1963 and 1965 and between 1989 and 1994. During his twenty-four-year silence – his protest against the military dictatorship that took root in Algeria – Mekbel turned to photography, earned a doctorate in mechanical engineering and worked for Sonelgaz.

With caustic humour, and in the perfect French that Mekbel had learned at French military schools, the last five years of 'Mesmar J'ha' savaged the Algerian regime and fundamentalist rebels alike.

The column made the newspaper he worked for, *Le Matin*, the best-selling daily in Algiers; it has lost more than half its circulation since he was killed. Both sides in the war had reason to want him dead. In an unfinished article found in his office, Mekbel wrote: 'I would really like to know who is going to kill me.' Before anyone else, he dared to formulate the central questions of the conflict: who is killing, and why?

Who killed Saïd Mekbel? It is unlikely that the well dressed young man who walked into the pizzeria that Saturday lunchtime will ever be arrested. 'Saïd antagonised both sides,' Marie-Laure says. 'The government as well as the FIS [Islamic Salvation Front]. I don't know which side killed him.' The

Armed Islamic Group (GIA), the extremist rebels blamed for most of the massacres in Algeria, claimed it murdered Saïd Mekbel because he was an 'infidel'. But his family, like many Algerians, see the hand of the *Sécurité Militaire* behind the GIA.

The Mekbels' small flat, in the drab high rises to the east of the Gare du Lyon, is decorated with Algerian Berber pottery and carpets. Saïd Mekbel's black and white photos of flowers and animals hang on the walls. His wife, often photographed in Algerian costumes, was his favourite model. 'He always said she looked like a movie star,' Hafid recalls. Marie-Laure shows me the last photograph her husband sent of himself, seven months before he was murdered. His sad, mischievous eyes peer over the top of his bifocals. His bushy moustache and mop of curly hair give him a comical look, like Charlie Chaplin or Groucho Marx.

'There are his glasses,' Marie-Laure says, pointing to the table at the end of the sofa. 'I wear them every evening.'

The manuscript of Saïd Mekbel's last column, published on the very day he was murdered, also lies on the table. His handwriting is easily legible, and he made very few changes to the text. 'He wrote his columns in his head first,' Marie-Laure says. 'He would start twisting a lock of hair on his temple with his fingers. Then I knew there was no point talking to him. He was gone, somewhere else, in his imagination.'

Marie-Laure and Hafid Mekbel are hurt by French indifference to Saïd's assassination. 'It's the same lack of respect they show for the tens of thousands of people who have been killed in Algeria,' Hafid says. But in Algeria, Saïd has not been forgotten. The Saïd Mekbel Theatre was inaugurated in Algiers this month, and a collection of his writings will be published later this year.

Saïd Mekbel's last column was a tribute to the courage of his fellow journalists, but it was also the chronicle of his own death foretold. Sixty-nine Algerian journalists have been murdered by fundamentalists and the government, it is commonly believed, and Mekbel's short text has come to symbolise their plight. It has been printed and reprinted. It hangs on the walls of newspaper offices, and has been committed to memory by his colleagues:

This thief who slinks along walls in the night to go home, he's the one. This father who warns his children not to talk about the wicked job he does, he's the one.

This evil citizen who hangs about in courtrooms, waiting for judgment, he's the one. This individual caught in a neighbourhood raid whom a rifle butt pushes to the back of the truck, he's the one. He's the one who goes out of his house in the morning unsure whether he'll make it to the office. And he's the one who leaves work in the evening, uncertain he'll arrive home.

This tramp who no longer knows where to spend the night, he's the one. He's the one they threaten in the privacy of a government office, the witness who must swallow what he knows, this bare and helpless citizen . . . .

This man who makes a wish not to die with his throat cut, he's the one. This body on which they sew back a severed head, he's the one. He's the one whose hands know no other skill, only his meagre writing, the one who hopes against hope, since roses grow out of dung heaps.

He is all these, and a journalist only.

The Mekbel family's story is also that of France's tormented, schizophrenic relations with Algeria. Because his paternal grandfather fought for France in both the First and Second World Wars, Saïd Mekbel was '*un enfant de la troupe*', entitled to a French military education. The son of an illiterate merchant seaman, Mekbel so impressed the French officers who taught him in Algeria that he was sent to France.

While his fellow Algerians were fighting for independence, Mekbel, still a teenager, was preparing for admission to the Saint-Cyr Military Academy. In 1957, he met Marie-Laure Ost, his neighbour in Strasbourg. She fell in love with the solitary, taciturn seventeen-year-old, whose sense of irony made her laugh. When Algeria won independence five years later, Saïd abandoned his shooting medals and military career to go home. And he asked Marie-Laure to go with him.

Marie-Laure's father, a construction site foreman, opposed her marriage to Mekbel. For decades, she had no contact with her family, and there were few Europeans left in post-independence Algeria. 'When the French were leaving, I arrived with Saïd,' she says. 'When you love someone, you have the impression that you can do anything.'

Saïd's family was also unhappy with the match, so the couple married in a civil ceremony in the war-damaged Algiers town hall, with only two witnesses. 'His family saw this *roumiyah* [a derogatory term for a Christian woman, going back to the Crusades] arrive with their son. It went down very badly. I didn't understand Arabic. I didn't know their customs. For example, any sign of affection between a man and a woman was an insult. I didn't know not to touch his hand in public.'

The Mekbels tried to teach their sons both cultures. They celebrated Christian and Muslim holidays. But as children, Hafid and his younger brother Nazim (who now lives in Perpignan in the south of France with his Algerian wife) still worried that France and Algeria would go to war again. 'We didn't know which side we would be on. We spent days talking about it, and in the end we decided we'd just refuse to fight,' Hafid says.

An angry young preacher named Ali Belhadj was the imam of the nearby Kouba mosque when Hafid was growing up. 'In 1979, Ali Belhadj came to see me and said: "Your mother has to become a Muslim." Nazim said we should say her name was Mariam [the Muslim version of Marie] so he'd leave us alone.' (Ali Belhadj, the deputy leader of the FIS, was imprisoned from 1991 until 2003.)

Hafid and Nazim Mekbel encountered prejudice in France too. 'Back in Algeria, I was the son of the *roumiyah*,' Hafid says. 'Here, I'm the son of an Arab. When I go to renew my French identity papers, they ask me why my father wasn't French.'

Except for occasional freelance articles for his father's former newspaper, Hafid is unemployed. Nazim finds short term jobs as a computer programmer.

The Mekbels live in their own little world now, with Saïd's manuscripts and their photo albums. Theirs is the fate of all exiles, but loss seems to have precluded them from building a new life. 'There is no tolerance anywhere,' Marie-Laure says sadly. 'Not in Algeria, not in France. I have the impression I'm living outside the real world; I create my own little world of tolerance that does not really exist. I try to forget, because if you think about these things you become too bitter. I have my pigeons, my flowers, my knitting, and my sons.'

2 May 1998

Lebanon

'I trust you, Lara.
Don't betray me.'

During his frequent trips to Paris, Rafik al-Hariri, the former Lebanese prime minister who was assassinated in Beirut yesterday, held court in the mornings in the mansion he purchased on the heights overlooking the Eiffel Tower. The house had been built by Gustave Eiffel for himself.

It was there that I saw al-Hariri for the last time, six weeks ago, and there that his widow Nazek yesterday received the condolences of al-Hariri's close friend, President Jacques Chirac.

When I saw him on 5 January, al-Hariri insisted it was an off-the-record chat. I was not to mention in print that I had spoken to him.

'I trust you, Lara,' he said. 'Don't betray me.'

He seemed seized by a kind of exuberance at the Syrians' increasingly difficult predicament in Lebanon. Since the attacks of September 11, 2001, Damascus has come under pressure from Washington, which accuses it of terrorism.

Some Lebanese believe that al-Hariri was behind the Franco-American-sponsored UN Security Council Resolution 1559 of September 2004, which demands an end to Syria's tutelage over Lebanon.

Rafik al-Hariri was a cautious politician. He left it to the rash Druze leader Walid Jumblatt to make anti-Syrian declarations. After resigning as prime minister last October, he began moving his Mustaqbal (Future) movement towards the anti-Syrian opposition.

'The opposition have about one-third of the seats in parliament,' al-Hariri calculated aloud. 'Even if we only win 46 percent of the seats [in legislative elections due this spring], I am sure that at least 4 percent will come over to our side, and we will have a majority. The Syrians will not be able to fake the results; the international media will be watching too closely.'

Hariri never said publicly that he would join the opposition. 'Beyond a doubt, I will be in the opposition,' he told me privately. 'I am playing it the Lebanese way. I have two deputies attending the Democratic Front meetings,' he said, referring to a grouping of Maronite Catholics and Druze Muslims. 'My radio and TV stations are giving them a lot of coverage. The ground is shifting. Syrian power is crumbling.'

That week in January, al-Hariri told me, the Syrians were making overtures to him. 'I want to give them one last chance,' he said. 'The Americans have told the Syrians that if there is violence in Lebanon, they will be held responsible. The US ambassador to Lebanon says they must leave quietly, in an orderly fashion. It's a dream, but it will come true.

'Syria is acting more and more like an occupying power, because they feel threatened,' al-Hariri continued. 'They are strengthening their grip on our country. [Syrian president] Bashar [al-Assad] is far less skilled than his father [Hafez] was. A year ago, President Bashar said: "I alone have the right to choose the president of Lebanon. No one else has the right to do it, neither the Lebanese nor the Syrians."'

In retrospect, the 1 October 2004 attempt on the life of Marwan Hamade, a Druze politician who had just resigned as minister of the economy, was a rehearsal for al-Hariri's assassination.

Was it the Syrians who blew up Hamade's car? I asked al-Hariri. 'At the very least, they let it happen,' he said. 'At the most, they ordered it.'

Although Damascus' reappointment of General Emile Lahoud as president of Lebanon led al-Hariri to resign, he secretly rejoiced in Bashar al-Assad's poor judgment.

'The Lebanese lobby in Washington are growing stronger; they have the ear of Bush. The French and Americans dreamed of doing something like [UNSC resolution] 1559. Bashar gave them a cause and a reason. This is the first time in the thirty years since Syria came to Lebanon that the international community decided they have to leave. The French and the Americans warned the Syrians not to reappoint Lahoud. I figured: if they want to commit suicide, let them.'

Iyad Allawi, the US-backed interim prime minister of Iraq, is half-Lebanese. His mother is from the Osseiran family, an aristocratic Shia Lebanese clan. Al-Hariri knew Allawi well. The US is leaning on Syria because it believes Damascus is contributing to the chaos in Iraq. Israel is also 'very important for the Americans', al-Hariri said.

'Lebanon fits perfectly into both of Bush's projects for the Middle East,' al-Hariri explained: 'the war on terrorism and democratisation. Bush thinks that to fight terrorism you must democratise. Instead of encouraging democracy, the stupid Syrians are reversing it. Bush feels these people are working against his big project. He wants to give Lebanon as an example. It will work.

'The Syrians are under tremendous pressure . . . . Bush figures that Syria is a weak country, and he intends to take care of it once the Palestinian question is settled. The Americans are threatening new sanctions against Syria. If the Europeans follow, it will be a disaster for Damascus.'

The fourteen thousand Syrian troops in Lebanon 'are not the problem,' al-Hariri told me. 'The problem are the intelligence services, the *Mokhabarat*.'

Hariri asked me to put down my pen when he told me how the Syrian General Rostom Ghazale, the head of military intelligence in Lebanon and the de facto ruler of the country, insulted him on the telephone, speaking to al-Hariri as if he were a servant. Al-Hariri hung up. Thereafter, Ghazale was polite to him, but continued to bully other Lebanese politicians.

15 February 2005

Merci, Cheikh Rafiq

I read this tribute to the Lebanese leader Rafik al-Hariri in French at a ceremony outside his home in Paris on 29 March 2005.

During the 1990s, when I was the Beirut bureau chief for TIME Magazine, I was fortunate to meet Prime Minister Rafik al-Hariri often. He was larger than life, with an immense heart. As the Irish police commissioner Peter Fitzgerald wrote in his report to the UN, al-Hariri was quite simply the most important character in Lebanese public life.

I returned to Beirut as it mourned al-Hariri's assassination, for *The Irish Times*. An old friend, a Christian from a modest background whose son was able to study medicine thanks to an al-Hariri scholarship, said to me: 'Lebanon will never see the like of him again.' I fear, alas, that this is true.

And yet, despite his success and the friendship of some of the most powerful people in the world, Rafik al-Hariri knew how to remain simple, authentic. In one of my first interviews with him, in 1993, I asked what it was like for the son of a citrus farmer from Sidon to become one of the richest men in the world, and the prime minister of his country.

'I never dreamed I would reach where I am now,' al-Hariri replied. 'I still think that I am in a dream.' His capacity for wonderment, his good humour and *joie de vivre* endeared al-Hariri to people.

With a word or a gesture, al-Hariri knew how to set right a misunderstanding, disappointment or sorrow. In 1995, TIME had planned to bring the eighty most influential American businessmen to Beirut for two days. Rafik al-Hariri participated whole-heartedly in the project. Several times, he received the top management from the magazine at his home in Koreitem. He organised a banquet for five hundred people. Engraved invitations had already been sent out.

A less generous man would have been furious when TIME, giving in to orders from the White House, cancelled the visit at the last minute. Sick at heart, I went to his office in Sanayeh to tell him the bad news. 'Don't worry, Lara,' he told me. 'It doesn't matter.'

Rafik al-Hariri could be a fierce adversary in business and in politics, but it never prevented him from being good. Since his death, I keep discovering people whom he helped discreetly, like the Lebanese woman I saw weeping at his tomb. He had paid for an organ transplant for her in France.

Al-Hariri was a warm person. The first time I saw him in Paris, after I had left Lebanon for good, he sensed my sadness and said to me: 'Beirut misses you, Lara. Come and see us.'

Another time, a colleague who was badly beaten on a reporting trip in Asia was surprised to receive a phone call from the prime minister, enquiring about his injuries. 'Shall I send my plane to fetch you?' al-Hariri asked.

In the 1990s in Beirut, close friends and I fell into the habit of laughing and saying 'Thank you, Sheikh Rafik!' each time we drove down the new highway, passed through the downtown that he was rebuilding, or arrived at the gleaming new international airport.

Forty days after his death, al-Hariri is more than ever omnipresent in Lebanon. Today, I repeat, from the bottom of my heart, but without laughing: for everything you did, for everything you were, thank you, Sheikh Rafik.

reproduced in L'Orient-Le Jour, *5 April 2005*

Search for Bodies Ends in Failure

It was an unseemly end for eighty-year-old Manaheel Jabr, flung over a blood-stained wall like a limp doll, grey hair falling around her shrunken black face, a collapsed ceiling pinning her down at the waist.

'It's the grandmother,' one of the onlookers gasped when the civil defence bulldozer finally pierced a hole in the rubble of what was until two weeks ago a three-storey house.

Mrs Jabr's corpse presented a terrible dilemma to the Lebanese Red Cross yesterday. Should they cut her in two, put the pieces in a body bag and take her to the hospital morgue, or leave her behind, in the hope that more powerful equipment could lift the concrete slab from her back – and would reach her before the dogs did?

It was late afternoon and the forty-eight-hour 'pause' in aerial bombardment promised by Israel was drawing to a close. The Red Cross's plan to retrieve eighty-nine bodies across the war zone was about to end in failure.

The Israelis, with whom the Lebanese Red Cross communicates via the International Red Cross, granted safe passage to only two of the six villages that the rescue workers wanted to visit yesterday, Srifa and Bint Jbail. And the convoy bound for Bint Jbail had to turn around because of bombing.

That left only Srifa, the site of the most dramatic devastation I have seen in this war. The entire Hay el-Birki neighbourhood, eighteen buildings by some accounts, was flattened at 2 AM on 19 July.

'The F-16s [fighter bombers] came from the west, the Apaches [attack helicopters] from the east,' said a local Hizballah official who identified himself as Abu Hadi.

It seemed amazing that bombs and missiles could chop buildings into so many millions of grey concrete pieces, a bed of rubble many metres deep, with only the occasional slipper or coffee pot to remind one that human beings lived here.

The field of ruins stretched to the horizon, reminding me of images of Second World War bombings.

Thirty of the eighty-nine names on the Red Cross list were in Srifa, eight in the house where we found Manaheel Jabr. Yet after battering away for four hours in the hot sun, the Red Cross and civil defence volunteers found only three corpses – one of them Mrs Jabr's – and a crushed skull.

It took the Israel air force minutes to flatten Hay el-Birki but it could be weeks or months before their victims are dug out. The technology used to destroy the neighbourhood was the most sophisticated in the world, the means to dig them out derisory.

At about 1 PM, a rusting Caterpillar bulldozer clamoured down the main street of Srifa belching black smoke and chewing up the tarmac. The driver stopped to put a white sheet with a Red Cross emblem on the roof of the cabin, in the hope of sparing it from bombardment.

For the past two days, Israeli forces have battled with Hizballah at Taibe and at Adayseh, just nineteen kilometres from Srifa. All afternoon we heard explosions, some frighteningly close.

'Israeli forces are trying to push in on the ground,' explained Abu Hadi, the Hizballah man.

'Hizballah is protecting Lebanon – mortars, RPGs and even suicide missions if necessary. We will not let them in. We are protecting the border of Lebanon.'

The bulldozer was joined by a digging machine with a scooped shovel. 'Stop, stop!' an upset Hizballah man with a walkie-talkie insisted as the bulldozer began pushing pieces of the former house down the hillside. 'This is not the way to do it. You will crush the bodies. The Lebanese army has better machines. We must wait for them.'

The Red Cross moved briefly to another address where civilians were known to have died. A medic in an orange jumpsuit placed a mattress over two black shrunken legs which stuck out from heavy rubble in the bomb crater.

'In Islam, we must respect a body,' said the Hizballah official objecting to the Red Cross operation. 'Either we wait for the Lebanese army machines, or we wait until the war is over and do it ourselves, even if there are only bones left.'

With infinite tact, the Red Cross persuaded Hizballah to allow them to continue work on the Jabr house.

The gruesome task had been easier on Monday, the first day of the mythical truce, when volunteers collected twenty bodies from cars and the streets of seven villages. 'Some are only bones and some are teeming with maggots,' said Muhammad Makke, head of the Red Cross in southern Lebanon. 'Some of their identities are known and some are not.'

Red Cross volunteer Kassem Shalaan, 28, lost 60 percent of the hearing in one ear when the Israelis fired on an ambulance in Qana on 25 July.

A man in the ambulance had a leg amputated by the missile, and his seven-year-old son, who had already suffered shrapnel wounds, is still in a coma, after the missile strike slashed open his head.

Shalaan took part in the body retrieval missions of the past few days. Is it true that dogs are eating corpses? 'Yes,' Shalaan said, turning his head to hide the tears. 'Especially people in the streets and cars. The ones that are buried alive are usually safe from the dogs.'

Whatever the outcome of this war, atrocities such as Srifa will poison Lebanese-Israeli relations for decades or even centuries.

Mahmoud Jabr, 56, lost six relatives in the bombing of Srifa; among them his brother, who owned the house that was partially excavated yesterday.

'There is not even a bullet in this village,' Jabr said. 'Israel forced the people to be Hizballah with their barbaric behaviour.'

Mahmoud Nejbi, 66, keeps returning to the rubble of another house, at the far end of the devastated neighbourhood. 'My twenty-seven-year-old son was smoking the *narguileh* and drinking tea with his friends when the air strike happened,' he said. 'He was a mechanic in Dubai and he brought his wife home to have their baby . . . . I would like to make a suicide attack on the Israelis . . . . Either the Israelis kill us or we kill them.'

2 August 2006

'I am very happy, because we are winning'

A woman of less cheerful disposition might have wept.

Three-quarters of Insaf al-Dirani's neighbours have fled, to escape the Israeli bombardment of southern Lebanon. The Shia Muslim district of Beirut was under attack again, after a week's respite. One hundred and sixteen Lebanese have been buried in the mass grave down the road from Mrs al-Dirani's apartment building, and ninety-three more bodies wait in the morgue.

When Mrs al-Dirani, a widow, invited me for tea yesterday, the Israelis were lobbing artillery shells onto the Naqoura road and Bourj al-Shemali, a short walk from her home on the southern outskirts of Tyre.

The racket of fighter-bombers and drones never subsided.

Perhaps only a Lebanese Shia could find cause for joy between a mass grave and the front line.

Joyous she was; positively bubbling. 'I am very happy, because we are winning,' the sixty-year-old former nurse explained.

Overnight the mood changed here. Hizballah had launched a record number of rockets at Israel the previous day, more than 230, but most of all, the Shia Muslim guerrilla movement had held out for three weeks, and they're still fighting.

But the damage . . . I said. *Malesh!* (Doesn't matter!) Mrs al-Dirani exclaimed. 'This is the price. Everything has a price, and the price of victory is blood. If you buy something from a shop, you pay for it. The price of land is blood.

'This is the first time that Israel is being defeated,' she continued.

Defeated? The destruction of Lebanon continues, and the television that is always on in Mrs al-Dirani's living room reported multiple ground incursions by some six thousand Israeli soldiers.

'Even if Lebanon is destroyed, Israel is defeated,' my hostess insisted. 'For the first time, their big cities are being hit. They haven't been able to advance on the ground. If they are brave, let them face Hassan Nasrallah's men.'

No one in Mrs al-Dirani's immediate family is a fighter. Her late husband was a teacher. Two of her sons are medical doctors. Her youngest children, Ziad, 27, and Mouna, 21, are studying geography and English literature at university. They are part of the Shia middle class, which is solidly behind Hizballah.

'Every day we destroy five Merkava tanks on the border!' Mrs al-Dirani says, carried away with exaggeration. 'The most important thing is that Hassan Nasrallah enjoys victory. If Hassan Nasrallah wills it, we are ready for our home to be destroyed today.'

'Be careful what you say, Mom,' her son Ziad interrupts, only half-joking.

To Hizballah supporters, secretary general Hassan Nasrallah is more than a hero. 'He's an idol,' says Mouna, the daughter. 'He's so self-confident. We trust him. Israel will count to a million before they attack Lebanon again. They are suffering.'

Ziad continues the effusive praise of the Shia leader. 'He knows his enemies very well. He second-guesses them.'

According to a profile in *L'Orient-Le Jour* newspaper, Nasrallah has spent a great deal of time studying liberation movements around the world.

Mrs al-Dirani tells of an interview on al-Manar, the Hizballah television station founded by Nasrallah: 'She was a woman with long hair, not wearing *hijab* [the veil]. She said, "After the war, I want a robe of Hassan Nasrallah, to smell the sweat, because he wore this robe when he was defending us. I want it to be cut into pieces and distributed to people here, to give them pride and dignity."'

Nasrallah's son Hadi was killed at age eighteen, fighting the Israelis. Nasrallah did not allow himself to weep when receiving condolences. 'My son was incredibly fortunate to die as a martyr,' he told mourners. 'I may suffer personally, but for the country, I am happy.'

'After his son Hadi was killed on the battlefield,' Ziad recounts, 'Nasrallah took the weapons and gave them to another son. I am sure that the sons of the government ministers are in London, Paris and New York now. But the sons of Hizballah are here, fighting.'

Israeli prime minister Ehud Olmert claims the war has turned people against Hizballah. 'Olmert's an idiotic idiot,' says Mrs al-Dirani. 'If people didn't love Hassan Nasrallah before, they love him now. Not only in Lebanon, but in the whole Arab world.'

Every few days, Nasrallah records a televised message mocking the US and Israel for thinking they can destroy Hizballah. The al-Diranis watch all the Lebanese and Arabic television stations – 'so we can see who supports us,' explains Ziad.

They like the Qatari station al-Jazeera best. 'If you watch al-Manar [Hizballah's station], you'd think we were already in al-Qods [Jerusalem],' Ziad continues. 'If you watch LBC [the Maronite station], you'd think the Israelis were already in Beirut.'

The al-Diranis insist that if Israel returned the occupied 'Shebaa Farms' to Lebanon and freed Lebanese prisoners, they would have no more quarrel with the Jewish state. They believe Israel covets all Arab land 'between the Euphrates and the Nile' – the equivalent of Israelis claiming that Arabs 'want to drive us into the sea'.

I briefly wonder whether Hizballah's welfare programmes might explain the widow al-Dirani's fervour. 'Hizballah helps people who don't have money,' Ziad says, almost insulted. 'We have jobs.'

'I give Hizballah ten thousand Lebanese pounds (€5.50) every month,' says Mrs al-Dirani. 'If I could give them more, I would.' Iran, she says, 'is a friend to us. And they are helping Hizballah.'

Ziad explains Iran's hold over Lebanese Shia. 'Iran is the only country where the Shia are in power. I like all the Iranian leaders. They have made Iran a strong country, and they don't do what Israel and the US tell them.'

Brother and sister disagree on the advisability of Hizballah giving up its weapons to a stronger Lebanese army, and on Syria's meddling in Lebanese politics, perhaps reflecting internal debate within Hizballah. As for talk of a multinational force, probably based here, they entrust the decision to Hizballah: 'Whatever Hizballah wants, I agree with,' says Mrs al-Dirani. 'They know what is best for Lebanon.'

4 August 2006

Fear, Blood, Rubble, Sorrow

Pope John Paul II once called Lebanon 'the remorse of the world'. The world *should* feel remorse for allowing the wholesale destruction of the Shia Muslim areas of this country to continue for more than a month now, while the UN Security Council could not even agree on a resolution calling for a ceasefire.

I lived in Lebanon from 1989 until 1996. To witness dead bodies being pulled, again, from the rubble of Qana, to see villages flattened by Israeli bombs and the country's proud new highways broken into pieces, is like watching the agonising death of a dear friend.

In Tyre, I went several times to an Internet shop owned by a Shia Muslim Hizballah supporter. Yet the picture posters on the wall were of Fayrouz, a Christian, and Lebanon's greatest singer, and Rafik al-Hariri, the Sunni Muslim former prime minister who was assassinated last year.

'Fayrouz is the beauty of Lebanon,' the owner explained. 'Al-Hariri was its strength.'

Before leaving Paris for Beirut, I attended a protest rally against the war. When they played Fayrouz singing 'To Beirut', tears flowed down the cheeks of the Lebanese around me.

'To Beirut, peace with all my heart,' she sang. 'From the soul of her people she makes wine,/ From their sweat she makes bread and jasmine./ So how did it come to taste of smoke and fire?'

Lebanon carried such a weight of tragedy before this war that the 1,100 new deaths and billions of dollars in devastation seem unbearable. I waver constantly between memories of past atrocities and present-day horrors. It is the same for the Lebanese. Everywhere I go, I see pictures of al-Hariri, whom I interviewed many times. And Samir Kassir, the journalist and writer, also a friend, who was murdered four months after al-Hariri.

So many places in Lebanon evoke unspeakable suffering. At the City Café in Hamra, I think of Lara Matar, killed by a car bomb on the road outside on her seventeenth birthday in 1989. She was an only child, and the grief of her parents, Ghassan and Maggie, was boundless. Now I'll remember the clients racing out, their bills unpaid, the screeching of brakes and blaring horns when Israeli missiles hit a disused radio tower nearby on Thursday.

In Qana, where I saw twenty-five corpses dug out of a bombed shelter on 30 July, I recalled old Saadallah Balhas telling me in 1996 how his wife, children and grandchildren were killed when the Israelis shelled the Fijian UN Battalion headquarters.

'I saw my children scattered like dead sheep around me,' he said.

In conversation, Lebanese have repeatedly mentioned photographs of pretty Israeli girls writing messages on 155mm artillery shells. 'From Israel and Daniele' and 'Nazrala [the Hizballah leader Hassan Nasrallah] with love' were inscribed on the weapons in felt pen.

'When I see Israeli children writing on missiles, I think it's in their character to massacre Arabs,' says Mohamed al-Husseini, a lawyer and the son of the mayor of Tyre. 'They teach their children to hate. Maybe they think they're taking revenge against the Nazis. But we're not Nazis.'

In a much-criticised statement, the US Secretary of State Condoleezza Rice said: 'What we're seeing here, in a sense, is the growing, the birth pangs, of a new Middle East.'

The Lebanese have taken to calling her 'Condi Candide', after Voltaire's character, who believed that everything was for the best in the best of all possible worlds.

The roads of southern Lebanon are littered with cars. Some stand perpendicular in bomb craters, or halved like melons, blown apart by missiles. Some crashed into walls, trees or other cars when their drivers were killed or wounded. There is dried blood in the broken glass, and it isn't difficult to imagine the same fate for oneself. Many of the destroyed cars have white sheets tied onto the roof or antenna.

I stopped at a shop in the battered Shia town of Nabatiyeh, in the hope of buying something to eat. But with no electricity for refrigeration, the cheese was covered in mould. The shopkeeper mocked the TV sign in white tape on the bonnet and roof of our car.

'You journalists!' he laughed. 'Do you really think that will protect you? They bomb children!'

Roland Huguenin, of the International Committee of the Red Cross, tells me that collecting bodies from destroyed vehicles is the worst thing he's encountered.

'Sometimes they lie there for ten days before anyone can get to them,' he says. 'You do it with gas masks, for the stench, and even then it is very difficult; you put the bodies in quicklime.

'Between Srifa and Deir Qanoun al Nahr, we found a car with a mother, father, two young children, a baby and a third adult. We couldn't get the driver out because he was pinned behind the steering wheel. It was getting dark and we had to leave him. It felt horrible, really horrible.'

If sorrow is a deep, dull knife blade, fear is a kind of stimulant, razor-sharp in intensity, nonetheless painful. I have rarely been more frightened than when driving from UNIFIL headquarters at Naqoura to Tyre, after waiting six hours for the Israelis to stop shelling.

As we set out, Sleiman, my interpreter and driver, slipped a cassette of prayers into the tape deck.

'I am not religious,' he said. 'I smoke and drink beer. But at times like this . . . .'

At times like this, I said, the more prayers the better.

We drove in silence for several kilometres. The first shell exploded just after we passed the white cliffs, to our right and behind us. It's a long way away, I lied, trying to reassure Sleiman. Don't speed up. A speeding car is guilty. Steady.

More than a dozen explosions followed, ahead, behind, on either side. I kept remembering what Captain Kevin McDonald, an Irish UN observer, told me when talking about the four UN observers killed by an Israeli bombardment: 'No one expects to be killed.'

One explosion was so close that Sleiman and I banged our heads against the ceiling of the old Volvo. I apologised for the expletive I'd shouted, and. Sleiman forgave me. When we heard the loud 'whoosh' of outgoing Hizballah rockets from the banana grove to the left, I thought it was all over, that the Israelis had the technology to pinpoint outgoing fire and bomb the place immediately. I asked myself what I was doing in southern Lebanon.

A few days later, the Israelis issued a blanket prohibition on all vehicles moving south of the Litani. The threat is taken seriously, and journalists walk now. On Thursday, I called a colleague in Tyre, who sounded shaken: he had just seen a man on a moped killed by a rocket fired from a drone.

Survivors say the bombing that killed thirty-two people in the Beirut district of Shiyyah on Monday night was sparked when a moped rider shot at a drone that followed him. Two days later, the Israelis dropped two bombs near the cemetery where twenty-six of the thirty-two victims were being buried. The crowd resumed chanting 'Israel is the enemy of God'. Then five more bombs fell. Pall-bearers and mourners abandoned the dead to run for cover.

It was the second time this week that bombing disrupted a funeral of victims of an earlier bombardment. Fifteen people were killed at Ghaziyeh, between Sidon and Tyre, in a bombing on Monday. Two more buildings were bombed during their funeral on Tuesday, killing at least six more people.

On Thursday, an Israeli jet dropped pamphlets over Martyrs' Square in downtown Beirut, ordering the residents of the Shia Muslim neighbourhoods of Hay al-Silm, Bourj al-Barajneh and Shiyyah, already bombed on Monday, to evacuate. Beirut is bursting with refugees from the south, and they have nowhere to go. Israel's response to 'terrorist operations' by Hizballah 'will not be confined to Hassan's gang of criminals', threatened the pamphlet, signed 'State of Israel'.

I was in the rubble of the former souk in Nabatiyeh when two civil defence workers invited me into a fruit and vegetable stall on the periphery of the destruction. They gave me fresh pears and spring water.

'The people of southern Lebanon have the whole case on their shoulders,' said Hassib Dagdoug. 'How are other Lebanese supporting us? With bread and sardines. In places where there are Sunnis and Christians, there is no bombing. This is a war on the Shia.'

With a few exceptions – a bombed bridge in the Maronite city of Jounieh, missiles fired at old water tankers in the Christian quarter of Ashrafieh – Dagdoug was right. That is why Shia refugees have flocked to Christian villages along the Israeli border.

Hizballah is so entrenched among the Shia population that some analysts say Israel would have to carry out a genocide against the Shia to eradicate Hizballah. Walid Charara, the opinion page editor of *al-Akbar* newspaper and the author of a book on Hizballah, uses Israeli academic Baruch Kimmerling's term 'politicide' to describe what Israel is trying to do to Hizballah. 'They want to destroy the conditions of its political existence, create a disaster zone so people are forced to leave,' he says. 'Today, it has become possible to make war on civilians without anyone reacting.'

Resentment between the Shia and Lebanon's other minorities is temporarily stifled by the war. 'The real danger begins after the ceasefire,' says Bahia al-Hariri, a member of parliament and the sister of the slain leader, Rafik al-Hariri.

Politicians such as Samir Frangieh, from the pro-Western March 14 movement, complain that Hizballah established 'a state within a state' in which Hizballah members were exempted from military service on the grounds they were serving with 'the resistance', and Hizballah used government funds to provide health care and social benefits to their followers, whose loyalty naturally went to the party.

'The state failed to protect these people when they were invaded and occupied,' counters Walid Charara. 'The March 14 group ignored and were contemptuous of the south. For years, Hizballah was fighting and dying while they had a nice life. And it continues.'

I call an acquaintance in Baabdat, a mainly Christian resort in the mountains above Beirut. She is a former journalist from the Sunni Muslim establishment, and has taken her four children to the family's summer home for safety.

'There's plenty of food, plenty of petrol; it's another world here,' she says. 'We have a swimming pool, a billiard table, ping-pong and babyfoot. The kids go cycling . . . . Deep down inside, everybody wants to get rid of Hizballah.'

A representative from the municipality of Baabdat knocks on the door, looking for donations for the refugees sheltering in the local school, so the wealthy Sunni housewife raids her medicine chest for the poor Shia.

'Nobody minds them,' she says. 'They're not allowed to put Hassan Nasrallah pictures on the wall, or play their resistance songs loudly on the radio.'

12 August 2006

III
YUGOSLAVIA

I first visited Yugoslavia in 1988, to do research on former UN Secretary General Kurt Waldheim's Second World War record in the German army. In the early 1990s, TIME Magazine sent me repeatedly to Croatia, Bosnia and Kosovo to report on the breakup of the country. I returned for The Irish Times in 1999 to cover NATO's bombardment of Serbia.

Sarajevo Waits for Winter

Mohamed Kresevljakovic, the mayor of Sarajevo, has finally made a decision he had been dreading: the 1984 Koševo Olympic stadium, symbol of the city's pride and vitality, would be turned into a cemetery for the victims of Serbian shelling and sniping. 'We don't have enough cemeteries. What else can we do?' asked Kresevljakovic, fifty-three, a former curator of historical monuments, as he sat in the cramped office where he has worked since his chambers were destroyed by an artillery shell. Already he had been forced to reopen disused graveyards dating back to Ottoman and Austro-Hungarian times to find resting places for an estimated eight thousand dead. 'In the Dobrinje suburb, people are burying the dead in their gardens,' he said. 'They have to dig graves at night, so the snipers won't kill them.'

Sarajevo, where a Serb assassin's bullet triggered the First World War, is taking its place on the grim list of twentieth century cities besieged and devastated. Exhorted by Bosnian president Alija Izetbegovic to 'maintain business as usual', Sarajevans go about their lives without flak jackets or helmets, with little sleep, subsisting on a spare diet of bread, rice and macaroni. Sanitation workers still collect garbage each day. Broken glass is stockpiled for recycling – some day, when the war is over. The players of the Sarajevo Football Club are considered so valuable a future asset for Bosnia that they are cosseted in the relative luxury and safety of the Holiday Inn, though it too is shell-battered.

For just about everyone else – the bankers, bakers, doctors and firefighters struggling to keep the city alive – survival is growing more difficult by the hour. The public transport system has run out of fuel; in any case, half its buses have been destroyed. Essential staff members either sleep in their offices or walk to work through streets raked by artillery or sniper fire. No corner of Sarajevo is safe. 'The Serbs are shooting into a fish bowl,' says a UN officer responsible for monitoring the artillery positions in the hills around the city.

According to the police, crime has more than quadrupled in the five months since the siege began. Armed robbery is the most common offence, followed by car theft and, not surprisingly, unlawful possession of weapons. With the government unable to bring newly printed Bosnian dinar banknotes through the siege lines, the deutsche mark and cigarettes are the only serious currencies. A single cigarette buys a newspaper, a packet three kilos of fruit. An egg, if available, costs one deutsche mark, or $1.40 – 10 percent of the average Sarajevan's monthly salary. Only three satellite phones – a call costs $40 a minute – are available to Sarajevo banks for international transactions.

'Sarajevo will survive because the spirit of its people will keep it alive,' says Dr Alija Agincic, as he changes the bandages of a twenty-six-year-old tram driver whose right hand was amputated. 'But I fear we will be a city of maimed people. Some patients would be better off dying. I have a ten-year-old boy here who has no face. He was playing in front of UN headquarters – the kids go there because the soldiers give them chocolate and Coca-Cola – when the shell exploded.'

Sarajevans have come to regard the West's failure to stop the siege as complicity in their slaughter. Agincic expresses the growing bitterness of his compatriots. 'Foreigners have been coming here for five months and gawking at our misery,' he says. 'They ask me what we need, and I tell them medicine, ambulances, weapons. But nobody has done anything to help us.'

Agincic's closest friend, Dr Sejo Sebic, died in a mortar blast last month as he queued for water in the Koševo Hospital courtyard. Five other doctors at Koševo have been killed, and the hospital has taken six direct artillery hits, which killed one patient and wounded eight others. 'We put two patients in each bed at night so we can move them to the safer side of the hospital,' says Agincic. The hospital is filled to capacity; many patients have no homes to return to when they are discharged.

Sarajevo's leading newspaper, *Vecernje Novine*, prints only five thousand copies these days, in contrast to a hundred thousand before the war. Its former fifty pages have been reduced to eight, two of which are taken up by death notices. Journalists in Serb-occupied areas of Bosnia risk their lives to transmit reports by ham radio. Editor Sead Demirovic says he is about to run out of newsprint.

At the Velepekara bakery, Kemal Mesak lies awake at night listening to the explosions and worrying about how long his flour will last. Working round the clock and with only two-thirds of its prewar staff, the city's main bakery has nearly doubled its production, to sixty tons of bread a day. Three bakers have been killed on their way to work.

Mesak, forty-nine, lives in his office above the bakery ovens, surrounded by pre-war national production trophies. Ethnically mixed Sarajevo was a microcosm of the Yugoslavia that the late Josip Broz Tito tried to create, and portraits of him still hang on the walls of many offices, including Mesak's. 'It's better that Tito didn't live to see this war,' he says. 'It would break his heart. Those were the best days of our lives.'

The 'brotherhood and unity' Tito tried to instil evaporated last April when Bosnia-Herzegovina received international recognition, sparking the siege. Although the new state was recognised by fifty-five countries, only Libya sent an ambassador to Sarajevo; his chancery has a shell hole in the roof. 'We knew that Bosnia would be attacked by the Serbs,' says Kemal Sokolija, dean of the electrical engineering faculty of the now closed University of Sarajevo, and a local opposition leader. 'But we thought that if we were an internationally recognised state, we could expect help. Unfortunately for us, diplomatic recognition made no difference.'

In the meantime, the firefighters do what they can to limit the damage. Eleven of 120 firefighters from Senad Podjorica's unit have been killed. He points to two holes in his frayed blue shirt. 'The shrapnel went in here,' says Podjorica, thirty-eight, gesturing towards his right side, 'and came out here' – over his stomach. He received first aid and returned to duty the same day. As he speaks, a sniper's bullet whizzes through the trees above his head. Podjorica ignores it. 'I'm in danger every day from fire, shells and bullets,' he says.

'One thing keeps us going. We think that if everybody does his job, we can keep this city alive.' Women and children are lining up behind a fire truck to fill their brightly coloured pails and jerricans with water. Electrical and water services were partially restored by UN soldiers in September, but there is not enough pressure to pump water to those who live on the hillsides or in high rise apartments. Pipes have been polluted by shell damage, and the Bosnian Institute for Public Health reports 2,512 cases of enterocolitis from bad food and water. Tuberculosis, typhus and hepatitis are also increasing.

It is frost rather than fire that now threatens the people of Sarajevo. With many windows shattered by gunfire and explosions, thousands of people are in danger of freezing to death in sub-zero winter temperatures. In a pitiful attempt to prepare for the cold, residents have begun felling remaining trees for fuel.

Throughout the wounded city, a sense of despair is growing. 'Whenever I talk to my people, I tell them what a fine city we will have after the war, to give them courage,' says the mayor. 'But sometimes I ask myself why God has spared me. It seems I am destined to watch my city die.'

TIME Magazine, *12 October 1992*

Stealth Fighter Crashes into a Time Warp

The torn wing of the F-117A Nighthawk Stealth fighter lay on a bed of burnt corn shocks in a muddy field at the edge of the village, a few metres from a broken wooden wagon. Its dull black surface was criss-crossed with what looked like bullet holes, as if it had been machine-gunned from above, but the bulb encased in the clear plastic wing light was unscathed.

Serb news reports about the downing of more than a dozen NATO aircraft since the war started on 24 March owed more to fantasy than fact, but here at last was proof of one.

The $45 million marvel had left Holloman Air Force Base in New Mexico with the 4450th tactical group of the 49th fighter wing last October, during an initial flare-up of the Kosovo crisis. It took off from Aviano base in northern Italy not long before it was shot down by the Yugoslav air force.

The proud, white stencilled emblem of a five-pointed star flanked by two stripes on either side was unscratched, but the ragged edges of the wing were a lasagne of the black linoleum-like outer coating fibreglass fabric, a tiny honeycomb of wires on wood, and yellow styrofoam.

It was just after 10 PM on Saturday night when the two thousand villagers of Budjanovci, 40 kilometres north west of Belgrade, heard the plane above them. 'We saw two lights in the clouds,' a local soldier said. His belted khaki-green uniform and pointed cap were the same as those worn by Tito's partisans in the Second World War.

His account implied that a Yugoslav MiG, not anti-aircraft artillery, downed the most advanced aircraft in NATO's arsenal. 'There was a big explosion. The fuel exploded. It fell to the ground and it burned until morning,' he added.

Yesterday Budjanovci was the most famous place in Yugoslavia. Twenty first century technology had crashed into a time warp, a village of six hundred ancient, crumbling houses in the Serb province of Vojvodina, near the Bosnian border. Here, peasant women wear headscarves, thick woolly socks and clogs. Prized pigeons nest in rooftops and the locals make *Sljivovica* brandy from the pink-blooming plum trees in their gardens.

The men piled on the back of tractor-pulled wagons to visit the black fuselage of the aircraft, protruding from a clump of bushes hundreds of metres across the fallow cornfields. The journalists were not allowed to approach the fuselage. 'NATO will come back and bomb this place, to destroy the evidence,' was the military press officer's feeble explanation.

Milica Lalosevic, 65, was in her cottage less than half a kilometre from the crash site, beyond a red-roofed, two-storey house and a yard filled with chickens.

'Every night we are waiting for the bombing,' she said. 'When we see and hear the doors slamming and the walls moving, we get dressed.' When she heard the racket in the sky above, Mrs Lalosevic wanted to run outside to watch, but her husband, Gavra, stopped her. It sounded like a plane turning around above them, she said. 'When we went outside, the plane was on fire. The whole of Europe was lit up by the fire. If a needle was on the grass, you would have found it.'

By coincidence, Yugoslavia's first triumph in the six-day-old war occurred on the eve of Serb National Day, the tenth anniversary of President Slobodan Milosevic's annulment of the autonomy of Kosovo and Vojvodina provinces. The F-117A wing quickly became a modern relic, ripped asunder, its pieces to be squirrelled away like treasure in the cupboards of local homes. Men sawed at the wing with knives, filling rucksacks with pieces of cake-like yellow styrofoam.

A farmer with a weathered face, missing teeth and dirt-stained fingers pulled a piece of the plane's black coating from his pocket. 'I know mechanics, and it is very simply made,' he boasted. 'The US military makes a lot of propaganda about how expensive it is, but it is only because of this material that the plane is invisible.'

The disappearance of the pilot also seemed a high technology miracle bordering on the mystical. None of the villagers or local soldiers saw him bale out, though one man claimed he'd found the pilot's equipment 4 kilometres away. NATO announced that the pilot was 'in good shape' and 'giving a full account' of what had happened. Equipped with a geo-strategic satellite positioner, he had, it was assumed, called in rescuers from nearby Bosnia.

But the Serbs were sceptical. It was hard to imagine where a pilot could hide in the vast, bog-like plain of freshly ploughed cornfields. 'I hope the poor bastard does not get found by peasants,' a Yugoslav official said, alluding to the Second World War, when enemy pilots whose parachutes were caught in trees were hacked to death by peasants.

It was one of history's reversals that Serbs once hid US pilots shot down by the Nazis. Until very recently, the ageing US fliers and their erstwhile Serb saviours belonged to an association that organised visits between the US and Yugoslavia.

Serbia's friendship for the US may never recover. Since Yugoslavia broke off diplomatic relations with the US, France and Britain last week, someone has painted swastikas on the door of the US embassy in Kneza Milosa Street, and the wall outside the French embassy says: 'US Servants – French Murderers'.

In Budjanovci, a sturdy peasant woman with angry eyes told me she would never speak to foreigners again. 'We will die here because of the Americans and English. They should be killing Albanians in Kosovo, not us.'

Serb forces, it seems, were attending to that. Throughout the weekend, refugees from Kosovo province arrived in Macedonia and Albania with terrifying stories of massacres and burning villages.

Among the victims was an Albanian human rights lawyer, Bajram Kelemendi, who was shot dead in the street in Pristina, along with his two sons.

Half a million ethnic Albanians, more than a quarter of the population, have now been displaced, NATO announced yesterday. The result of this war could be the fulfilment of the Serbs' fondest wishes: the mass expulsion of close to 2 million ethnic Albanians from Kosovo to neighbouring countries.

The federal information minister, Milan Komnenic, provided the only commentary on the slaughter in Kosovo. After asserting in a press conference on Saturday that Belgrade 'has become a symbol of resistance to barbarism', he accused NATO of mounting 'an unthinkable aggression' against 'a sovereign country which never attacked anyone, which was dealing with an internal matter'.

He called Hashim Thaci, a leader of the Kosovo Liberation Army and a signatory of the Rambouillet peace accord, 'America's favourite terrorist', and said that Thaci had called upon Kosovo Albanians 'to leave their houses on fire to create a pretext for massive NATO air raids on Serbia and Montenegro'.

So after accusing the Albanians of rigging a massacre at Račak in January,

Yugoslavia is now accusing them of destroying their own villages.

The shooting down of the F-117A fighter provided a temporary morale boost for the Serbs. Egged on by the presence of television cameras, they jumped on the aircraft wing, waving Yugoslav flags.

Back in Belgrade, thousands attended an open-air pop concert marking Serb national day. They burned US flags and chanted obscene slogans about US mothers to the tune of Serb football songs.

In the first days of the war, air raid sirens sounded *before* the bombers reached Belgrade. But several times at the weekend, the howling sirens were heard *after* loud explosions, indicating that the early warning system which officials had vaunted has been damaged.

Residents of the capital seemed especially frightened on Saturday, after Friday night's bombing of the Avala munitions dump. During a late afternoon alert, fellow passengers in my taxi urged the driver to run red lights and speed past the defence ministry and telecommunications buildings because they feared they might be targets.

Stranded pedestrians huddled in the entrances of buildings. Wolf-like dogs tore rubbish bags from a trash skip in one of the city's finest boulevards. But amid the noise and panic, the tall, handsome young couple walking nonchalantly down Balkan Street were an apparition.

Belgrade Serbs claim they do not understand why NATO is punishing them, although some theorise that the US wants the precious minerals of Kosovo's Trebca mines. They exclude the possibility that the West would wage war for moral, humanitarian reasons.

'What about the Kurds?' a Serb friend asked over lunch in a deserted fish restaurant on the river. 'There are 25 million Kurds, and less than 2 million Kosovo Albanians, so why don't they give the Kurds a country?'

Two hundred thousand Bosnians were killed before the US finally stopped that war in 1995; two thousand people, mostly Albanians, have been killed in Kosovo.

Somewhere in the back of their stubborn minds, the Serbs suspect that by going to war for Kosovo, the West is trying to redeem the honour it lost in the Cambodian, Rwandan and Bosnian genocides.

29 March 1999

Kosovo Refugees Die Under NATO Bombs as the Serbs Expel Them

I filed this article to The Irish Times *before NATO's responsibility for the deaths of seventy-three Kosovar refugees was confirmed. Two weeks later, NATO bombed a second convoy, killing another fifty refugees.*

Colonel Slobodan Stojanovic of the Yugoslav army was holding an improvised press conference by the side of the road outside Velika Krusa, fifteen kilometres north west of Prizren.

We had just passed another burned-out Albanian village with a dynamited mosque, and the colonel stood among the wreckage of one of four ethnic Albanian convoys that had been destroyed, the Serbs claim by NATO, on Wednesday.

There was a bomb crater, a rusty wagon spilling clothes and bedding on to the asphalt, a blood-stained flour sack, a second wagon, and the tractor that had pulled it thirty metres off the road. For some reason, there were also dozens of sun-bleached animal skulls in the grass nearby.

NATO had systematically attacked these convoys, Colonel Stojanovic was saying. Serb and foreign journalists, photographers and television cameramen crowded around him, and only a few of us turned to see what happened next.

Two large coaches caked in mud and dust came towards us from the north west, heading towards Prizren. The dark brown blinds were pulled down, but through the front and back windows, peering through the cracks below and between the sunshade curtains, we glimpsed the faces of Albanian women and children.

It was a haunting image of dispossession and forced expulsion, of women separated from their men, of an entire people chased from their comfortable, middle class, European homes into the hardship of refugee camps. I suspect the bus turned right at Prizren and headed for Vrbnica, the border post with Albania, where its sad human cargo would be dumped.

In a two-day journey through the war zone of southern Kosovo, I saw four such buses, all packed with Albanians. In Urosevac, two empty buses passed us, driving in the direction of Pozeranji, where I had just witnessed a crowd of some two hundred Albanians, mostly women and children, standing in the town square with all their belongings.

Across the width of southern Kosovo, from Bujanovac to within a few kilometres of the Albanian and Macedonian borders, I saw thousands of torched Albanian houses, some of them still burning. We also passed several Serb villages around the Brezovica ski resort, where every house had been burned by the Kosovo Liberation Army since the war started.

I was to hear within hours that ten thousand more Albanians crossed the borders yesterday in what the United Nations High Commissioner for Refugees called the Serbs' 'resumed expulsion with full force' of ethnic Albanians.

One of the mysteries of our trip was why the Belgrade authorities allowed us to witness this new surge in 'ethnic cleansing'. I concluded that they believed they had more to gain by showing us the results of a bombardment which even NATO can still not explain.

In one surreal moment, an official was telling us that although the Nazis had made Belgrade the first *'Juden-frei'* capital in Europe, no Serb ever collaborated in the Jews' Second World War deportation. At that very moment we passed an Albanian village with yet another burning house. All eyes, including the official's, were on the burning house, yet no one mentioned it.

In the course of our thirty-three-hour journey, not one Serb journalist asked about the burning houses and buses packed with Albanians. I thought they had deliberately blinded themselves to their government's wicked policy, or that they accepted it with equanimity.

But after we left the first bomb site at Velika Krusa, we passed more burning Albanian houses. Tears flooded down the cheeks of the Serb woman journalist sitting next to me in the bus. We shared no common language, so she scribbled a note.

'You'll find someone to translate this for you,' she wrote at the top of the piece of paper. 'Dear Lara, there are a large number of us who do not accept that the Kosovo/Metohija [the Serb name for Kosovo] problem should be solved this way. Where are the people? Why are their houses and cattle abandoned? Why are they being punished? All the children in the world are the same, they should be allowed to play and laugh. God, when will the innocent stop suffering, regardless of which nation, which religious confession and which race they belong to?'

The innocent were suffering in Prizren Hospital, where we saw the remains of six Albanians who had been killed in one of the convoy air attacks on Wednesday, and eleven wounded men and women.

The wounded lay between rough blankets in airless rooms without sheets or pillowcases. Four frightened little girls with fair hair and big eyes sat on one bed in the room with their mothers. A dark-haired young woman with blood-stained bandages on her left arm stared at the wall, then pulled a blanket over her arm to hide it from the journalists.

One woman with leg wounds spoke angrily in Albanian, but it was a measure of the abyss between Serbs and Albanians that we could find no one among the doctors, police or officials travelling with us to translate her words.

A wounded man named Esmet Sulija, a forty-six-year-old father of three, spoke enough Serbian to say that his family had been 'advised' to leave their home in Molitce three weeks earlier, when the war started. They had sheltered in a place called Dubros, but were told to move again on Wednesday.

According to Sulija, the Serb police merely showed him the way from Prizren to Djakovica, but did not accompany his convoy of five tractors. With five policemen with assault rifles standing in the hall outside, it would have been surprising if he had said anything different.

'I was driving a tractor pulling a wagon with thirty-five members of my family,' Sulija said. 'The airplanes came over and bombed three times. My sister-in-law and daughter-in-law and two others were killed. Eleven other people were wounded.'

After being expelled from their homes, after dying in terror under air attack on Wednesday, the dead of the Djakovica convoys suffered a final indignity. In the Prizren Hospital morgue, three women, two men, one of them headless, and a seven-year-old girl were loosely wrapped in blood-stained sheets and left on the concrete floor of a room with cobwebs and peeling plaster. Two of the corpses had numbers stuck on them. I could not help thinking that the dead would have been treated with more respect had they been Serbs.

The Prizren dead and wounded were taken from Velika Krusa, the first bombed convoy site. At Gradis, a few kilometres further north west on the road to Djakovica, we found a man's leg, still wearing a sock and shoe, and an old, white-haired man with a blood-stained face slumped dead against a tree.

The roof of a cream-coloured mini-van was pierced by bomb shrapnel, its front truncated like the passenger train we passed at Grdelica, destroyed in a NATO air raid on Monday.

NATO bombs were exploding over the hill with a loud 'pop, pop, pop', and wisps of grey-brown smoke rose as I wrote the details in my notebook: clothes, a box of disposable razors, family photographs, the battered remains of a red tractor, a crashed white Mercedes . . . . In addition to the two bomb craters, there were holes in the earth over a wide area immediately west of the road, the sort of strafing splash-pattern left by the cannon of the heavily armoured US A-10 'tank-buster' aircraft.

The Serbs claim that NATO used A-10s to attack the convoys. NATO claims that an F-16 pilot accidentally struck a 'possible' lead tractor of a convoy at Mija, north of Djakovica. But we saw five bomb craters amid destroyed convoys in three locations south of Djakovica.

When pressed to release the pilot's video of the bombing, the NATO spokesman, Jamie Shea, yesterday said he would like a 'rain check' while the matter is clarified.

Amid the carbonised corpses, amputated limbs, severed head and a row of less damaged bodies laid out on blankets, there were no answers, only questions. As dusk fell, contrails of NATO bombers criss-crossed the sky to the north west, and we walked among these Albanian victims accompanied by the steady drumming of a NATO aerial bombardment just a few miles away.

Could NATO have killed seventy-three of the very refugees it was meant to protect, as the Serbs claim? And if so, what possible error of judgment or technical failure could explain such a bloodbath?

17 April 1999

NATO Bombs Television Station

A dead man hung upside down in the pancaked rubble of the Radio Televizija Srbije (RTS) building, his brains oozing out of the top of his head. The body of the station's make-up artist, the close friend of an interpreter for a British television network, was charred beyond recognition. A limp, dead hand emerged from the ruins.

Dust and smoke swirled in the searchlights as yellow-helmeted firemen pulled away the wreckage. There was a strong odour of burning plastic – electrical cables or videotape? – as hundreds of stunned Serbs watched from behind police lines in Tasmajdan Park.

'Why is NATO doing this?' a part-time RTS employee asked me. 'Don't they realise that this will really make people hate them?'

At least ten people were killed when cruise missiles struck the state-run television building in central Belgrade at 2.06 AM yesterday, but the death toll is expected to rise. About a hundred journalists and technicians were working when the explosion occurred, and yesterday afternoon firemen still struggled to remove the roof of the four collapsed storeys of the network's main control room and tape recording centre. Survivors moaned or tapped from beneath concrete slabs. One man could be freed only by amputating both his legs.

RTS had anticipated the bombardment and within six hours was broadcasting from another location, showing images of monasteries and historical paintings, then reports on its own destruction. The patriotic songs and marching soldiers were back on air – Tony Blair called the station 'a recruiting sergeant for Milosevic's wars' – so NATO had killed at least ten civilians for nothing.

A NATO spokesman first mentioned the station's possible destruction in a briefing two weeks ago. RTS was 'the heart of Slobodan Milosevic's propaganda machine', he said. But if the station agreed to broadcast six hours of

Western television each day, it might be spared. Another NATO spokesman, Jamie Shea, said that RTS was *not* on NATO's target list. But the question of the station's fate kept cropping up, and the NATO commander, General Wesley Clark, reportedly led those advocating its destruction.

On Monday 19 April, the CNN office in Belgrade received a telephone call from an executive in Atlanta. The White House had told the US network that RTS would be destroyed, despite the risk of civilian casualties, and that CNN should cease operating in the RTS building.

A few hours later, Goran Matic, a Yugoslav minister without portfolio, held a press conference where he invited foreign journalists 'to see the building that makes NATO tremble'. The television studios on Takovska Street 'will be bombed tomorrow', he predicted. He was wrong by three days.

Western correspondents did not take Matic seriously. They did not believe that after more than a hundred Serbs and ethnic Albanians were killed in NATO bombings of Aleksinac, the Grdelica passenger train and the Prizren refugee convoys, NATO would deliberately target a radio and television station.

At Matic's press conference, an Australian journalist asked how Serb officials could possibly believe that NATO would do anything so absurd as attack a building where hundreds of civilians were known to work around the clock. 'Absurd?' Matic responded. 'The assault on Yugoslavia was absurd. The attack on the train was absurd. The attack on the convoy was absurd . . . .'

Yesterday, Serb officials claimed that the attack on RTS was an attempt to muzzle the international press too; after all, they noted, foreign television networks transmitted their videotape from the destroyed building. Earlier, Serb media widely reported British government criticism of the BBC correspondent John Simpson and his reporting on NATO's 12 April bombing of the bridge where a passenger train was hit.

Serb television *is* biased and pro-Milosevic. It has emphasised NATO strikes against infrastructure and civilians, but rarely reports attacks on Serb military targets. And it has completely ignored the Serbs' 'ethnic cleansing' of Kosovo Albanians. It refers to Western heads of state as plotters, 'fascists' and 'blood-thirsty criminals'.

Propaganda videos show the US Secretary of State, Madeleine Albright, wearing a Nazi helmet, her face becoming a skull with flames shooting from the eye sockets. In other clips from the *NATO u Blato* (NATO into the Mud) series, Adolf Hitler transmogrifies into President Clinton, and Hitler pats a little boy on the head, calling him Javier Solana.

Uncomfortable as they were at Serb attempts to equate them with RTS journalists, Western correspondents in Belgrade, some of whom had been working in the RTS building, were asking yesterday how NATO could claim moral superiority after killing journalists and technicians because it did not like the content of their broadcasts.

The attack was condemned by the International Federation of Journalists, but Western leaders tried to justify it. A British cabinet minister, Clare Short, said, 'The propaganda machine is prolonging the conflict – this is a legitimate target'. The NATO spokesman, Jamie Shea, compared the attack with the strikes of the two previous nights that had destroyed Milosevic's party head-quarters and home – without casualties. 'There will be no sanctuary for those aspects of the regime which are spreading hatred and creating this political environment for repression,' Shea said.

Rajka, a Serb woman living across the street from the RTS building, noticed fire trucks around the television station on Thursday night and could not go to sleep for fear it would be bombed.

Note the fire trucks: the Serbs knew the building was to be destroyed but, like NATO, they were willing to sacrifice the journalists inside rather than back down. Rajka talked with a neighbour and watched television until 2 AM. She had just tiptoed back into her own flat to avoid waking her family when she was jolted by the explosion.

'It's a thing that only happens to you once in your life,' she said. 'I went to the balcony and I saw a huge cloud of dust where the building was . . . . What happens next?'

Other targets that were bombed early yesterday give an indication of what NATO has in mind for Serbia's immediate future. The main post office and telephone exchange in the southeastern town of Uzice were bombed, putting eighty thousand telephones out of order. Two hours after the RTS building was destroyed, NATO aircraft bombed power transmitters at Resnik and Zemun Polje, depriving most of Belgrade's suburbs of electricity. NATO is celebrating its fiftieth anniversary 'with blood-stained hands', the Yugoslav foreign ministry spokesman, Nebojsa Vujovic, said. 'This is a campaign to bomb the Serbian people into submission.'

24 April 1999

Arkan: A Symbol of All That Was Wrong with Yugoslavia

The last time I saw Arkan was at the Writers' Club in Belgrade. The courtyard was lit by battery lamps that night at the end of May, NATO bombing having shut down the nearest power plant. The explosions were so frequent that even the restaurant's most devoted clientele began slinking home.

The remaining customers and white-coated waiters fell silent when Zeljko Raznatovic, the Serb militia leader, politician, football club owner, convicted bank robber, assassin and indicted war criminal, better known by one of his early aliases, 'Arkan', strode into the little garden with his third wife, the pop singer Ceca. They emerged from the penumbra like an evil omen, a symbol of all that was wrong with Yugoslavia, of all that would continue to be wrong with it when NATO's war ended.

Ceca, a beautiful young woman with long dark hair, wore a powder-blue trouser suit and glittering jewellery. In Belgrade, Arkan was said to have cured her of a cocaine addiction, and to keep her under close watch lest she stray. She was accompanied by her sister, and seemed to enjoy the public appearance. Arkan sat in the back corner of the restaurant, facing the entry like a self-conscious cowboy who fears being shot in the back.

The couple's two bodyguards, in twin skinhead haircuts, black T-shirts and shiny grey suits, sat at the end of their table. A Range Rover with two more gunmen waited in the dark street outside. Manda, the guard who was killed with Arkan in the lobby of Belgrade's Intercontinental Hotel on Saturday, must have been one of them.

I had seen Arkan once before, at Ceca's open-air concert in the Trg Republika at the end of March, two days before the international tribunal in The Hague announced that he was wanted for war crimes. The former British defence secretary, George Robertson, had just called him 'an obnoxious thug' and said Arkan's Tigers militia were 'flaunting their wares' in the streets of the Kosovo capital, Pristina. He would only go to Kosovo, Arkan responded, if he could kill British soldiers. Throughout the war, Arkan insisted that his 1,500 militiamen, who had raped and pillaged their way through parts of Croatia and Bosnia in earlier conflicts, were not present in Kosovo. But the Tigers were known to occupy a whole floor of Pristina's Grand Hotel, and I saw a man in a Tigers T-shirt leaving with the rabble that pulled out of Kosovo before NATO's arrival.

By appearing at Ceca's Belgrade concert to cuddle their small children in front of the TV cameras, and by showing up in the best Belgrade restaurants, Arkan was building his alibi. He was also, in a sense, using the Western press as a human shield. The couple abandoned their garish, wedding cake house in the rich suburb of Dedinje for the duration of the war.

A Serb opposition newspaper editor described the baby-faced Arkan to me as 'the most dangerous man in Yugoslavia'. Ostensibly his wealth came from a casino and the ARI bakery and ice cream plant he owned, but he was deeply involved with the Albanian as well as the Serbian mafia. Arkan's father, a colonel in the Montenegrin secret police, had used his influence to bring his delinquent, bank-robbing son into the late Marshal Tito's intelligence service, where Arkan excelled as a hit man. One of his most prominent victims was the manager of a Croatian oil company who wrote a book divulging Tito's secrets, whom Arkan personally murdered in Germany.

Belgrade sources described Arkan as a sort of secret weapon, a ruthless killer whom Slobodan Milosevic's regime held in reserve for future use. His flamboyance was unusual, and ultimately fatal, for a man who knew so much and had so many enemies.

17 January 2000

IV
Iran

Real Bodies, Unreal Words

A middle-aged man named Farid was going from body to body in a cold storage depot in Bandar Abbas when we arrived to view the remains of the victims of Iran Air Flight 655. He was clean-shaven, with wire-rimmed glasses. Tears flowed down his cheeks as he lifted blankets off burned and mutilated bodies in the 'unidentified' row of corpses, searching for three close relatives.

It was a cold, vault-like room the size of a basketball court. Farid was oblivious to the bright lights of the American television crews. He ignored the dozens of journalists who crowded round to record his suffering.

That morning's Gulf newspapers had quoted President Reagan's emphatic 'yes' when he was asked whether the United States had apologised sufficiently for downing the Iranian plane. The victims were not yet buried, but President Reagan had said in a letter to Congress that he now 'regarded the matter as closed'.

Amid the cheap plywood coffins, those clinical statements from Washington were hard to take. We followed the example of the Revolutionary Guards who held a cloth over their noses to reduce the smell of decaying bodies.

Many of the victims seemed almost untouched by the explosion that had hurled them thousands of feet into the water. 'Would you like to see a woman?' an Iranian official asked me. 'Come, you are a woman, you look at her.' He lifted a coffin lid and pulled back a sheet of plastic. Forty-year-old Zahra Khorasanipour from Shiraz was a striking woman. Her long chestnut hair had been carefully combed to show off her beauty. A two-inch gash under her left eye was the only indication that she had died violently.

The sight of Leila Behbehani, a three-year-old from Kuwait, would also stay with me. The girl was wearing a turquoise party dress; she had been on her way to a wedding. Most of the corpses bore peaceful expressions, but Leila Behbehani seemed to have died crying.

We were half a world away from the Pentagon briefing room where Admiral William Crowe had given the first account of 'the tragedy'. A tragedy it certainly was, but the repeated use of the word gave the downing of the Airbus an aura of inevitability, put it on the level of a hurricane, an earthquake, some kind of natural disaster.

Our press tour of the cold storage depot and interviews with Iran Air staff – all professional, all fluent in English – lent an almost obscene character to suggestions that the plane might have been on a kamikaze mission. The words that rang true were those of Captain Will Rogers III of the Vincennes when he said: 'This is a burden I will carry for the rest of my life.'

We all knew how cruel the Iranians could be, how willingly they had sacrificed their youth in the war and massacred their domestic opponents. But the chasm between Iran and America could not be measured in terms of religion or political system, of time zones or miles.

When we looked over the corpses and the scraps of fuselage and engine cowling scored by a missile, the arguments about transponder signals seemed immaterial. The human remains and the plane's wreckage were evidence that – whether or not Captain Mohssen Rezayian, the pilot of the downed aircraft, heard the warnings transmitted to him – Iran and the United States seemed doomed to continue their dialogue of the deaf on conflicting frequencies and channels.

Iranians with whom I spoke maintained that had Iran shot down an American airliner, US bombs would have fallen on Tehran. Without exception, they seemed convinced that the Vincennes had shot down their plane deliberately.

Iranians have an unparalleled faith in American technology and intelligence-gathering and were quick to suspect the United States of plotting. But Iranian belief in America's innate evil has been matched by America's apparent certainty that its action was understandable and excusable. Polls showed that the majority of Americans blamed Iran for the disaster.

The US government qualified its announcement on 11 July that it would pay compensation to the relatives of victims with a statement that 'ultimate responsibility' lay with the Iranians for refusing to end the Gulf War. Vernon Walters, the US ambassador to the United Nations, has promised to 'defend the circumstances under which this occurred'.

There is a deeply disturbing aspect to all these official statements. They assume that America's version of events has to be the correct one.

Moorhead Kennedy, a former US diplomat who, as head of the economic section of the embassy in Tehran in 1979, was held hostage for 444 days, has forgiven his former captors. He says the United States has 'a mythical and imaginary view of the world in which we are always right'. But sometimes an event like the downing of the Airbus 'teaches people that we need to work together more than we need to fight each other', and 'if that happens then maybe some good will come of this'.

For many, though, it is easier to support US seamen defending themselves against 'fanatical' Iranians than to question how a missile crew, programmed with fears of suicide attacks, could have slaughtered so many innocents.

International Herald Tribune, *14 July 1988*

Chador Gives Way as Attitudes Soften in Iran

When I met Roya at an Islamic conference in Tehran eleven years ago, she was a convinced revolutionary. But she felt embarrassed when officials running the conference objected to the mid-calf black dress I was wearing.

My black socks were too transparent, they said, and my ankles were showing. In a pique, I bought the ugliest, sack-like black *manteau* – Iranians adopted the French word for this version of the chador – I could find, and I still wear it here.

Roya thought it was wrong that anyone should tell a foreign journalist how to dress, but she was sure of her own taste. I'll never forget her emphatic declaration: 'I love my chador.'

Before the revolution, she explained, she tried to enter the Intercontinental Hotel in Tehran in a chador and was prevented from doing so by the Shah's police. The chador was her badge of faith and defiance.

My friend was eighteen when the Shah fell and Ayatollah Khomeini returned from exile in 1979. Over the years, I have watched her, and the revolution, move from dogmatic idealism to faltering faith and self-doubt.

When Roya met me a few days ago at Mehrabad Airport, she was wearing high-heeled boots and a stylish trouser suit with a wool cape from Paris. Not a hint of the once-loved chador.

When I asked Roya about the transformation of her *hijab* (Islamic covering), she instead told me of the changes in her own life. Back in the 1980s, she said, 'I was very happy with myself, because I believed in the revolution'. But in the 1990s she began to ask questions. 'The war with Iraq was over, so the government had no more excuses. Why didn't our economy improve? Why did the government still control our television and radio? I started thinking about all the things you have in the West, and wondering why we couldn't have them.'

Harassment by the 'Islamic' vigilante *komiteh* added to Roya's disillusionment. In the mid-1990s, she was turned around on her way to Darband, a mountain area where young couples like to go climbing. Her sister and a young man were arrested for meeting in a public park at midday to talk. 'I realised that these things had nothing to do with Islam,' Roya says.

Iranians have a strong sense of personal dignity, and Roya is no exception. When she travelled abroad with her husband, a businessman, customs and immigration officials were rude when they saw her Iranian passport. 'I was insulted outside the country and I was insulted inside the country – and I helped make this revolution to have respect.'

The mullahs have taught their people 'to make all the world Muslim and to serve Islam', Roya says. But somewhere along the line, she rebelled. 'Religion should help you have a better life,' she says. 'I wasn't born to serve Islam. What about my wishes, my youth?'

When Roya and her husband discuss visiting Europe, she tells him she would like to travel without her *hijab*. 'I am tired of being different,' she says. 'I want to retire. For a while, I stopped praying. My husband was very worried. I started praying again, because it was less hassle. But I'm not praying like before, and I feel hypocritical.'

Although *hijab* is still obligatory in Iran, attitudes towards it are changing. The sculptress and university professor Zahra Rahnavard wrote in a recent newspaper article that Iranian women suffer from a high rate of osteoporosis because so little sunshine reaches their skin. She said that dark colours cause depression, and urged women to wear bright colours, so that society will grow accustomed to it.

Roya took me to her favourite *manteau* shop, 'Diana' in Haftetir Street, so I could see the latest styles. A saleswoman named Minoo proudly showed us coats with satin cuffs and collars and *guêpière* lace trim. There were *manteaux* with gold or silver embroidery; rhinestone and gold buttons for evening. A blue and white pinstriped version imitated a man's business suit. The fashions are cut much closer to the body, and safari suit-like models with four pockets are very popular, Minoo said. So are the thigh-length jackets which younger women wear over trousers. 'You would never have got away with this ten years ago,' Minoo said. 'They have to ease up, because women wouldn't take it any more. It's been much freer since President Khatami was elected [in May 1997].'

Hijab rules are based on verse thirty-one, surah twenty-four of the Koran: 'And tell the believing women to lower their gaze and be modest, and to display of their adornment only that which is apparent, and to draw their veils over their bosoms, and not to reveal their adornment save to their own husband.' God willing, Minoo told me, *hijab* rules may one day be abolished.

Roya has heard rumours that some progressive mullahs advocate making it optional. 'Maybe we will lose it little by little,' she says. 'The first step is wearing dresses instead of *manteaux*, and bright colours.'

I would have expected Roya, now forty, to be happy at the changes sweeping Iran. But she, like much of the population, has lost her bearings. 'I was happier then,' she says of her youth. 'I was so sure of everything, and I had so much hope. Now I feel middle-aged – and confused.'

23 February 2000

Iran's Lost Generation

Azadeh, Morvarid, Marjan and Golshabeh sit on benches outside Golestan shopping centre in west Tehran, watching people. The four young women are the closest of friends, all aged between eighteen and twenty-two. The centre, in an upper middle class neighbourhood near a university campus, is one of the few places where young people can meet in the capital without being harassed by fundamentalist vigilantes.

'Look at those guys!' Marjan says, giggling and pointing at two young men who turn back to glance at her. She has an impish, mischievous face, and her friends call her 'the satanic one'. On this cold February day, the girls wear grunge-style baggy jumpers and trousers beneath their black headscarves and loosely fastened *manteaux*, intended to preserve the modesty of Iranian womanhood.

Golshabeh, the eldest of the four, the reliable one whom her friends call 'the driver', wears Nike runners with her tracksuit, but her friends prefer the chunky mountain boots so fashionable in Tehran.

One of the boys is a weightlifter, wearing a tight, short-sleeved T-shirt, despite the cold. 'He's showing off his muscles!' Golshabeh says. 'Oooh. Only a girl of fifteen or sixteen would be impressed by a guy like that!' Marjan remarks with mock disgust.

Anywhere else in the world, the four girls would be ordinary college students on a break between classes. But the young women, all of whom voted for President Mohamed Khatami's Islamic Participation Front on 18 February, have bottled up a lifetime of frustration and despair. 'We voted for the bad to avoid the worst,' Golshabeh says. 'There'll be a few less mullahs in parliament.'

Azadeh's father manufactures refrigerators. Morvarid's is a car salesman. Marjan's mother teaches in a primary school and her dad makes tyres. Golshabeh's father is a manager in a cigarette company. None has known poverty, but one has been lashed with a whip, and the others have seen friends drug themselves and attempt suicide. 'Everyone in our generation is very sad,' Azadeh says.

'The other day we were listening to Siyavash Qomaishi's *Eyes that are Waiting* and we all started crying – because the eyes are waiting to see something good, something new, and there is nothing so far.'

The disillusionment of Iranian youth was a strong theme in this month's general election campaign. 'We must begin to respond to the aspirations of the young – if not, we will have anarchy,' Dr Mohamed Reza Khatami, the younger brother of President Khatami who led the winning reformers' list, predicted. Half of Iran's population of 61.9 million are under the age of thirty. More than a third fall into the rebellious, sixteen-to-twenty-five-year-old bracket.

President Khatami owes his own election to young voters. But he knows they are a time bomb. He and his new parliament are now their only hope.

The youth of Iran are a disorganised, pent-up force. In recent years they have alarmed the ruling clergy by pouring into the streets in their tens of thousands. They did it when Iran qualified for the World Cup in 1997. They rioted for a week last July, and they have turned the annual Halloween-like *chara shanbeh souri* holiday in March into a huge protest demonstration.

Iran's other invisible youth army are the unemployed – 20 percent officially, but at least 30 percent according to experts. Close to a million young people enter the job market every year, and there are nowhere near enough jobs for them. Between 6 and 8 AM each day, crowds of young men can been seen on Tehran's main squares: day labourers, hoping to find work in the construction industry. Until recently they came from small towns outside the capital. But the economic crisis has grown so severe that men from border areas are looking for work in Tehran. The problem is aggravated by the world's highest refugee population – nearly 3 million Afghans, Iraqi Shias and Turkish Kurds.

In the Iranian middle classes, the children of the 1980s grew up indoors, because of fear of the revolutionary *komitehs* and Iraqi bombardments. 'In many cases, it was a very Westernised environment,' says Kianoushe Dorranie, a journalist who writes extensively about the problems of Iranian youth. 'The mothers stayed at home, making themselves up and trying on scanty outfits. Little girls of four or five used their mothers' make-up a bit more than was natural. The boys saw their fathers as models, and the fathers stayed home smoking opium and drinking in front of the children, who learned very early to separate completely what happened inside and outside the house.'

Over the past few years, and especially since President Khatami's election, the young have taken to the streets. On Thursday nights, the beginning of the Iranian weekend, carloads of teenage boys and girls drive up and down the road known as Jordan (its pre-revolutionary name) or Africa, looking at one another.

Through open car windows, they hand one another slips of paper with telephone numbers, then arrange to meet later, out of sight of the police. A similar rite takes place in Gisha Street, near Tehran University, except that the students there are walking.

Lack of freedom is a constant refrain among Iranian young people. One of the most striking examples was the trial last October of four university students who wrote a play about Shia Islam's 12th Imam. The play was deemed blasphemous. The students were threatened with death sentences. This week they were pardoned.

Back at the Golestan shopping centre, Azadeh speaks mostly of freedom. Ironically, her revolution-era name means 'freedom'. She has coloured her hair – several inches of which show beyond the edge of her black scarf – a fair honey colour, to match her topaz eyes. She plucks her eyebrows and shapes her long nails. Her friends call her 'the beauty'. 'At high school, they wouldn't have let me get away with it,' she says. 'But at university the teachers assume I'm married.' Married women are allowed to colour their hair and pluck their eyebrows to please their husbands; single girls are not.

'We want very simple freedoms – things any wise person would accept,' Azadeh says. 'For example, if I wear mascara at the university, they make me take it off. They don't respect us. They won't let us talk to boys.' That morning, the 'behaviour committee' had threatened Marjan for letting her punk-style fringe protrude from under her scarf.

The four friends admit to having met boys by 'cruising' Jordan Street. 'We have no choice,' Azadeh says. 'If we didn't do this, what would we do? The *komiteh* would come and take us.' Three years ago, when Azadeh was still in high school, the vigilantes found her in a parked car with her boyfriend. Her parents had to pay the equivalent of sixty-five euro to obtain her freedom from the 'Judiciary Committee of Guidance' in Vozara Street. But before she was released, she had to lie on a table, to be whipped ten times on the back by a woman. Her boyfriend, Hessam, received fifteen lashes.

Azadeh's eyes fill with tears as she tells me the story, and Morvarid, 'the little one', puts her arm around Azadeh's shoulder to comfort her. 'For a month afterwards, I couldn't talk,' Azadeh says. 'I was in shock. When I pass that building it still gives me bad memories, and I try not to look at it.' She considers herself lucky that she was not taken to a doctor to have her virginity confirmed. She and her friends have just seen *The Girl with the Sports Shoes*, a popular new Iranian film which begins with the heroine being taken to the doctor by the *komiteh* after she is caught with her boyfriend. The film heroine is shown looking out of a window, dazed and humiliated.

Iranian newspapers often tell of young people who die of drug overdoses. Drug dealers ply the pavement of Arya Shahr Square in west Tehran, and Almahdi Park in central Tehran, every evening.

Hashish from Afghanistan, said to be the best in the world, is cheap. It costs less than two euro a day to maintain a hashish habit.

'A lot of our friends smoke "bang",' Azadeh admits, using the Iranian slang for hashish. 'If our lives weren't so restricted, if we lived in a normal place, we wouldn't do these things. We use "bang" to be able to laugh. We use drugs and do crazy things like driving too fast. We don't know what is right and wrong.'

A young man wearing blue jeans, with greased black hair and sunglasses, asks if he can join our little group. He is Mike, twenty-two, from Texas. His mother is Iranian and he has spent the past year in Tehran with his grandmother and sister, finalising marriage arrangements with his Iranian fiancée. Mike has been attending underground 'techno rave' parties in houses outside the city.

'You can find anything you want there – ecstasy, cocaine, heroin, alcohol. Even in America they don't have such parties. The men who give them are real gentlemen, businessmen in their thirties, guys from rich families who drive Mercedes and BMWs.'

In Mike's mind, the 'gentlemen' who throw techno rave drug parties are good Samaritans, trying to alleviate the oppressiveness of life in Tehran. 'They invite their friends, and their friends invite friends. A guy brings his girlfriend and she uses drugs. Once she uses it, she gets hooked and then she doesn't have the money for it. Those girls, their lives are ruined.'

Mike has decided to return to the US. 'In Texas, on Saturday and Sunday you get a six-pack of beer and go to the beach with your girlfriend. In Iran on the weekend you get some drugs and sit in a room and get high – there's nothing else to do here.'

But like young people everywhere, Iranians want to be in fashion. 'I like techno music,' the 'driver', Golshabeh, says. 'Venga Boys, Cat Girls, the Spice Girls, Tony Braxton's "Unbreak My Heart". We used to like Celine Dion but we had too much of *Titanic*.' In poor south Tehran, they buy Iranian-made jeans and mountain shoes. In better-off north Tehran, the jeans are American, the shoes Timberland, Doc Martens or Caterpillar. The boys wear rap-style baggy jeans, the girls skimpy tank-tops at their parties.

In two hours of conversation with the young women at Golestan shopping centre, I heard tales of *komiteh* brutality, narrow-minded university professors and strict parents. Not a single happy story. Suicide is widespread among Iranian young people, and Marjan is haunted by the memory of a girl she met two years ago, while visiting her aunt in hospital. 'She was so beautiful,' Marjan said, still in wonder. 'Long black hair, a little nose and blue eyes. The doctors all came to stare at her. She had cuts all over her arm, and I asked her what had happened.' The young woman was from Shahra Rey, a small town south of Tehran, and she had tried to slash her veins with a broken bottle. 'She had seven brothers,' Marjan explains. 'She said, "Whatever I do, my brothers give me a hard time." It was the fifth time she had attempted suicide, and she said she'd keep trying until she succeeded. One of the psychiatrists came and said, "I'm going to help you". But the girl told her, "No, the next place I'm going is the Ekbatan buildings."' The Ekbatan buildings are the Golden Gate Bridge of Iran, a high rise housing complex near Mehrabad Airport, famous because so many young women go there to kill themselves.

The friends have named their group 'four crazy girls'. They do everything together and sneaked off to Morvarid's parents' cottage in the mountains last Tuesday afternoon to celebrate her boyfriend Kamyar's twenty-first birthday. 'We don't smoke or drink, we just laugh and play cards,' Morvarid said. To avoid problems with the police, the girls drive in one car, the boys in another, and they come home early in the evening, so their parents won't get suspicious. 'But it's a risk,' Azadeh says. 'A big risk. We do what we want to, but always with fear.'

The four have missed their afternoon classes, but they don't seem to mind. They are nice girls who still believe in God, but never go to a mosque or pray. They are against pre-marital sex but admit to a lot of hugging and kissing with their boyfriends.

Their group friendship, a widespread phenomenon among Iranian teenagers, gives them strength. 'I love my girlfriends more than my family,'

Marjan says. They all insist they love their country too. They just can't stand the regime they've had until now. Iran is like another planet, Azadeh says. 'But I hope it will change for the next generation.' At twenty, she says she feels old already. 'We are escaping from the university. We are escaping from the house. We are looking for something new, and we don't find it.'

I am sorry to leave them in such sadness. But as the 'four crazy girls' walk away arm in arm, their laughter drifts back across the esplanade, like music, like a hint of promise. Their generation is a lost generation, which barely dares to hope in President Khatami and his reformers. To save his country, he must save them.

26 February 2000

Awaiting Mehdi and the End of the World

The thousands of Iranians who flock to Jamkaran mosque every Tuesday night don't think of themselves as superstitious or politically exploited. They are not even aware that intellectuals in north Tehran and some reformist clergy are alarmed by the Mehdi revival.

The new president, Mahmoud Ahmadinejad, shares their fervent desire for the return of Mehdi, the 12th Imam, who disappeared in Samara, Iraq, in 941 AD.

Ahmadinejad has brought his entire cabinet to pray in the shrine here. Rumour has it that Ayatollah Ali Khamenei, the supreme leader of the Islamic Republic, sends his assistant to Jamkaran every week to have his appointment book approved by Mehdi.

For Mehdi never died. He has been wandering around the earth for 1065 years 'doing his job as an imam', one believer tells me. He is the Christ of Shia Muslims, the name they utter in moments of despair, the one who suddenly appears in human form to rescue them from the worst difficulties.

But because Mehdi is hidden, you mustn't tell anyone you've seen him. It is forbidden by the *hadith* (sayings of the prophet Muhammad), as is claiming you know the date of his return.

Hossein Afshar Tous, 71, brings his wife Effat, 60, their children and grandchildren to Jamkaran mosque every Tuesday to pray for the return of Mehdi. The family arrives early and picnics on the esplanade in front of the mosque. Tous, a wheat farmer from the countryside south of Tehran, is a true revolutionary.

He proudly shows me his *basij* (militia) membership card and his credentials as a village councillor.

When the new moon rises every month, Tous kisses the image of Ayatollah Khomeini on the ten thousand rial banknote by the light of the moon, for good luck.

As we eat pistachios with tea, Tous tells me how a thief came in ancient times to steal carpets from the mosque. Because it's a holy place, he ran around in circles and never found an exit.

Tous met Imam Khomeini in his dreams once, a few months after the revolution. 'Imam was wearing shoes without heels, so I took a hammer and nails and put heels on. He asked me how many children I had and said I would be rewarded. A few days later, the *komiteh* gave me five hectares of land.'

Before the Shah fell, Tous worked with an American oil company. 'The American engineer used to urinate in front of us and yell at us,' he recounts. 'We Iranians know how to overcome people with ruse. One day, I was driving with the American in the desert. I stopped the car and said it was broken. He started yelling, so I told him to get out and look under the bonnet. I drove away at high speed.'

The Jamkaran pilgrims pray for other things besides Mehdi's return: a theology student from nearby Qom has come to thank Mehdi for curing his nervous disorder, caused by too much study.

An Afghan Hazara refugee asks Mehdi for better treatment in Iran. 'They won't let us attend university,' she complains. 'They are rude to our children in school, and we are Shia like them.'

One tale says a mullah used to gather up the little letters left by women in the dry well where Mehdi allegedly hid from his enemies. Many of the letters said, 'Mehdi, send me a husband'. The mullah would send a man to the address on the note, for a temporary 'pleasure marriage'.

Two middle-aged sisters and their mother have driven six hours from Isphahan to pray at Jamkaran. 'I am asking Mehdi to destroy America,' says Shahrbanou, 45. 'She means only the bad Americans,' her sister Khadijana, 52, explains, worried I'll be offended.

'We all love Ahmadinejad,' says Shahrbanou. 'He's a believer. He is with God. In the time of [former presidents] Khatami and Rafsanjani, Islam was going to die.'

At Imam Sadig University in Tehran, Professor Mohammad Hadi Homayoon is delighted to hear me say there's a Mehdi revival.

'It started with our revolution,' he explains. Homayoon believes that 'practically every verse in the Koran' alludes to Mehdi. By reading between the lines, one can know the fate of the world.

Before Mehdi returns, Homayoon says, 'the world will grow very bad, full of injustice, wars and epidemics. This will pave the way.

'Imam Mehdi will begin from Mecca. The internal situation in Hijaz [Saudi Arabia] will be chaotic. He will go from Mecca to Iraq to al Qods [Jerusalem], where Christ will join him. The Christians who believe in Christ will believe in Imam Mehdi and they will pray together.'

Islam has no battle of Armageddon, but the small minority of humans who know good from evil but who choose evil – the *mustakbireen* ('maybe Jews', Homayoon says) – will fight Mehdi, Christ and the faithful. 'It will be a real war,' Homayoon says. 'Maybe with guns, planes, tanks and missiles. I'm not sure.'

Does the professor think the looming war between the US and Iran is the war of the end of the world, the war with the *mustakbireen*?

'Personally, I believe it,' he answers. 'It may be the day we are waiting for. I hope for the least possible bloodshed.'

Ahmadinejad's election was seen by many as a sign that Mehdi's return is imminent.

'I think that he believes as I do,' says Homayoon. 'He believes strongly in Mehdi. After the war, there will be one world government, an Islamic Republic of the World, and everyone will live in peace.'

Ahmadinejad's enemies say that he and George W. Bush, a born again Christian, are two of a kind. Professor Homayoon rejects the comparison, saying Bush doesn't really believe the end of the world is nigh. 'He pretends, but he's not sincere. If he was a real follower of Christ, he wouldn't do what he's doing.

'He and his entourage know the Islamic revolution is spreading throughout the world, and they want to stop it, to prevent the end of time. He is among the *mustakbireen*. This gang is what we were waiting for.'

20 April 2006

V
AFGHANISTAN

US Dollar Smooths Rugged Way Over the Old Silk Road

The border guard in the emerald-green uniform shook his head.

Bekobod was not an international crossing point. We would have to go back to Tashkent. 'Give him $50,' our driver whispered. Minutes later, we were stopped by a second guard, whom we mistook for a Tajik. He too was an Uzbek, though wearing bright yellow and brown camouflage, and he too wanted a crisp $50.

A colleague on the Paris-Tashkent flight and I decided to share the cost of a car and driver to Dushanbe, but we didn't realise how costly it would be. When we reached the third border guard, I commented on his US-issue 'chocolate chip' combat fatigues; 'I'm an American boy,' the Tajik grinned, baring a mouthful of gold teeth.

That was when it started to get unpleasant. Two unsmiling Tajiks, in yet another variety of green camouflage and with pistols at their hips, ordered my colleague into their cinderblock hut and clanged the metal door shut. I suddenly remembered my Paris travel agent reading the Quai d'Orsay advisory to me. She could not sell airline tickets to Tajikistan 'in view of the instability in the country, including the taking of hostages'.

While I was wondering what to do if the French correspondent was kidnapped, the border guards demanded to see his Uzbek currency declaration. The Uzbeks, Tajiks and Afghans have caught on to the fact that the journalists swarming into their countries in anticipation of US military action carry large amounts of cash. The old Silk Road across central Asia is bandit country, and most of the bandits wear uniforms.

The two guards split the pile of $100 bills and started to count them. 'How much do you want?' my friend wisely asked, in the hope of preserving at least some of his reporting budget. Fifty dollars each, they answered. We left quickly, but seeing more uniforms ahead wondered if it was harder to go forward or go back.

In the end we pressed on to Dushanbe, a twelve-hour drive on a rutted dirt and asphalt track, through jagged, three-thousand-metre peaks and cliffs with drops so sheer I had to close my eyes for long stretches.

Our old Lada broke down twice in this wilderness, and I noticed the taxi's licence plate holder. 'In God We Trust' it said, in English.

It was a joy to arrive at the former Soviet Intourist Hotel in Dushanbe, despite the omnipresent smell of cockroach powder, the ten-minute wait for the lift and dysfunctional telephones and plumbing. Another vestige of the former Soviet Union is the *dejou mara*, or floor-key lady. In the old days, she recorded every coming and going for the KGB. These days, her main concern is the Afghanistan-bound journalists who filch hotel towels.

Tajiks call the policemen who ply the leafy boulevards of Dushanbe BDAs – which stands for 'Give some money to your brother' in Tajik. The average Tajik earns less than $20 a month, but a police shakedown can cost up to $100.

Local drivers and interpreters have more than doubled their fees since the influx of journalists started soon after September 11th. The Tajik foreign ministry requires that every reporter obtain a Tajik press card (price $40), though it serves no purpose. They've issued over five hundred.

The next step is the Afghan embassy, run by the mainly Tajik United Front, where hundreds of journalists are clamouring for a lift on a clapped-out former Soviet MiG helicopter to the Front's enclave in northern Afghanistan – and the chance of an encounter with a Taliban MiG. The rebels have few choppers, and they need them to resupply their seven 'pockets' of territory, with which they have no contact by land. The television networks, with their thick wads of cash, take priority.

So like the characters in the film classic *Casablanca*, we wait, and wait, and wait. From dawn until dusk, on a parking lot outside the Dushanbe Military Airport. Your correspondent almost made it onto a flight yesterday, but a sandstorm descended over northern Afghanistan and Tajikistan, coating everything in reddish dust.

At the United Front's military headquarters at Hoza Bahuddin, they told us, the dust was 'so thick you can't see your hand'. Poor Afghanistan has waited twenty-four years for the world to sort out its problems, so perhaps we should be patient.

Sadly, central Asia is rich in potential conflicts. Tajikistan called off its own civil war of three years only after the Taliban came to power; the Tajiks were afraid the Taliban would gobble them up if they didn't stop fighting each other.

And any resident of Dushanbe will tell you he's got an axe to grind with the Uzbeks. The Soviets gave the magnificent ancient city of Samarkand to Uzbekistan in the 1920s, and the Tajiks would like it back.

3 October 2001

Into Afghanistan's Heart

In Afghanistan, the heat at noon is oven-hot, choking. At night the icy winds blowing down from the Hindu Kush chill through you. For sustenance there is nothing but rice, gritty bread, goat meat and tea. The only toilets are stinking holes. Village children collect cow dung for winter fuel. They stare with saucer eyes, their bare feet caked black with dirt, their coughs tubercular. Men who stop rare vehicles look wild, with matted beards and hair, ranting that they will go with you to Panjshir, shaking a Kalashnikov in the air.

What ought to be highways are little more than paths, where it takes an indestructible Russian jeep to climb over rocks the size of television sets, forge rivers, negotiate slipshod bridges of logs and stone, slalom through sand so powdery it rises like steam and must be removed with windscreen wipers. Along the way, an abandoned Land Cruiser makes you wonder what happened to its passengers; there can be little doubt about the fate of the cars and trucks lying at the bottom of the ravines. Or the Soviets, who between 1979 and 1989 were constantly ambushed by Ahmed Shah Massoud's men in the Panjshir Valley. Dozens of carcasses of Soviet tanks and vehicles litter the valley floor; trophies, proof of the pleasure these tough people take in destroying invaders. It is difficult to imagine what new hardship the US and Britain can visit on the world's most punishing country.

I spent three days driving through the northeastern enclave held by the late Commandant Massoud's 'United Front'; conditions are even worse on the Taliban side of the front line. In Faizabad, where my journey began, the local United Front potentate has cornered the market on four wheel drive vehicles and interpreters since journalists began flocking to Afghanistan in the wake of September 11th. Last week, the three-day journey cost $700; this week it's $1,500. Two colleagues and I found one of the last available interpreters in northern Afghanistan. 'My name is Orush. It means "danger",' he proudly told me.

Orush's grievance with the Taliban, like most of the Afghans I encountered, was personal. 'We were living in Kabul in 1996. My father was a policeman,' Orush said. 'He fled to Faizabad before they came to the apartment. When I said he wasn't there, they threatened to kill me. They stole our car. It was a new Toyota, worth $2,000.'

Like all United Front supporters, Orush refers to the Taliban as 'terrorists'. One of the big questions facing the West is whether the United Front would be significantly better. Orush defends the forced isolation of Afghan women. 'They like wearing the burqa,' he told me. In three days, his most passionate condemnation of Mullah Omar's regime was that they stole the family's new car. For Commander Rolam Jailani, whom I met a day down the road at Iskozar, on his way to 'liberate' Kabul, it was also personal: the Taliban burned down his house.

There was something particularly sad about Azizullah, the United Front soldier we spoke to as we loaded the jeep. His age, twenty-three, is exactly that of the Afghan war, and like most of the Afghans I met, Azizullah looked a dozen years older. He had just returned from two months on the front at Taloqan and was proud that his unit had captured a hundred Taliban. But five of Azizullah's friends were killed, fifteen others wounded.

His wrist is scarred from a Taliban bullet, but he can still fire a Kalashnikov. 'It's impossible to eat or sleep on the front line,' he told me. 'We had only bread and water, nothing else. Most of the people are hungry in Afghanistan; this is the main problem.' Azizullah has been fighting since he was fifteen. 'Afghan people like fighting,' he continued. 'But if there was peace, I would throw away my weapon. I am one of the government forces and I am very poor. I don't have a house.' His monthly salary of 50,000 Afghanis comes to about $1.20.

At the first checkpoint we passed, a soldier wearing a US army surplus uniform with the name 'De burg' still penned on the pocket flap pretended to read our travel permit, upside down. 'Dear military officer of the Islamic State of Afghanistan,' it begins. 'Three foreign journalists want to go to the Panjshir. Please help them. Mohamed Nazir, Chief of the President's Foreign Relations Office.'

The presidential seal at the top shows a Moghul dome with two flags embraced by laurel branches. The president in question is Professor Burhanuddin Rabbani, who was chased out of Kabul by the Taliban in 1996. He majored in Islamic studies in Kabul and at Al Azhar, the seat of Sunni Muslim theology in Cairo. Rabbani's Afghan government is still the only one recognised by the United Nations, but his 'Islamic State' is an odd creature, repressing women almost as much as the Taliban, ensuring no government services other than defence. The 'Islamic State' still grieves for its real leader, Massoud, assassinated by Osama bin Laden's followers on 9 September 2001. Black flags fly throughout the enclave. A poster of 'the martyr Massoud' with his head thrown back and a red rose shedding tears of blood is omnipresent. Nearly every vehicle has a picture of Massoud taped to the front windscreen.

In a village called Hazrati Saïd, I met a pharmacist named Golam Omar, another refugee from the Taliban's 1998 conquest of the Shomali plain. He has not fought for three years, 'but I will fight now', the mild-mannered, bespectacled pharmacist said. 'We needed this,' he said of the US intervention. But didn't it sadden him to kill fellow Afghans? Omar reiterated a theme I hear often: 'Afghans never kill other Afghans. I killed foreign terrorists,' he said, alluding to the Arabs in Pakistan who joined bin Laden's forces.

We stopped for the night at what Orush called a 'hotel', a mud hut with a jute-cloth roof. The three owners brought plates of rice, which we ate with our fingers by the light of a sputtering lantern. The BBC was reporting the death of four UN employees in Kabul, civilians who worked in mine-clearing. A French correspondent and two photographers, disguised as women wearing burqas, had been arrested by the Taliban. It was the third night of the US bombing raids over Afghanistan, which the innkeepers had learned of only that day. They weren't really interested – the price of rice in Faizabad was their first question to our interpreter and driver. I was the only woman among eleven people who climbed into sleeping bags on the floor. Although I kept my long black coat and headscarf on, the Afghans stared at me as if I were an extra-terrestrial.

They had probably never seen the face of a woman outside their immediate families. Just after they snuffed out the lantern, torrents of rain began pouring through the jute ceiling, in a country that has known three years of drought. 'No problem. It's just one night,' Orush said.

We shared a breakfast of tea and bread with hundreds of United Front soldiers at a truck stop at Iskozar. The first fighter I spoke to fretted that the Americans were destroying Kabul, most of which is already in rubble. 'Who will rebuild it?' he asked me. 'Will the Americans pay for it?' The men sat cross-legged on thin mattresses on the floor, their Kalashnikovs in front of them, on the edge of a red vinyl cloth that served as a table. Some wore daggers on their belts. They pointed out an ethnic Pashtun soldier named Nasrullah.

'He's a Taleb [the singular of Taliban],' they joked. There were fifty Pashtuns in their unit of four hundred, they boasted; the United Front constantly tries to refute its image as the party of Tajiks.

If they met the Taliban in the trenches around Kabul, how would the 'army of the Islamic State' know the difference between Mullah Omar's men and their own fighters? 'They all wear *longi* [turbans],' the men laughed. 'And they have long beards and long hair,' another chimed in. 'We can tell from their speech,' a third said. Later, when we asked a goatherd to clear his animals from the road, Orush told me he was a Taleb. How did he know? 'He has a Pashtun accent,' the interpreter responded.

The unit commander, Rolam Jailani, supported the US intervention 'if only Taliban and military are killed. But I don't agree if civilians are killed, because they are Afghans.' Jailani fought the Soviets throughout the 1980s and boasted gleefully, in front of his two teenage sons, 'I killed a lot of Russians'. But wasn't it strange that 'infidel' Russia is now the United Front's ally? Not at all, Jailani said. 'The Russians are out of Afghanistan, and they help us.' Perhaps it was little different from the US government's flip-flop regarding Osama bin Laden and the Taliban. When the latter came to power in 1996, Madeleine Albright said it was 'a positive step'.

The high mountain to the Panjshir Valley is dotted with Soviet bomb craters, now lakes of sapphire-blue water. For all the desolation of this country, there are moments of great beauty: villagers harvesting golden wheat on a mountain plateau; the apparition of a horseman on a white Arab stallion who stops to stare at us from the riverbank.

The road gets slightly better as we jolt towards Kabul. There, on the opposite bank of the Panjshir river, are Massoud's collection of spent missile cases fired at the Taliban; more trophies. Three of the Front's helicopters, one of which bombarded Kabul on the night of September 11th, wait on the tarmac at Astanah. At Bozarak, the Front has assembled an impressive array of Soviet-made materiel.

And these are not rusting carcasses, but functioning weapons: fifteen T-54 and T-55 tanks, ten Katyusha rocket launchers, a dozen Kamaz trucks (used as troop carriers), a surface-to-surface missile, towed machine guns, and a dozen heavy artillery pieces.

It seems foolhardy to leave so much weaponry lined up in the open. The

Front obviously no longer fears the Taliban air force. One day soon, they believe the US and Britain will attack the Taliban's frontline positions, just a few dozen kilometres away. And that will be the signal they are waiting for, the signal to advance on Kabul.

13 October 2001

Smoking Hash While the US Bombs Fall

After more than a week of US and British bombardments, the evening ritual is well established. For the best view of the bombing of Kabul, you must arrive at the mountain village of Toap Dara before sunset, then wait on the roof of the local 'Islamic State Army' outpost as the temperature falls ten degrees every hour.

Hamid, my interpreter, and I somehow ended up discussing the will of Allah versus human initiative as we drove up the slope at twilight, in full view of the Taliban guns on the top of the mountain.

'Everything that happens is God's will,' Hamid said. 'That is why a Muslim is never afraid.' Moulana Nezamuddin, the village mullah, stood on a pile of stones, his hands cupped behind his ears, to chant the evening prayer call.

We climbed to the roof of a house abandoned by an Afghan who had fled to Pakistan. The rusted cab of an old truck, embedded in the mud building, served as a watchtower. Through binoculars, I could make out a Taliban tank on the crest to the southeast, and a Taliban radio antenna swaying on the peak directly above us.

'These binoculars have drunk the blood of many Taliban,' a mujahed named Ismael boasted to me. 'It doesn't let Arabs or Pakistanis or Chechens survive.'

The crack of gunfire raced down the mountain towards us, and the mujahedeen laughed as I ducked behind a wall. 'The Taliban see there are many of us on the roof,' one suggested. 'It's their way of saying "Welcome to Toap Dara".'

The procession of headlights from Kabul started at 6 PM, a long necklace snaking towards us, then stopping in the Taliban positions on the far side of Shomali Plain. The Taliban military feel so confident the US will not bomb their frontline positions opposite the United Front that they take shelter there every night. 'Everyone knows this; everyone sees them,' Hamid said. 'So why doesn't the US attack them? It is very suspicious.'

There were a few sparks – rockets fired by the United Front at the Taliban convoy – and the headlights went out briefly. At the northern end of Shomali, towards Panjshir, something burned bright yellow.

Below us, near Bagram Airport, another explosion left a crimson glow. In the midst of this soundless light show, we could hear the Taliban firing a heavy machine gun at a mujahedeen position on the mountain range where we sat.

'Why weren't they targeting *us*?' I asked the hirsute commander, Golpatcha. 'They used to shoot at us a lot,' he said. 'Now they are still firing, but not at us; we have some indications they want to defect to our side.'

The 'foreign ministry' of the United Front had insisted on sending a guard with us. I had mistakenly assumed it was to protect us from the Taliban, or bandits on the road. But the guard was there, I soon realised, to protect us from the Islamic State of Afghanistan's own fighters.

As night fell and we watched the chain of Taliban headlights, the gunmen began puffing away on hashish cigarettes. An American photographer's supply of juice cartons disappeared. 'These people are not trustworthy,' Hamid whispered. 'Do not leave your belongings.' The hash-smoking guerrillas never went to school, he added. 'They know only the Kalashnikov. They like to steal, especially from foreigners.'

The Afghan capital was 35 kilometres due south, a halo diffused from behind the screen of a low mountain. Our light-fingered mujahedeen compan-ions were by now so high on hashish that they giggled like schoolgirls as they sat waiting beside us.

At 9 PM, arrows of red tracer bullets and sparkling anti-aircraft fire rose up from the city. With the first bright flash of an American bomb, the muja-hedeen cheered and roared with laughter. 'Kill the Taliban! Kill the Taliban!' they shouted. A few more flashes over the following hour, then nothing.

When I picked up my shoulder bag to go, the mujahedeen shrieked. Here was something more frightening than Taliban bullets or American bombs: a scorpion the size of a man's hand, quickly crushed under Ismael's heel.

Hamid had napped with his head on the bag, and drew the obvious con-clusion: 'You see, Missus Lara, Allah wants me to survive.'

On the road back to Jabal Saraj, Hamid, 28, told me how he'd abandoned medical school in Kabul because the faculty no longer had the means to train physicians. He left the capital a few weeks ago, in the hope of making his way to Europe via the United Front's 'free' enclave.

The guerrillas' laughter at the bomb explosions had enraged him. 'My mother and father, four brothers and sisters, are all in Kabul,' Hamid said. 'Maybe the bombs fell on them. These country people don't understand. My friends and family are Afghans too.'

17 October 2001

No Peace While There Are Foreign Hands

Commander Ahmed Shah Massoud was about to climb into a helicopter for Tajikistan when his press attaché pulled him aside. Could the leader of the United Front, the internationally recognised government of Afghanistan, spare just ten minutes for two Arab journalists? They'd been waiting nine days.

The 'cameraman' set his equipment on a table opposite Massoud and fidgeted with it for a long moment. 'What would you do with bin Laden if you returned to power?' the 'correspondent' asked. Massoud burst out laughing, and the camera exploded. Afghanistan's most charismatic warlord, 'the lion of Panjshir', was killed instantly, though the Front tried to keep his death secret while its new leadership was established.

Two days later, bin Laden's followers destroyed the World Trade Center. Massoud's assassination is believed to have been the sign for them to attack. The murder was calculated to destroy domestic opposition to the Taliban before American retaliation. For Afghans, the death of Massoud, not the destruction of the World Trade Center, marks the beginning of the war between the US and the Taliban.

Massoud is buried on a high promontory in his native Panjshir Valley. To the north, the river flows through the yellowing autumn trees of Bazarak town. The spires of the Hindu Kush soar to the south, the majesty of nature in contrast with the poor dwellings, the cheap red bricks they're using to build Massoud's still domeless mausoleum. His followers have named the promontory Tapa Salare Shaheedan, 'the hill of great martyrs'.

It is sunset, and a beautiful European woman alights from an aid agency jeep. She wears mourning clothes: a long black dress and a white headscarf that flutters in the breeze. The driver walks a respectful distance behind her as she stands on the earthen bank around the half-finished tomb, looking down on the grave, meditating. A strange, heavy-sweet scent rises from the flowers growing over Massoud's remains. A mullah squats against the wall of the mausoleum, reading the Koran. The woman turns to go, and she is weeping. 'Commander Ahmed Shah Massoud helped our hospital very much,' she says. 'I cannot talk now.' She floats away, an apparition, one more element in the growing mythology of Massoud.

The guards at the tomb keep a visitors' book with entries in French, English, Chinese and Japanese, as well as the Tajiks' language, Dari. The messages, many of them from Western journalists who had interviewed Massoud, are gushing. It seems ironic that Massoud was so admired abroad, when his constant refrain was the danger of foreign intervention. 'We want good relations with foreign countries, but we do not want to be under their control,' says the Massoud quotation outside his tomb.

'While he was alive, there were no foreign hands in Afghanistan,' the twenty-two-year-old guard tells me, apparently forgetting ten years of Soviet occupation and the Pakistani influence on the Taliban. 'We follow his way by cutting foreign hands from Afghanistan. As long as there are foreign hands, there can never be peace in Afghanistan.'

Among the men coming to pray at the graveside, I come across another crucial ingredient of myth-making: the premonition. Hafizullah, 60, a cousin of the 'great martyr', last saw Massoud a week before he was murdered. 'He was swimming with his son and nephew in the Panjshir river, and while they were swimming, he told his son, "This is the last time I will swim with you". That night he woke his wife at 1 AM and told her, "I will not be here long. Soon I will be martyred."'

When I ask the name of Massoud's widow, the interpreter refuses to translate the question. I insist, and receive only embarrassed silence in reply. In Afghanistan, there is a taboo against speaking any woman's name. In villages, the mere mention of a female leads to fights between her relatives and the imprudent speaker. Despite Massoud's 'progressive' Islam, the women in his enclave do not exist, even in name. Massoud had three wives, a Western Afghan expert told me, warning that I risked being expelled from 'free Afghanistan' if I reported it.

Still trying to understand Massoud's hold over his followers, I spoke to another of the men emerging from the domeless mausoleum. 'Massoud was a champion,' he said. 'If you want to know who he was, look at all the burnt-out Russian tanks and vehicles.' As if on cue, he points to the carcass of a T-55, lying at a slant on the mountainside, just thirty metres from the tomb.

But if Massoud was such a great man, I ask, why is the United Front enclave so poor, without plumbing, electricity or paved roads, only gunmen and weapons? The great man's cousin, Hafizullah, answers, 'It was better to finish the fight first.'

27 October 2001

Trapped in a War That Every Afghan Dreams of Escaping

Several times, as I clung to the gearshift of a Russian jeep hurtling alongside deep ravines, contemplated life as a hostage in the upper Panjshir Valley and felt my toes going numb hiking over a snowed-in mountain pass, I thought of Haji Qadir.

I'd interviewed the former governnor of Nangarhar province before his brother Abdul Haq, a hero of the *jihad* against the Soviets, was executed by the Taliban last week.

Sitting cross-legged on blue velvet cushions, Qadir stuck a bare foot out and clamped his own ankle with both hands, simulating an animal trap. 'If the Americans continue in this way,' Qadir said, 'the day is coming when they will be caught like the Russians.' Afghanistan does not welcome visitors.

At best, its people accost foreigners with the insistence of beggars. Their cruelty to one another is legendary; in the past decade, thousands of prisoners were dumped in wells and blown up with hand grenades, or left to suffocate in shipping containers in the desert.

Westerners go there at their peril. Three French colleagues and I hired a worn-out Russian jeep, the best we could find in Jabal Saraj, for the journey through the Hindu Kush mountains to the Tajik border.

After six hours, our driver Emon announced that the gearbox was broken. Each time we started up a steep slope, he threw the jeep into first gear and shouted '*mocambi*', the signal that I was to wrestle the lever down.

That night we stopped in a remote village where we were given dry bread and tea in a cramped mud hut.

A few hours later, I woke to a terrible racket. While Céline, Rémi and I slept in our sleeping bags, Jean-Baptiste discovered we were prisoners. He shook the wooden door and shouted, as the villagers who had shut us in with a padlock laughed.

Jean-Baptiste eventually broke a plank and prised off the padlock. In the morning, the owner of the hut demanded to be paid for the damage.

By then we had other worries. A storm overnight left the village mired in mud, and the first snow on the peaks above us. Several hundred men from the 01 division of the 'Islamic State Army' were, like us, heading north. Emon the driver followed two Kamaz army lorries.

We advanced slowly, waiting in the cold each time the trucks broke down or got stuck. At one stop, the division commander Mohamed Akram introduced himself and we took souvenir photos, not realising we were about to trek over the mountains together.

At 4,900 metres, the Anjoman Pass is higher than Mont Blanc. The surrounding peaks average 6,000 metres. Most years, the first snow falls in early November; we were unlucky. The pass remains snowed in until midsummer.

The Kamaz trucks and our jeep driver put on snow chains, but as we approached Anjoman it was obvious we could not drive through fifty metres of snow. It was already 3 PM and we had to decide: hike over Anjoman at the risk of freezing in a new storm or darkness, or turn back to Jabal Saraj, where we might wait weeks for a helicopter.

A soldier named Shesdat carried my canvas bag with the strap across his forehead. Another fighter, Shirin Agha, wore my computer across his chest, its strap forming an 'X' with his Kalashnikov webbing. Several dozen of us set out in single file through the snow. In running shoes, I worried about frostbite, until I realised that one of the mujahedeen wore sandals with socks; another, sneakers with no socks. Despite the support of Iran, Russia, France, India and the grudging assistance of the US, the United Front is as impoverished as Afghanistan itself.

In the afternoon light, with a half-moon rising, the snow-covered mountains were so spectacular that we were seized with a kind of euphoria. The mujahedeen plunged Kalashnikovs and rocket launchers into the snow in lieu of walking sticks. Once we'd started the icy descent, a reckless soldier abandoned the snaking path to race headlong down the mountainside, shouting 'Commando, Commando'. An old soldier with a grey beard struggled under a heavy machine gun. Each time he slipped on the ice, the others laughed without mercy.

Another fighter fell far behind. Word reached the front of the procession that his shoes had broken. Commander Akram found a spare pair and placed them on a rock, then fired his Kalashnikov in the air to show the hapless soldier where the shoes were.

It was dark when we reached an army encampment on the far side of Anjoman. We hired another jeep, and reached the northern capital of Faizabad the following afternoon. By chance, the first Antonov in ten days was preparing for take-off. We half-pleaded, half-stormed our way on to the plane, which was ferrying thirty of President Burhanuddin Rabbani's bodyguards to Tajikstan, en route for training in Iran.

We hadn't realised that the transport aircraft was bound for the Russian air base at Kurgonteppa, not Dushanbe. When the Afghan bodyguards had disembarked, there were eleven journalists and aid workers left.

We had no authorisation to fly to Dushanbe, or to leave the air base, a Russian colonel informed us. For despite a decade's independence, Russia still runs Tajikistan. We would have to spend the night on the tarmac at Kurgonteppa, the colonel threatened.

I'd met a man in Jabal Saraj who had paid $1,500 for a Tajik visa. When he flew to Dushanbe last year, the Russians arrested him at the airport, threw him into a crowded, lice- and flea-infested cell for twenty days, then dumped him over the Afghan border.

Frightened though he was, the Afghan was about to restart the desperate process, in the hope of reaching Europe.

But we were privileged Westerners, playing Scrabble as we waited for the Soviet-era bureaucracy to sort itself out. A decrepit bus with a Tajik bodyguard who looked like a sumo wrestler eventually came for us. 'They call me Hurricane,' the bodyguard boasted.

Hurricane saw us through highway checkpoints with gates like level crossings, designed by Moscow decades ago to control the masses. Dushanbe was the last stop before showers, food, and beds with sheets and *sans* fleas.

About the same time, Commander Akram, Sheshdat and Shirin Agha would be arriving on the front line at Taloqan, trapped in a war that every Afghan dreams of escaping.

31 October 2001

VI

IRAQ

Clear Memories of Dark Days

In the third week of March 2003, Iraq counted the days until George W. Bush's ultimatum expired, as if waiting for the Apocalypse. The Pentagon had threatened the most intense, sustained bombardment in modern history. US officials said they would retaliate with tactical nukes if Saddam used chemical or biological weapons.

Over the preceding months, the residents of Baghdad had grown to accept the idea of their annihilation, as if they were to be punished for failing to overthrow their dictator. When the bombardment finally started, a few hours after the passing of the deadline Bush imposed for Saddam and his family to leave Iraq, it was almost a relief. Iraqis who had the means to escape had fled. Those who remained stocked up on mineral water, fuel, battery lamps, tinned food and gas masks. The government distributed rations for six months in advance. In the last days of the countdown, I saw tearful civil servants empty desk drawers in ministries marked for destruction. Anticipating the looting that would seize the capital when the regime fell, merchants hid their goods and bricked up shopfronts.

Until the regime fell on 9 April, its henchmen indulged in the usual threats and bluster. The wives and mothers of US servicemen would 'cry tears of blood', warned Saddam's psychopathic son, Uday.

I saw a woman weep tears of blood on 2 April in Hilla, a hundred kilometres south of Baghdad. She was Samira Murza Abdel Hamza, a forty-eight-year-old housewife, and she'd been wounded by US cluster bombs in an attack that killed some sixty civilians. Shrapnel had lodged in both Hamza's eyes, turning them bright red. Fragments of metal had pierced her chest and knees.

Uday Saddam Hussein and his brother Qusay would be gunned down by US Marines in Mosul four months later. Uday's prediction that Americans would not be safe 'anywhere in Iraq or in the world' has, alas, come true. True, too, the Iraqi government's declaration that Saddam Hussein was born in Iraq and would die in Iraq.

The US fired the opening salvoes at dawn on the morning of 20 March, bombing a disused farm on the outskirts of Baghdad. (It was still 19 March in Washington – the reason the date varies.) In the centre of the capital, anti-air-craft artillery rattled on for half an hour, accompanied by barking dogs, chirp-ing birds and the muezzin's prayer call. Saddam went on television to announce that 'the insane Bush . . . has started a war against Iraq'. But the dawn bombardment was just an appetiser, a distant clap of thunder before US forces got down to serious business on the night of 20 March, the night of 'shock and awe'.

As deafening explosions shook the city, huge golden fireballs spread across the presidential complex on the west side of the Tigris river, then burned like bonfires all night. It was a spectacle of unimaginable violence, but because we could not see the US bombers and warships that were launching the cruise missiles, it seemed like a natural disaster, perhaps a volcanic eruption. From the Palestine Hotel, across the Tigris from the complex, some three hundred journalists transmitted this sound and fury to the outside world.

Almost daily for three weeks, officials from the Iraqi Ministry of Information would show us bombed-out buildings, the wounded and dying. The bombard-ment rarely let up, but was especially heavy at night. The Iraqis burned tyres and oil inside berms – parallel earthen containment banks – in the hope of dis-orienting US missile guidance systems. The smoke mixed with desert sand-storms, turning Baghdad into a sinister twilight zone where men wrapped keffiehs around their faces to breathe, and cars used their headlights even at midday. Jet engines roared constantly in the sky overhead. Explosions were so frequent that no one noticed unless they were nearby.

On 26 March, US missiles struck morning traffic in Ash-Shaab, a neigh-bourhood of car repair garages in northwest Baghdad. Seventeen people were killed, including a mother and her three children, two restaurant workers, a mechanic, the owner of an electrical shop and the neighbourhood beggar.

I would see worse things in the course of the war, but the attack on Ash-Shaab stuck in my mind. Dirty rain, saturated with smoke and desert sand, coated my face, clothing and notebook. In the muddy devastation of Abi Taleb Street, oil from the mechanics' shops swirled in sickening pools with the vic-tims' blood.

Hisham Danoon, a dazed building supervisor who had seen four men cut to pieces by the missile, pointed to a hand lying in the mud. 'That was my friend Tahar,' he said. The hand was yellowed, no doubt by tobacco. Its fingers curled, and it was crimson red at the wrist where it had been severed. I thought of a chicken chopped into pieces by a butcher's cleaver. 'There is Tahar's brain,' Danoon continued, pointing at a viscous mound between two shards of corrugated steel roofing.

At Ash-Shaab, I learned days later, a Belgian colleague saw a Scud missile launcher in a side street, a fact US forces used to justify the attack on the civilian district. Fifty-five more Baghdadis were killed in a similar attack on the Shu'ala market two days later.

On 3 April, US forces reached the outskirts of Baghdad. That night, at the onset of a twenty-four-hour battle for Baghdad's airport, the electricity and running water went down. The regime had tried to keep its military casualties secret. The following day there was no attempt to hide the dozens of maimed and bleeding men who filled the Yarmook Hospital to overflowing.

The southern and western parts of the capital were now the front line. Burned-out Iraqi armoured personnel carriers, gun batteries and jeeps dotted the roadsides like dead insects. Soldiers and militiamen were everywhere. Army lorries drove past with corpses stacked in their flatbeds. Within days, I would see the blackened, bloated remains of motorists who'd been killed by US tank fire as the invaders secured a key interchange on Dora highway.

On 7 April, I was awakened by the clatter of F-18 bombers, the whinnying of A-10 'tank-buster' aircraft, artillery, and small arms fire. The Americans had arrived in central Baghdad, and were taking over the presidential complex, which they would turn into the Green Zone, their occupation headquarters.

Again, the journalists in the Palestine Hotel were placed front row centre. We watched some thirty Iraqi soldiers flee their bunkers and artillery emplacements to run along the bottom of the river embankments as US Bradley armoured fighting vehicles took position above them. An Iraqi wearing only white pants and a vest appeared to have been caught sleeping.

Three journalists were killed on 8 April, the last full day of Saddam's reign. Tariq Ayoub, a Jordanian correspondent for al-Jazeera television, was broadcasting from the roof of the station's office, on the west bank near the presidential complex, when a US aircraft fired a rocket at him. Al-Jazeera had received assurances from the US government that it would not be attacked.

Two US Abrams tanks moved onto Jumhurriya bridge. One trained its turret on the Palestine Hotel and fired a shell, killing Taras Protsyuk, a cameraman for Reuters television, and José Couso, a cameraman for the Spanish channel Telecinco.

The US military did not admit that it had killed the journalists until France 3 showed its videotape of the tank firing, followed by the hotel shaking two seconds later.

The ninth of April will forever be the anniversary of *al-suqut*, the fall. West Baghdad, al-Karkh, was now secured by the Americans. But Baghdad Risafa, the east bank, where the Palestine Hotel is located, still hovered in limbo. Another US division approached via Saddam City, the Shia slums in the northeast of the capital.

Though fighting continued, especially on the bridges, we decided to visit the Saddam Medical Centre. Nothing in three weeks of war had prepared me for what I saw in the hospital lobby. The wounded were lined up on trolleys and on the floor. Some were bandaged or covered in burn cream. Others waited with open wounds to be treated. Limbs dangled by pieces of bone or flesh. An orderly pushed pools of blood with a mop.

Dr Khaldoun al-Bayati, the director of the hospital, was the heroic captain of a sinking ship. He had not slept for six nights, and did not know where his wife and children were. US troops on the far side of the river kept lobbing shells onto the hospital grounds, because it was located opposite the defence ministry, and the Iraqi army had hidden armour in the oleander shrubs outside. With each explosion, shrieks of terror punctuated the moans of the wounded.

We waited for a lull and sped back to the Palestine Hotel. My Iraqi 'minder', a colonel in the *mokhabarat* (intelligence service), ran away to hide at his sister's home. I talked to the Arab fighters who sat cross-legged under the portico of the Palestine. They were afraid the local population would lynch them, and contemplated surrender to US forces. 'Why does this always happen to the Arabs?' an Algerian asked me.

Saddam Hussein claimed there were thousands of Arabs eager to sacrifice themselves for his regime. These hungry, thirsty fighters had been abandoned by their Iraqi commanders. But they vanished before the Americans arrived. Later, when Arabs began carrying out suicide attacks, I wondered if they were the men I'd talked to on 9 April.

The Americans were coming. In the afternoon sun, I walked down Yassir Arafat Street until I saw the endless line of sand-coloured tanks and armoured personnel carriers rolling towards me. Their supplies were strapped onto the sides of the armour, like camels in the desert. Wearing goggles, helmets and body armour, the soldiers trained their M-16s at the Iraqis who watched from the roadside.

Looters swarmed in the wake of the US convoy. The first one I saw, a teenager in a grimy tracksuit, pushed a medical X-ray machine down the pavement. As the Americans set up in the Palestine Hotel, the looters fanned out through the city, sacking government ministries, embassies, UN offices. Arsonists set fires that burned for days across the city. The Americans did nothing to stop them.

Several hundred Iraqis gathered on Ferdoos Square, outside the Palestine Hotel. They tore the plaque off the base of Saddam Hussein's statue, then attacked it with a sledgehammer. US Marine Sergeant Leon C. Lambert from Colorado asked his commanding officer, Lieutenant Colonel Bryan McCoy, for permission to tear down the statue. It was, McCoy said, a job for the Iraqi people. The people tried for forty-five minutes, so McCoy relented. The Iraqis placed a cable, noose-like, around the neck of Saddam's effigy, and Sergeant Lambert's M88 tank retriever tugged at the statue. It cracked at the shins, teetered, and slowly fell. The mob stamped on it, hacked off its head and dragged it around the square with a chain.

The world had its iconic image of Saddam's fall, but Iraq's nightmare was only beginning.

15 March 2008

Baghdad Under the Bombs

President Saddam Hussein's monumental Palace of the Republic rises above lush gardens, a couple of kilometres as the crow flies from my hotel room balcony. The first time it was attacked by US cruise missiles, on the night of 21 March, huge flames devoured its façade, and I expected to see a pile of ashes in the morning.

But my report of the destruction of the immense complex, like oft-announced US-British successes in southern Iraq, was premature. The burn marks are there on the side of the stone structure, and part of its roof is missing. Though no one seriously thinks the Iraqi leader is inside, the US still bombs the palace almost daily, and motorists instinctively speed up when they pass it.

Saddam's palace is a fitting allegory for Baghdad itself. For the first days of the war, the capital played dead. The streets were deserted, and shopfronts blocked by metal shutters, if not completely bricked up. The bombardments have not diminished – on the contrary, they are more frequent – but a strange thing has happened two weeks into the war: battered, limping, at only a fraction of its pre-war pace, Baghdad lives.

Red and white Chinese-built double-decker buses ply their regular routes. Boys on donkey-drawn carts hawk cooking gas and kerosene. At the Shorja market in the city centre, there are tonnes of powdered baby milk on offer, fresh lettuce, oranges, tomatoes, bananas and cigarettes.

Judging from the number of Iraqis nervously puffing away, tobacco consumption has doubled.

The tailors' shops in al Rashid Street are closed – 'People don't need clothes during a war', an official explains – but street vendors have hung camouflage T-shirts, militia and army uniforms from the fence along a major traffic circle.

For some reason I haven't fathomed, Baghdad has more barber shops than anywhere I've been, and most of them are still open. [*I later realised it's because most Iraqi men over age forty dye their hair black. This preening was not interrupted by the war.*]

Yesterday I saw water tankers emblazoned with the words 'Baghdad Municipality. Keep Your City Clean' hosing down streets and watering plants in three areas of the city.

'We're still working, every day,' Sa'el Hussein, the deputy mayor in charge of the capital's water supply, roads and city planning, told me. 'Collecting rubbish and sweeping streets is our way of resisting.'

A former brigadier in the Iraqi army who trained as a mechanical engineer in the northern city of Mosul, Hussein wears a green militia uniform and proudly shows me his revolver. 'I spend four hours a day on guard duty in the street,' he says. 'I sleep here [in the municipality building] at night, to set an example.'

Life in Baghdad is a strange mix of normality and terror. Several times, I've seen boys playing football on vacant lots, as I drove to the site of bombings. Blue-uniformed traffic cops wear helmets with camouflage netting and wave Kalashnikovs as they shout at cars, 'Keep moving. Keep moving'. Iraqis stopped respecting traffic lights when the war started – surprising, in a country where the tiniest infraction brings swift punishment.

'As long as there is bombing, people shouldn't stop at intersections,' the deputy mayor explains. 'Because the Americans concentrate on any accumulation of cars; they consider them a target. We haven't made a formal announcement, but those with military experience know this.'

The air raid alert was on when I arrived at the municipality, and listless men filled the lobby. 'I send the staff to the ground floor during air raids,' Hussein explained. It was pay day for his 9,000 employees. All receive their salary, the equivalent of $10 on average, including women who stay at home with their children, and men whose places of work have been destroyed. Construction projects, like the massive Saddam Hussein Mosque, stopped with the first bombardments.

The deputy mayor's biggest concern is potable water. 'We have fourteen water purification and twenty-three sewage plants in Baghdad,' he says. 'One of the water plants received a direct hit, but others have been damaged by cut pipes and cables.'

Though the 1,600 employees of the city water company produce 2,250,000 cubic metres of drinking water each day, there's a chronic shortage, 'because of the embargo,' Hussein says. 'We've had no hard currency for new plants, and chlorine has been scarce since the last war.' Now he fears US bombers will target electricity plants, without which he cannot pump water.

Despite the municipality's efforts, and the resumption of morning traffic jams downtown, the siege of Baghdad has already started in the minds of the capital's inhabitants. Middle class Baghdadis have retreated into their homes.

Idle teenagers complain that Iraqi television no longer shows films – only imams citing Koranic verses about *jihad*, and patriotic anthems. Cinemas are closed, and Baghdadis now make a sport of standing on rooftops, trying to spot US cruise missiles and bombers.

The last internet cafés shut down last week. So did international phone lines, after six telephone exchanges were bombed. With Iraq's isolation from the outside world almost total, daily newspapers give pride of place to anti-war protests from Djakarta to California, and Iraqi claims of heavy US and British losses.

Every day, there is an entire page of gruesome photographs of civilian dead and wounded. For once, the poor quality of the printing is a mercy.

The government has ordered all bakeries to remain open; bakers continue to receive daily deliveries of wheat flour and oil from the trade ministry. Most economic activity is linked to the war. Television aerials are the hottest-selling items on the pavements of Jumhurriya Street. Iraq's last remaining television station blinks on and off as the US bombs its transmitters.

The government has improvised mobile broadcasting stations, but their signal is weak; hence the need for better reception. With a cheap Chinese antenna, which costs nearly a month's wages, Iraqis can watch the Arabic service of Iranian TV. Sorting out fact from fiction in news reports from neighbouring countries is as great a challenge as deciphering their own government's propaganda.

The items stacked for sale on the pavements downtown speak volumes about how poor Baghdadis hope to survive: jerricans for fuel and water; plastic sheeting to replace broken windows; kerosene lanterns; battery lamps that can be charged from mains electricity, for use during power cuts.

The rich long ago acquired water tanks and generators. Luxury shops and restaurants shut down for the first twelve days of the war, but a few are beginning to stir, sniffing a long conflict and the possibility of profit. A supermarket that specialises in gourmet pre-cooked meals reopened this week, but its shelves are almost empty.

'I can't sell fresh food because it will spoil if the electricity goes, and I am not restocking because I worry about looters,' the owner says.

The office of the deputy mayor is cluttered with relics of past achievements and unfulfilled dreams: a scale model of a Spanish water-pumping station; a plaque commemorating the completion of the 'Saddam Quarter' housing project in 1985; the map of the 'Baghdad Comprehensive Transportation Study', including ring roads and a metro, drawn up by Scott Wilson Kirkpatrick and Partners of West Byfleet, Surrey.

The walls are papered with Polish architects' impressions of a master plan for 'new Baghdad'. Since the plan's conception in 1989, the paper has faded, the edges curled. 'I want Baghdad to be as it was in history, the bride of the east, under the Abbassid caliphs, in the thirteenth century,' Hussein says. Until two weeks ago, he was working with Baghdad University on a new 'master plan', target date: 2027.

Now, from the sixth floor of the municipality building, Hussein contemplates columns of smoke, stretching across the city. Baghdad is burning; the blackest smoke is from the oil fires lit by Iraqis to confuse US bombers. White or grey smoke usually indicates a newly bombed target.

Our conversation is interrupted by a loud explosion. The windows rattle and the floor vibrates, and I wonder which fantasy is more deluded: the deputy mayor's vision of a glorious city, or the US-British determination to impose 'freedom and democracy' on this tortured country.

2 April 2003

'Yours, guiltily'

I received a difficult request from Dublin the other day, to write about my daily life here. It's not that there isn't plenty to say about explosions and danger, blackouts and water shortages, bad food and grotty hotel rooms. All of these are much as you'd expect.

But however challenging the assignment, Western journalists are privileged people, even in this war zone. US bombers are less likely to target our hotel. Wads of $100 bills can perform almost any miracle, short of stopping a cruise missile or healing a wounded civilian. So let me apologise from the outset for trying to describe my life here . . . .

Saturday is my day off, because *The Irish Times* isn't published on Sunday. So on Saturday morning, I listened to the BBC, breakfasted on biscuits and Nescafé, then enjoyed a glorious cold bath and hair wash. My hotel had been without water for thirty-six hours, and it felt fantastic to be clean.

A joke during the Lebanese civil war had it that Beirutis were the happiest people in the world, because they knew true joy every time the water and power came back. Here too, simple things bring inordinate pleasure: being able to recharge your sat-phone, laundry that you'd given up on, a good night's sleep.

The BBC was reporting that the risk of chemical warfare had never been higher, so I pulled the suitcase holding my €300 Finnish gas mask from the top of my hotel room cupboard. I'd attended a nuclear-biological-chemical training session for journalists in January, but it had been almost as incomprehensible as the manual that came with the gas mask.

'Tell me something practical,' I had pleaded with the French briefers. If there was a chemical attack, they said, get the hell out of the area. If that wasn't possible and you were in a tall building – and I'm thinking of my seventeen-floor hotel – go to the roof. A friend in Paris suggested I paste a sticker with my name and blood type on the mask's plexiglass visor, and I washed the drinking water bottle with the special screw-in nozzle before leaving.

But my preparations ended there, and I thought I'd devote my leisurely Saturday morning to learning how to use the gas mask. The only section I understood was 'using the drinking device', so I filled the canteen with bottled water, then tried ridiculous contortions to trap the transparent straw inside the mask with my tongue and teeth, as per instructions. Impossible. I stashed the mask back on the top shelf and decided to worry about chemical weapons if, and when, the problem arose.

After giving up on the gas mask, I thought I'd stock up on supplies. A pack rat mentality comes naturally in war; you buy anything that might prove useful. Shopping enables you to talk to people and see what is going on in the city. And it brings more of those small pleasures, like finding the computer diskette I needed to clear the memory on my Toshiba, or a bar of Nivea soap to replace the skin-peeling variety provided by the hotel.

Since the battle for Baghdad started at the weekend, most shops have shut down. Tension rises by the hour, along with the number of armed men in the streets.

The search for an open grocery store took me to the southwest of the city. When I saw a *duschke* anti-tank gun and pieces of wreckage at an intersection, I realised we had wandered on to the front line. Two burned-out Iraqi army trucks smouldered beside the boulevard; a charred BMP armoured personnel carrier lay at the base of a scorched palm tree. Hundreds of Iraqi soldiers were in the area, sheltering next to walls, riding in the back of open lorries.

I felt sheepish over my cheery Saturday morning fussing and grooming, while this battle was going on just a few kilometres away. A pick-up truck, its back gate open, drove by with four militiamen perched on the sides, their guns pointed outwards. The bed of the truck was layered with bodies, two deep, under blankets. A naked foot stuck out.

Back at the Palestine Hotel, dozens of Iraqi police cars were speeding by, their sirens on, their occupants waving Kalashnikovs out of the windows as they headed for battle. The information minister was holding a press conference, a staple of daily life here, in which he claimed that the Republican Guard had taken the airport back from the Americans.

There was a terrible racket outside – anti-aircraft artillery – and everyone ran to the window. 'He's shot down! He's shot down!' the Iraqis exulted. Then we saw the contrails of a US jet zig-zagging – the pilot had escaped after all. By nightfall, it was the turn of the Republican Guard to circle the hotel in pick-up trucks, joy-shooting to celebrate their 'victory' at the airport.

No description of life here would be complete without the noise. The best words are comic strip onomatopoeia, written with an exclamation point: 'Crash!', 'Bang!' and especially 'Boom!' Some of my more macho colleagues claim they can hear the difference between incoming and outgoing artillery fire, between Tomahawk cruise missiles and laser-guided bombs. The only sounds I recognise with certainty are jet engines and, because it's so distinctive, the drum-rolling detonation of cluster bombs.

I barely notice the noise now, unless an explosion is particularly loud or close by. Earplugs enable me to sleep for hours at a stretch. In Baghdad, detonations are part of the background, along with ambulance sirens and the thrum of the television networks' generators.

Visually, the night of 21 March was the most dramatic violence I have witnessed in more than two decades as a reporter. From my balcony, I watched as building after building was enveloped by giant bubbles of golden flame. I couldn't help thinking of my late mother, who believed the world would end with the battle of Armageddon.

On an infinitely smaller scale, the anti-aircraft artillery that fired as I drove past it a few days ago was fascinating. The guns could have been US Civil War cannons. The analogy that came to my mind, of white lizards' tongues, was so strange that I left the word 'lizard' out of my copy.

The present in Baghdad constantly takes me back to other wars: the crashing of cruise missiles in the dark is familiar from Belgrade; the devastated *mokhabarat* building I saw last week looked like the former US Marine headquarters in Beirut, destroyed by a suicide bomber in 1983.

On Friday night during an air raid, a raucous group of Iraqi children, doubtless the progeny of high-ranking officials, rushed into a lift in the Palestine Hotel, giggling and pushing and jamming the system. There was a loud detonation as the door finally closed and one cried out *'Oumi'* ('Mamma'), to be slapped in the face by a sibling. In 1991, at the Meridien Hotel in Dhahran, spoiled Kuwaiti children behaved the same way.

Several times over the past two and a half weeks, I've thought of that scene in *Lawrence of Arabia* where Omar Sharif and Peter O'Toole watch an artillery bombardment at night, from a distance. 'Pity those poor bastards, under that,' Sharif says. 'But they are Turks!' O'Toole protests. 'Pity them all the same,' says Sharif.

When you hear a bombardment, you can't help feeling sorry for anyone near it. But subconsciously, there's a selfish undertow, a gratitude that it's someone else, not me.

Feelings about 'the big picture' are equally contradictory. In moments of weariness, you want the bombardment to end immediately, no matter what, no matter how. At other times, out of dread of the sheer violence of it, you want to postpone the final battle indefinitely, forever.

War breeds irrational fears and superstitions. Before the electricity went out last Thursday night, I kept fighting the urge to turn out my hotel room lamps, in the absurd belief the light might attract a US bomber. Am I tempting fate, I sometimes wonder, by wearing a red pullover? Is it better to joke about private fears or keep quiet?

For twenty-five years, Guillaume Apollinaire's *Alcools* has been my *livre de chevet*, the thin volume of poetry that I keep on the nightstand. It was with me in the Saudi desert in the previous Gulf war. Most nights I lie in bed in Baghdad, with a battery-run halogen miner's lamp on my forehead, and read a poem or two.

Poetry, I know, is no antidote for this madness. All the more reason to read '*La Chanson du Mal-Aimé*' for the umpteenth time, turn out my miner's lamp and hope, selfishly, that the explosions will be far away, at least until morning.

8 April 2003

On the Last Day
of Saddam's Misrule

The last day of Saddam Hussein's regime started with the usual deadly ruckus of bombing, artillery and gunfire, and reports that US troops were converging from the north and south east of Baghdad towards the city centre.

Some invisible frontier had been crossed overnight. Downstairs in the Palestine Hotel, almost none of the information ministry officials who helped, bullied, bored and financially exploited foreign correspondents showed up for work.

Outside, white sheets hung from the balconies, a reminder of the two cameramen killed when a US Abrams tank fired a shell at the hotel inhabited by the foreign press the previous day. A reminder, and a plea to the advancing Americans: 'Don't shoot. We're journalists.'

My minder reported for duty, albeit late. 'I was almost martyred twice,' he panted. 'I nearly drove into three American tanks near the Yarmook Hospital, and four more in Haifa Street.'

As we headed up Yassir Arafat Street in Karrada, I noticed that the militiamen, police and Saddam Fedayeen who'd ruled the streets had vanished. 'It is useless to carry a gun against a tank,' my minder said. Until yesterday, he was a staunch supporter of the regime.

City services broke down last week and piles of rotting garbage lined the streets. In a bakery queue, I asked a middle-aged, middle class Baghdadi how he felt. The minder was out of hearing range, but it will take time to break the conditioning of thirty years of dictatorship.

'Maybe I can tell you soon,' the man answered. 'We are afraid.'

The baker was not frightened. He walked out carrying bags of hot, fresh bread for me, grinning broadly. US troops were already in the slums of Saddam

City, a few miles up the road, and he knew it. We could hear the loud 'c-r-r-u-m-p' of outgoing artillery fire, and shooting, but the baker's joy outweighed fear or intimidation by the minder.

'I am very, very, very happy,' he announced. Then he turned to my imposed escort and taunted him, in an extraordinary show of bravado. 'You are from the Ministry of Information, I believe. The ministry has been bombed! Yesterday, I saw your minister drive by in an old car, not a limousine, and he looked very upset!'

Most of east Baghdad was still nominally in the hands of the regime, but we saw not a single soldier. The bridges were undefended. We stopped at Saddam Medical Centre, across the street from the bombed-out defence ministry. Two military tents were pitched between the hospital and the riverbank, and an armoured vehicle was parked beside an oleander shrub ten metres from the hospital.

In the Adnan annex – named after Saddam Hussein's late uncle, Adnan Khairallah, whom he allegedly had killed in a helicopter crash – we found a scene worthy of Hieronymus Bosch's *Tryptych from Hell*. The twenty-foot-wide corridor of the outpatient department had been turned into an emergency room. The first patient held his arms upwards, paralysed in an arc, covered in burn cream. His face was so badly burned that I had to look away.

On another hospital trolley, doctors were performing an emergency tracheotomy to stop a man suffocating in his own blood, which poured on to the floor. An orderly tried to push the liquid away with a sponge mop into a pool of blood and discarded tubes and syringes in a side hall. Everywhere there were burned and bleeding men, weeping, groaning, unconscious.

'The Baghdad Hospital has no water and no power, so we've taken over the burden,' said Dr Khaldoun al-Bayati, ear, eye, nose and throat specialist, and the hospital's director. 'Yesterday more than 150 severely wounded people were admitted. We are short of anaesthetists, so they have to wait for surgery. We performed five brain surgeries, and each operation takes three hours.'

His teaching hospital for postgraduate medical students normally takes cases on referral. 'Now we are a frontline emergency hospital,' he noted, 'operating on electrical generators and with insufficient water.'

Dr al-Bayati's home in north Baghdad had been destroyed in a US bombardment. 'I have two little twin daughters,' the hospital director said, holding a hand flat to indicate their height. His voice broke and his eyes filled with tears. 'I told them I might not see them for a time, that I had a humanitarian mission . . . .'

The Abrams tanks on the far side of the Bab al-Moaddam bridge began firing, dangerously close to the hospital. We followed a trail of blood back into the makeshift emergency room.

'This man is dying, at this moment,' Dr Sabah Sahib said, nodding towards a large, middle-aged man covered with shrapnel wounds. The man heaved forward, then fell back with a thud. 'When the shelling stops, there will be a new rush,' Dr Sahib predicted.

We made our way through the hospital trolleys, loaded with men whose limbs hung by shreds of flesh, men with disfigured faces. In the lift to the eighth floor, a young surgeon struck up a conversation. 'We are running out of dressings, IV fluid, antibiotics and anaesthetics,' he said. 'We had a three-month supply, but it's almost gone now.'

Dr Sahib accompanied us through room after room full of wounded men, hundreds of them, all with hollow, vanquished eyes. There were few uniforms in sight – a pair of black army boots on a window ledge, a couple of men wearing the black trousers of the Saddam Fedayeen – but most of them looked like soldiers.

The 'fierce resistance' so often cited at US military briefings led to this: a terrible beating, broken bodies, for those who fought and survived. The scenes at the Adnan Hospital help to explain why the will to fight went out of Baghdad yesterday.

The rooms were so overcrowded that beds were crammed into central aisles, so one had to walk sideways to talk to patients. I asked why there were so few women and children when doctors kept insisting that most of the victims were civilians.

'They often don't survive, so they don't come to hospital,' Dr Sahib answered, unconvincingly.

There were, of course, exceptions: a five-year-old boy, wounded in the family car during an air raid, with a brick at the end of a rope to hold his broken leg in traction; a pretty nine-year-old waiting for an operation on her legs after she was caught in the bombing of Mansur.

The patients were terrified by the tank bombardment we could hear so close by. On one floor, half a dozen women had been moved into the windowless corridor to make them feel safer.

A nurse wept on a bench in the crowded hospital foyer. Dr Sahib showed us to the door, stopping to listen to the tank fire and gunfire as if testing the wind. Just inside the door, a child on a trolley was receiving a blood transfusion.

As we sped back towards the Palestine Hotel, I saw armed Iraqis for the only time yesterday: four militiamen with rocket-propelled grenades, waiting at the eastern end of the Bab al-Moaddam bridge. But when the time came, a few hours or, at most, a few days later, would they really want to die for a regime that so many had already abandoned?

I suspect that the bridge defenders will try to escape, like the dozens of 'Arab volunteers' I found sitting in front of the Palestine Hotel. There were Syrians, Palestinians, Jordanians and Algerians among them. Iraqi officials had claimed that there were six thousand volunteers, half of them determined to commit suicide in 'martyrdom operations' against US soldiers.

Though some now claimed to be students or agricultural labourers, a few admitted that they had come to defend Iraq against American invaders. Each time they tried to leave Baghdad, they claimed, US forces turned them around.

'This is a very sad day. Iraq will be occupied,' an Algerian told me. As he spoke, an American aircraft dropped a bomb on the other side of the Ishtar Sheraton, a few hundred metres away. The crowd that always mills under the Palestine's portico scattered. The Arab volunteers didn't budge; they'd seen worse in combat.

Before he tore up his government identity papers, asked to be paid and went into hiding at his sister's home, my minder read the regime's awful newspapers with me, for the last time.

Saddam Hussein's photograph was on every front page, up to the last day. *Al-Iraq* quoted Mohamed Saïd al-Sahaf, the information minister who had earned the international sobriquet of 'Comical Ali'. 'The Iraqi people will defeat the aggressors,' the headline proclaimed. 'The Americans and British are lying to the media to hide their casualties.'

'This cloud will pass,' said the banner headline of *Ath-Thawra*. It, too, made al-Sahaf's last press conference the front-page lead. *Babel*, the mouthpiece of Saddam Hussein's eldest son, Uday, said: 'This is the day of sacrifice, so be on your guard for this fire, and cut its tail . . . . The Great Iraq continues its steadfastness.'

At that very moment, looters were rampaging through Uday's office in the building housing the Iraqi Olympic Committee.

10 April 2003

Surreal Scenes as Marines Have Their Big Day

From a distance, the US armoured column looked strangely like a camel caravan, edging down the Baghdad boulevard in the afternoon heat, stretching south as far as the eye could see. The M1-A1 Abrams battle tanks, armoured personnel carriers and Humvees were coated in dust, with backpacks and boxes of MREs (Meals Ready to Eat) roped to the sides of the armour.

There seemed to be some indefinable connection between these Marines, exhausted but alert after their twelve-hour journey, and the Arab tribesmen who had won praise from the now-deposed dictator for shooting at helicopters with hunting rifles.

The Marines' imminent arrival was heralded with a festive mood in Yassir Arafat Street. An open-air restaurant served chicken schwarma sandwiches, while the solid, Sunni Muslim bourgeoisie watched from their balconies. Many of the women and children were venturing out of doors for the first time since the war started. Men standing on the pavement looked solemn, but most smiled and said they were happy when I asked them. One woman just gave me a dirty look, then turned back in to her building.

That was when I saw the first looter, a teenage boy in a grimy blue tracksuit pushing a medical X-ray machine down the pavement. A man emerged from a side street carrying clothes racks from a shop; most merchants have stored their goods elsewhere, and that was probably all he found.

'I am happy we got rid of the tyrant,' said a man from the neighbourhood with whom I had grown acquainted. 'But I'm worried about the rubbish people, who will come in the night to steal from us.'

The 'rubbish people' he referred to are Shia Muslims, the majority in Iraq, who have suffered discrimination since Ottoman days. Saddam Hussein's regime oppressed them terribly, and now the Shia want vengeance.

The fender on the minesweeper of the Abrams tank going by had 'USMC' painted next to the Arab image of a heavily made-up woman's eye. Until then, I hadn't been able to talk to the Marines, because they couldn't hear me. But a passing gunner pulled his helmet off to call to his comrade on the next vehicle.

'Where are you from?' I called to him, and he shouted back: 'I'm from Texas, Ma'am.' Sergeant Adam Palacios, of 1st Tank Bravo Company, 1 Division of the US Marine Corps, was from George Bush's home state; how fitting.

How did it feel to be in Baghdad? 'It feels great,' he said. 'I didn't expect people to be so happy.'

In the past three weeks, the unit has seen combat in Basra and Nassiriyah, cities where several dozen Marines were killed or taken prisoner.

Corporal Christian Rojas, from Georgia, stood guard in Sa'adoun Street, a toothbrush tucked into his chest webbing to clean his M-16. He looked younger than his nineteen years and offered a banal account of what he will probably remember as the most momentous days of his life. 'We've just been clearing,' he said.

What did he mean by 'clearing'?

'Firing tank shells and heavy machine guns.' At buildings or people? 'At people,' he answered in a neutral tone.

What *kind* of people? 'Some were civilians. Some were in uniform. Most of them surrendered,' he said. I assume that by 'civilians' Sergeant Rojas meant militiamen in civilian clothing. Being in Baghdad was 'cool', he added.

'We got up at 5 AM,' Sergeant Bartholomew Bochenski, from Connecticut, told me. 'We were about five miles south of the city. We didn't know we were coming in today. Then we started seeing big buildings, and I kept hearing stuff on the radio about securing the Palestine Hotel.'

Was he worried that Iraqis might hate the US for the civilian casualties they suffered? 'It goes through my mind once in a while,' Sergeant Bochenski admitted. 'But this is war.'

The same sentence – 'This is war' – was the standard excuse of the Iraqi information ministry director each time Iraq did something bad.

As I walked past a tank with the words 'Kitten Rescue' painted on its barrel, a matron in a headscarf and her grey-haired husband, wearing an Arab *galabiyeh*, shuffled nervously along the pavement, cringing as if they thought the tank would fire on them. They carried a few groceries in a plastic bag and kept as close as they could to the wall. The woman shook a white cloth over her head the whole time, and when they cleared the street corner, the old couple scurried to their apartment building.

The Marines' arrival at the Palestine Hotel, in the heart of residential east Baghdad, upstaged their taking of the main presidential complex across the Tigris two days earlier, because it signified the final collapse of government authority. And the presence of hundreds of journalists provided a direct line to world television screens.

A crowd was gathering in the adjacent square, dominated by a huge statue of Saddam Hussein, holding his right hand aloft in the manner of Kim Il-Sung. First, a young man tore off the brass plaque bearing the president's name and the date of his inauguration. Another took a sledgehammer to the base. Others arrived with a ladder, to hang a noose-like rope around the neck of the effigy. But the crowd should have reckoned with the stubbornness of the dictator. He built his statues as he built his palaces and bunkers: to last. At one point, the young men grew frustrated with their failure to topple the statue and covered its head with a US flag. It would take hours, and the help of a US tank retriever, to finally topple the likeness so that Iraqis could trample on its head.

Among the men who swarmed about the statue was Mustafa Abdullah, 47. He approached me and pointed to his shoes. 'Jacques Chirac, Jacques Chirac,' Abdullah kept saying, lifting first one foot, then the other. The soles of one's shoes are considered unclean in Arab culture, and the insult was clear.

Poor Jacques Chirac. Like the 'human shields' and the 'Arab volutneers', the French president defended what he thought to be a just cause. Mixing his French metaphors, Abdullah told me that 9 April was the Iraqi taking of the Bastille, the new equivalent of 14 July 1789.

What was his profession? 'Official,' he replied. He worked for the government and he was celebrating the collapse of the regime? Yes, he said. He was very happy. Like hundreds of thousands of Iraqis, perhaps millions, Abdullah will no doubt be rehabilitated, 'de-Saddamised'.

It will take time, or the proven arrest or death of Saddam Hussein, for Iraqis to believe that his rule is really over. I asked one happy man in Sa'adoun Street where he thought Saddam had gone. 'Maybe he is dead, or he escaped to Mosul. Many army people come from Mosul, and they love him.' The Russian embassy in Mansur was another rumoured destination, along with Saddam's home town, Tikrit.

In days to come, phenomena like the unexplained fire which blazed in north Baghdad last night, shooting thousand-foot flames on to the dark skyline, will inevitably evoke the fate of the Iraqi dictator.

US Secretary of Defence Donald Rumsfeld said the looters who descended like vultures on downtown Baghdad were 'just letting off steam'. The looters stole a television camera, and the cameraman's money, and threatened to shoot this correspondent when I tried to enter a ministry they were sacking.

Returning to the Palestine Hotel, I asked my taxi driver to drop me a block away from the Marines so they wouldn't open fire on his battered old car. To my surprise, there were still more looters, dragging a coffee table, a transistor radio and coat trees out of the culture ministry. At the oil ministry, the thieves despaired of starting the minister's Mercedes, so they stole its tyres and uphol-stered seats, stripping it down to a skeleton.

A US Marine corporal could see the looting of the culture ministry from Ferdoos Square, but it didn't seem to bother him. A Shia family carried an air-conditioning unit out of another building. Were these apartments? 'No,' the father replied, '*mokhabarat*' (the intelligence service). No wonder there was no sign on the building. The inhabitants of Zaim Street stood in their gardens, watching the plunder to either side. A few doors down, a woman with tears in her eyes spoke to me from her doorway. 'This is not good,' she said. 'The war has been awful.' She nodded first towards the US Humvee, then at the looters. 'The Americans are down the street, and look what these people are doing.'

The Marine corporal watching the looting was Kevin Bird, from Tennessee. 'We didn't expect to be here so quickly,' he said. I asked him how he thought Iraqis saw US forces. 'They seem strangely comfortable,' he replied.

But as I walked up the hotel drive, I passed a Yugoslav Reuters photographer whom I knew from the 1999 war. One of his close friends was killed and two others wounded in the US attack on the hotel on Tuesday, and the photographer looked devastated. By chance, a woman from al-Jazeera, whose correspondent was killed in a rocket attack on the same day, sat crying nearby.

Indoors, the Palestine's manager was pleading with Marine officers to protect his hotel. He'd obligingly used his master key to let them search all the rooms used by the Iraqi Ministry of Information.

Protecting the journalists that another unit had attacked the day before was not unlike the challenge facing the US throughout the country. Winning the confidence of people you've bombed isn't easy. But keeping peace between Iraqis could be even harder.

10 April 2003

Saddam's Regime is Toppled

By nightfall, President Saddam Hussein's regime was as smashed as the black statue of the fallen dictator in Ferdoos Square, symbolically wrenched off its plinth by a US tank retriever and hundreds of Baghdadis. All trace of Iraqi government authority in the capital vanished. There were few signs of resistance, though some explosions were heard in the evening.

The occupation of most of Baghdad by US troops was met with a strange mixture of joy and terror, as poor Shia Muslims from the slums of Saddam City swarmed into the city centre to help themselves to the contents of shops and government buildings.

With US forces saying they had no instructions to prevent looting, residents of central Baghdad organised themselves into armed vigilante committees to protect their property, and that of neighbours who had fled the bombing.

Though tens of thousands of Baghdadis turned out to greet the Americans in the streets, the 'liberation' of the capital was tainted by doubts that Saddam had really fallen, and especially by fear of anarchy in the city.

The mobs that tore and burned his omnipresent portraits did so more in vengeance than in celebration.

A seemingly endless column of US tanks, armoured personnel carriers and Humvees drove northwest on Sa'adoun Street, arriving at Ferdoos Square by late afternoon.

The Marines of 1st Tank Bravo Company said they encountered no resistance in their day-long journey from south of Baghdad, but their tank turrets swept constantly from side to side, and in the back of each armoured personnel carrier a dozen Marines were staggered, facing opposite directions with their M-16 assault rifles poised.

Many of the men, women and children who lined the pavements waved and flashed 'V for victory' signs. Happy families, eager to set eyes on their liberators, drove towards the invasion force, waving white flags.

There were tragic blunders. I saw a civilian car, waving a white flag, with a wounded person lying across the back seat and blood dripping onto the street, timidly attempt to approach the armoured column, then turn back in fear. French colleagues from *Libération* and *Le Parisien* saw an old Iraqi man driving a blue car, with his wife in the passenger seat, shot in the head because he drove too close to US troops.

At the same time, the last Iraqi military and intelligence officials to leave could be seen loading their cars with personal belongings. The type of goods in a car – bedding and suitcases, or appliances and office furniture – was the best indication whether motorists were fleeing remnants of the regime or looters.

The Americans placed tanks and armoured vehicles, some flying the Stars and Stripes from their antennae, at each corner of the Palestine Hotel, one day after a US tank from a different unit had fired a shell that killed two cameramen. I picked up a taxi farther down Sa'adoun Street, in what is now no man's land.

An Iraqi gunman fired a volley as we sped round towards the Ministries of Industry and Education, where whole families were looting computers, photocopiers, desks and electric fans.

One boy's arms overflowed with telephones. Two women in chadors pushed a trolley towards the ministry, and a horse-drawn cart pulled up to take its share of the plunder.

I tried to walk into the building, but men shouted at me to turn back, making a shooting gesture and threatening to kill me, then claiming the Americans had given them permission to take what they wanted.

A few blocks away, back in Sa'adoun Street, Majid Hamid and Hamid Sultani, friends from the neighbouring Jadriya district, followed the American column on rickety bicycles. They'd seen a mob take over United Nations offices.

'We're protecting the houses of our neighbours who left,' Majid Hamid said. 'We have Kalashnikovs and we won't let looters in our street.'

The cyclists, a mechanical engineering student and a spare car parts dealer, sent their families to Jordan and the United Arab Emirates before the war started.

'We think America loves peace,' Majid Hamid said. Hamid Sultani agreed, adding that 'Saddam Hussein and Osama bin Laden give Islam a bad image.'

As terrified employees stood by, a mob stormed into the lobby of the Palestine Hotel, minutes before the US military vehicle gave the final tug to the Saddam statue outside.

The rough-looking men from the Shiite suburbs cried 'Allahu Akbar, Allahu Akbar', then smashed, tore or burned every portrait of Saddam they could get their hands on.

A young woman wearing an Islamic headscarf retreated into the coffee shop, clutching her baby and weeping.

10 April 2003

Distressed Iraqis Exhume Their War Dead

Dozens of Iraqis peered through the wrought iron fence towards the former Saddam Children's Hospital, but none of them stayed very long. The stench drove them away. Inside the hospital grounds, civil defence workers and volunteers from the local mosque wielded shovels in the noonday sun, exhuming bodies buried more than two weeks ago, in the last days of the US assault on Baghdad.

Most of the diggers had white paper surgeons' masks strapped across their lower faces; a few wore gas masks, of the type that were meant to protect us from Saddam Hussein's chemical weapons.

Mohamed Haitham, 33, removed his gas mask to talk to me. 'We exhumed five yesterday, seven today,' he explained. 'The ones today were Syrian fighters, killed at Celebration Square. They will be buried in the foreigners' plot at Kharkh Cemetery.'

'Their names will be there, if anyone ever looks for them. There are another twelve or thirteen Iraqis buried here. We'll wait until their relatives claim them before we dig them up.'

Black clouds of flies vibrated around us, and Mohamed Haitham's anger exploded. 'I would like to blow up this vehicle,' he shouted, pointing at the US Humvee with the name 'Thunder' painted on its window. 'I would like to commit suicide in front of this vehicle. We dug up children and old men here.'

In three weeks of war, doctors said, two hundred Iraqis died in the hospital, including thirty children. It was in the last, desperate days, when there was no electricity to run refrigeration units, that they dug the mass grave.

One by one, the corpses were removed from their temporary resting place and laid gently on a flatbed lorry. Pieces of bodies were put into black plastic bags; those still intact were wrapped in white sheets.

Two grey-haired brothers, Adnan and Musa Khazal, clutched handker-chiefs to their noses as they walked from grave to grave, pulling little scraps of paper from soft drink bottles shoved upside down into the earth. Each paper recorded the place and date where the body was found and, when possible, its identity.

'We are looking for our brother Alaaeddin,' Adnan said.

'He was forty-two, an engineer. The tanks fired on his car in Celebration Square in Mansour on 6 or 7 April. We found his car, but not him. We want to bury him in the family plot, in Ghazali Cemetery.'

For fifteen days the Khazal brothers have searched through lists of dead and wounded in all of Baghdad's main hospitals, mosques and *husseiniyas* (prayer rooms). 'We even looked at the al-Rashid and Zafaraniya military hos-pitals,' Adnan continued. 'His widow is very upset; she has four children, aged two to twelve, and she doesn't believe her husband is dead.'

Private Thomas Spencer, 25, of the American 3rd Brigade, 3rd Infantry Division, manned a heavy machine gun on the roof of the Humvee. Did he realise how upset the Iraqis were, exhuming their war dead? 'I dunno. I guess some people are happy and some people are sad,' Private Spencer shrugged. 'We're just trying to help them. But the smell bothers me.'

23 April 2003

Unspeakable Savagery
on the Streets of Baghdad

The little bundle wrapped inside plastic sheeting is dwarfed by the adult-sized plywood coffin. Two-and-a-half-year-old Fatima Ala'a's aunt crumples to the ground outside the Baghdad city morgue when she sees the viscous, grey-green blob teeming with maggots.

Another relative sprays insecticide on the corpse, to fight off the onslaught of flies. 'They kidnapped her seven days ago,' says Fatima's uncle, Walid Mohamed. 'A neighbour's family did it, the sons of Um Ashraf and Abu Ashraf. They wanted money and we didn't have it. Someone else was demanding money from them, so they turned on us. Another neighbour noticed a bad smell in his house. That was how we found her, in the sewer. I recognised her hair barrettes and her black trousers with the green polka dots. Though she was very small, I think they raped her.'

Fatima's father Ala'a Abed, a nightwatchman, stands to one side, as if in a trance. The little girl was his eldest child. He has only an infant son left. The Shia family from the district of Sayadieh did not have enough money to take Fatima to their holy city of Najaf for burial, so they buried her in Baghdad yesterday.

'We blame the Americans for not taking security seriously,' her uncle Walid says.

A trip to the Baghdad city morgue and forensics institute makes clear the depths to which human beings can sink, the unspeakable savagery that reigns on the streets of the Iraqi capital.

As I talk with Fatima's family, a white jeep backs up to the door of the autopsy room, its tailgate open. A man keens over the body of his brother, shot dead hours earlier. 'Oh Ahmad Mohamed,' he wails. 'Where are the people who believe in the holy books, in the Koran and the Bible?'

The morgue receives between twenty and thirty bodies each day, less than during the peak killing season of July and August, but still three times the number of daily fatalities prior to the US occupation.

'The Americans should issue a new law, that any murderer they catch will be hanged,' says Dr Sa'ad Kadim, a forensic pathologist. 'When Saddam Hussein fell, we were happy, but after the looting and killing took hold, we lost heart.'

Police brought 667 bodies to the morgue in the month of September. Of those, 372, including fifty women, died of gunshot wounds, says Dr Qais Hassan, also a forensic pathologist, and the director of the morgue's statistics department.

In August 2003, 518 Baghdadis were shot dead, compared to ten fatal shootings in August 2002, before the invasion and occupation.

The statistics tell the story of Baghad's descent into cold-blooded mayhem. In all of 2002, 174 people died of gunshot wounds in the capital. This year, until the end of September, pathologists recorded 2,173 deaths by firearms in Baghdad alone, almost all of them since May.

The institute closed down for ten days when the regime fell in April, so dozens if not hundreds of deaths during that period were not counted.

'It's a disaster,' Dr Hassan says. 'At the end of the war, the Iraqi army left weapons all over the place. US forces could have collected them, but they didn't do it. Security is getting a little better, because there are more Iraqi police now.'

Dr Hassan estimates that up to a quarter of fatal shootings are caused by US troops. 'Twenty days ago, Iraqis were joy-shooting at a wedding party in Baghdad and the Americans thought they were being attacked. They opened fire and killed a twenty-one-year-old woman, the five-month-old daughter she was holding in her arms and the woman's eight-year-old brother.

'At the end of July, a family were driving past a power station guarded by the Americans in the Suleikh district. Something exploded near a generator and the Americans fired at the car. They killed the father – I remember, his name was Adel – his twenty-year-old son and daughters, aged nineteen and thirteen.'

Dr Hassan says it is easy to tell the difference between Iraqi and US bullets. 'This morning, the police from Mahmoudiya station brought in this man,' he says, holding up the papers for twenty-six-year-old Sa'ad Mohamed. 'I found

American-type bullets in his body. They are long and narrow and do far more damage to internal organs than Iraqi bullets. They make big laceration wounds.'

Sa'ad Mohamed had five bullets in his chest, head and arms. 'I don't know if he attacked the Americans,' Dr Hassan says.

When asked by Western journalists, the Coalition Provisional Authority (CPA) and US military officials have repeatedly said they do not know how many Iraqi civilians have fallen victim to the extreme violence of post-war Baghdad. But every month, Dr Hassan says, US representatives in the health ministry across the street ask their Iraqi counterparts to request the statistics from him.

It is not clear whether the silence of the CPA regarding civilian Iraqi deaths is due to a deliberate cover-up or merely to the bureaucratic failure to pass on information within the CPA.

In the small alley behind the forensic institute, outside the blue metal doors leading to the autopsy and refrigeration rooms, the tragedy is unending. The cheap coffins lined up on the ground are lent by mosques. Since Muslims are buried in a shroud only, the coffins are recycled after each trip to the cemetery.

A man removes a blood-soaked piece of cardboard from one coffin, a blood-stained blanket from another, preparing them for the next victims.

A middle-aged man stands calmly amid the moaning and wailing and bustle of families crowding around the clerk's window to pay the ten thousand Iraqi dinars (about €4.30) fee for a death certificate.

'I am waiting for my daughter's body,' he whispers. 'She was standing by the gate to our house and someone shot her.' Water used to mop the floors inside the morgue floods into the alley, which reeks of the sour, butcher shop smell of death.

Policemen carry in a man's body, covered by a blanket. Two bloodied feet, bound at the ankles, protrude from under the rough fabric. 'We found him in the street in Baghdad Jediedeh at 7 AM,' Lieutenant Arkan Khalil says. 'The thieves cut his legs, but he died of strangulation. We think they stole his car. We found no identity papers. It's a miserable situation. These things never used to happen.'

'When the victim has no papers, we write "unknown" in the records,' Dr Kadim says. 'It happens with three or four out of every twenty victims. Families come here looking for missing people. We keep them in the refrigerator for one month, and then Muslim charities or the municipality bury them.'

A Toyota police pick-up with a double cabin backs into the courtyard with two partially covered bodies in the back. They are car thieves, shot by the man they tried to rob.

'Most of the deaths are related to car theft,' Dr Kadim continues. The owner of a new Opel car handed over his keys to thieves in Haifa Street and ran.

When the thieves realised that he had used an electronic zapper to block the door locks, they pursued him and shot him; the Opel owner's body too found its way to the city morgue yesterday morning.

Revenge is another frequent motive. 'It's from the previous time,' Dr Kadim explains. 'A lot of those killed are former Ba'ath Party members, intelligence and security officials. We know because their relatives tell us.'

Musa Ahmad has come to collect the body of his cousin Haidar Sabah, 32. 'The neighbours saw him dying in the street and went and told his mother. He was shot four times in the legs and lower abdomen. He was his widowed mother's only son, and we had to stop her from throwing herself in the river. The two of them lived alone together.'

Sabah sold electrical supplies in the Shorja market. 'He was a scrappy guy, always getting in fights,' Musa said. 'I think it was revenge. But only God knows.'

10 October 2003

The Ghastly Results of a 'Licence to Kill'

At 11.59 AM on 8 April 2003, Samia Nakhoul, the Gulf bureau chief for Reuters news agency, saw an orange flash as a US M1 Abrams tank on the Jumhurriya bridge fired at the Palestine Hotel.

Seconds later, Nakhoul recalls, 'I was hit by a lid of fire, as if someone threw hot iron at my head. I felt my face burning and the blood pouring out.' Under bombardment, Nakhoul's colleagues drove her to three hospitals, searching for a brain scan. In the first emergency room, she learned that Taras Protsyuk, a cameraman for Reuters, had died.

For weeks, Protsyuk and Nakhoul had gone on stories together. 'I wanted to go home to my husband. He wanted to go to his family,' Nakhoul says. 'When I heard that Taras died, I felt, "That's it". Things will never be the same again.'

That night, as Nakhoul decided to risk brain surgery in Baghdad, she learned that a second television cameraman had died. He was José Couso, from the Spanish channel Telecinco. Though Nakhoul survived several operations and resumed work for Reuters, she still suffers from headaches, nightmares and panic seizures. On 17 August 2003, another Reuters cameraman, Mazen Dana, was killed when a US tank fired on him in broad daylight from thirty metres. 'I felt like I was being attacked again,' Nakhoul says.

A fine journalist who has covered many wars, Nakhoul would be the first to admit that a reporter's life is not inherently more valuable than anyone else's.

Yet the killing of journalists by US forces in Iraq is emblematic of much that has gone wrong with the US occupation: the lack of co-ordination and communication, a propensity to lie and refuse to accept responsibility, rules of engagement which are, in the words of Amnesty International, 'a virtual licence to kill'.

To mark the anniversary of the attack on the Palestine Hotel, the International Federation of Journalists has declared today an international day of protest and mourning for media casualties. Twenty-one journalists have died in Iraq in the past year.

At least seven of them were killed by US forces. Tariq Ayoub, a reporter for al-Jazeera television, was killed by a US rocket on the same day as Couso and Protsyuk.

The targeting of al-Jazeera had one important point in common with the attack on the Palestine Hotel: like several of the journalists staying in the hotel, al-Jazeera forwarded its building's map co-ordinates to the Pentagon, and received assurances that it would not be attacked.

The Pentagon and the US Central Command in Doha knew that the Iraqi government had forced all foreign journalists to live in the Palestine Hotel. Anyone who listened to the radio or watched television knew that it was a media headquarters, like the Commodore Hotel in Beirut, or the Holiday Inn in Sarajevo.

Jean-Paul Mari, a correspondent for the *Nouvel Observateur* who helped to carry our wounded and dying colleagues out of the Palestine Hotel, devoted months to an in-depth investigation. His report, entitled 'Two murders and a lie', was published earlier this year by Reporters Without Borders.

Mari concludes that responsibility for the attack lies with General Buford Blount's 3rd Infantry Division command, for failing to tell unit commanders and soldiers that the Palestine Hotel was the media headquarters. Captain Philip Wolford, the commander of the Alpha 4-64 armoured company, who authorised the firing of the tank shell, did not know there were journalists in the hotel.

The Pentagon's criminal negligence almost had more horrific consequences. Wolford called in an air raid on the Palestine Hotel, which would have killed dozens more. On learning that his unit had wounded journalists, twenty minutes after the tank shell was fired, he cancelled the air raid.

Explanations for the attack went through an evolutionary process not unlike the lies about Saddam Hussein's weapons of mass destruction. Less than two hours after the attack, General Blount claimed there were snipers firing at US troops from the hotel. More than two hundred journalists were witness to the fact that not a shot was fired from the hotel, and that there had been a long lull before the tank fired at it.

The following day, the official version began to slip. Military sources said mortars were being fired from the *area* of the hotel, not from the hotel itself, and that Iraqi 'spotters' were using large buildings to watch US troops.

Sergeant Shawn Gibson, the African-American soldier who asked permission from Wolford to fire the fatal tank shell, said he saw a man with binoculars on a balcony. In the abridged 'report' released by the Pentagon in August, the man with binoculars became 'a hunter-killer team'.

The story of 'direct firing' from the hotel was a lie from the beginning. The US military eventually admitted there was no firing from the hotel. The US army statement issued on 12 August 2003 concluded that firing a 120 mm high-explosive tank shell at the hotel because Sergeant Gibson saw the glimmer of a camera lens was 'a proportionate and justifiably measured response . . . fully in accordance with the rules of engagement'. A US 'investigation' into the death of cameraman Mazen Dana came to the same conclusion.

The family of José Couso has filed a lawsuit in Spain against three US soldiers for 'war crimes' and 'murder'. Reuters news agency, the Committee to Protect Journalists, and Reporters Without Borders maintain pressure on the Pentagon to release the full text of its inquiry into the killings.

I asked Lieutenant General Ricardo Sanchez, the commander of US forces in Iraq, why soldiers who kill Iraqi civilians and foreign journalists are invariably cleared of wrongdoing. General Sanchez replied: 'Young soldiers on the ground have to make decisions. When they feel threatened, they always have the right to shoot.'

Except that everyone in Iraq feels threatened, all the time. Firing a tank shell and calling in an air raid because a soldier thinks he sees a man with binoculars is one of thousands of examples of the profligate use of lethal force. If the US military wants to be trusted, it urgently needs to reappraise its rules of engagement.

8 April 2004

When the Danger for Journalists is Omnipresent

Rory Carroll, the young Irishman and *Guardian* correspondent who was kidnapped in the Shia Muslim slums of Sadr City yesterday, is one of a handful of Western journalists who are based full time in Iraq. He came to Baghdad from Johannesburg last January to work for one year, after which he is to resume his job as Africa correspondent.

When we had dinner on Monday night, Rory told me he'd already booked his flight out at 10.15 AM on 21 January. In the meantime, he was looking forward to covering Saddam Hussein's trial. He intended to stay in Baghdad through Christmas and New Year's Eve.

As a permanent correspondent here, Rory is on the roster of journalists allowed to enter the courtroom for Saddam's trial. The order was determined by lottery, and he drew number fourteen. Since only four can attend at one time, he knew he would not get into the trial for weeks. Rory initially planned to go to the Convention Centre in the Green Zone and watch the trial on television there. There would be Iraqi politicians to talk to. But he changed his mind and on Tuesday night told colleagues he would watch it on television in Sadr City with a Shia Muslim family who had suffered under Saddam's rule.

Rory is one of the best-informed correspondents working in Iraq. Before anyone else, he explained how British troops in Basra had bought peace with the local Mehdi Army and Badr Brigade militias by incorporating them into the British-trained police, then turning a blind eye while they fought each other and terrorised the local population. We talked about the assassination in Basra last month of an Iraqi stringer who worked for the *Guardian* and the *New York Times* – an event that deeply disturbed him.

Rory is also one of the most generous correspondents I've met. He volunteered to share the trial pool reports from the permanent press corps with me. He listened carefully to my queries about what one could and could not do in Baghdad. I know a Shia sheikh in Sadr City who is close to the popular leader, Moqtada Sadr, and speaks English, I told him. On the telephone, the sheikh said it was too dangerous for him to come to my hotel – he thought he might be kidnapped on the way – and Rory understood perfectly my reluctance to go to Sadr City.

'Interesting question,' Rory mused. 'I haven't been to Sadr City for a while. [Sheikh] Moqtada's people usually don't start working until late afternoon, so the system we'd worked out was that our driver and interpreter would drop by the evening before and tell them we'd be coming in the morning, as a courtesy.'

I was weighing two other offers of interviews: a meeting with the Sunni politician Saleh Mutlak, and an offer through friends to go to the home of pro-Saddam Sunnis in Aadamiya, another Sunni neighbourhood that is a stronghold of the insurgency.

Mutlak should be all right, Rory said. One of the US networks went to see him the other day. Aadamiya was dodgy for Western men, but women reporters had gone in and out, wearing *hijab*. The thing was to get quickly out of the car, walk straight into the house, not linger in the street.

As my interpreter put it: 'If we go to Sadr City, there are criminal gangs but no terrorists. If we go to Aadamiya, there are terrorists but no criminal gangs.'

The difficult thing about working in Iraq, Rory rightly said, is that 'the risk-to-reward ratio is totally skewed'. In most war situations, you have a sense of where you can go safely, and what the risk is. In Baghdad, the danger is diffuse and omnipresent. It is impossible to say whether a given press conference or interview is 'worth it'. But if you stop going out of your hotel, you stop learning.

Last weekend, Rory went to Falluja with a US unit to cover the referendum on the constitution. Falluja has been one of the most violent cities in Iraq almost since the beginning of the occupation, and I was impressed by his courage. He and other 'embedded' journalists were dropped off by US armoured vehicles a few hundred metres from polling stations, then walked there on their own.

'Don't you ever get scared?' I asked Rory. The new 'shaped charges' which the insurgents use in roadside bombs worry him, he said. Before, a roadside bomb might damage an armoured vehicle and wound those inside. Now the shaped charges, which concentrate explosive power in a smaller area, destroy the vehicle and kill everyone inside.

I was trying to arrange an 'embed' with US forces in Amariya, a request which has since been denied. 'Amariya is good,' Rory said. 'There's a lot going on there.' He explained, as the military press office had not, that I would enter the Green Zone by early evening and sleep in the Convention Centre.

'I'll lend you my sleeping bag,' he offered, adding with a laugh, 'I'm afraid it's smelly.' Rory knows the routine by heart; early in the morning, the US helicopters take you out from the Green Zone, even if the base you're visiting is just a few kilometres away.

Rory thought the security situation might be improving. 'It's been a long time since there was an attempted kidnapping,' he said. 'Some of us are even thinking about going out to restaurants again.'

I was surprised to hear that Rory still goes to Warda and the Honey Market, grocers that sell imported food. 'It's one of my few contacts with real life in Iraq,' he said. 'I don't want to give it up.'

With his slightly ginger hair, he could be mistaken for a Kurd, he said. But his 'employees' – his interpreter, his driver, and the two men who followed in a 'chase car' – invariably blew his disguise by insisting on carrying his grocery basket.

The French ambassador to Baghdad was on my flight from Paris to Amman last week. He scolded me and other journalists who were coming to cover the referendum and Saddam's trial, saying: 'You're taking enormous risks. You must know that there are spies in every hotel, tipping off the kidnappers.'

'He's right,' Rory said (though I don't believe the men who seized him in Sadr City yesterday were tipped off by his hotel). 'I buy a lot of chocolate bars, and I give them to all the hotel guards,' he laughed. 'Because I always hope that when it comes time to sell a journalist, they'll think, "Oh, not him. He's the nice one who gives me chocolate."' I hadn't thought of chocolate, I said, but I tip generously, and am careful never to have rows with anyone, for the same reason.

Most foreign correspondents here use a chase car, the idea being that the second car can alert you by cell phone if you're being followed. When I arrived in Baghdad this time, I discussed the possibility with Kassim, *The Irish Times* interpreter. 'Iraqis know about the chase car now,' he said. 'It just makes you more visible, and it multiplies the number of people who know where you're going.'

We decided not to hire a second car. But we use three different cars, depending on the day. To try to ease Baghdad's horrific traffic jams, the government has instituted an odd/even number plate scheme. When we've been uneasy about appointments, we take a powerful BMW, in the hope of outrunning kidnappers. We also leave a note on my desk, with the names, phone numbers and address of the people we're going to see.

These preparations are an integral part of working here. So is attention to clothing. 'Have you noticed that Iraqi men wear baggier jeans, higher up on their waists than Westerners?' Rory asked me on Monday night. 'And they tend to wear striped pyjama-like shirts.' He had gone to Iraqi shops and bought local clothing.

He's also noticed that Iraqi men carry their personal belongings around in plastic shopping bags, so for example when he walks those perilous few hundred metres from the car to the entry of the Green Zone, he carries computer, notebooks, pens and cell phone in a plastic bag.

'Some of the American correspondents have got the swarthy, unshaven Arab look, even the clothes,' Rory said. 'But then they can't resist carrying that chic reporter's bag, and the effect is spoiled.' Rory and I then had a detailed discussion of *hijab* or Islamic dress, which I began wearing in Iraq when the situation turned nasty in April 2004.

Until this trip, I'd never given much thought to the details. Rory agreed with me that Western journalists never seem to get the *hijab* right. 'Most Iraqi women don't wear full *abayas* [long robes],' he observed correctly. I had realised that my black cotton *manteau*, a pocketed, big-buttoned sack that I bought in Tehran years ago, stood out here.

The women who frisked me when I went into the polling station last Saturday asked me, *Intie iraniya?* ('Are you Iranian?') It was Kassim who suggested I change headscarves. I'd chosen the least conspicuous ones before leaving Paris, but they were still coloured. He lent me a black scarf belonging to his wife. During those long hours in Baghdad traffic, I immediately noticed the difference: no one looks at me.

Or at least I hope not.

20 October 2005

Saddam Shows Old Power as he Defies Judges

It is one of the great mysteries of human nature: how and why do people persist in loving a dictator who has brought them to ruin? In a modest villa in a Sunni Muslim district of Baghdad inhabited by former officers of Saddam Hussein's armed forces, Marwa, 24, her sister Warda, 22, their widowed mother Nadia, 51, and visiting cousin Omar, 21, watched the opening session of Saddam's trial yesterday.

Photographs of the family's late father, husband and uncle, a brigadier general who died before the 2003 US invasion, decorate the living room walls. Three Korans are stacked on a shelf. The family are low on petrol, but they don't want to miss a minute of their hero's performance, so they leave the generator running all morning, to power the television.

It is nearly 1 PM, more than three hours late, when the first grainy images of the Kurdish judge, Rizgar Mohammed Ameen, appear on screen.

'That's Barzan,' Omar says. Saddam's half-brother is speaking, but the sound is cut. 'This is Taha Yassin Ramadan, the deputy prime minister . . . .' Then Saddam Hussein walks into the courtroom, wearing an open-necked white shirt and dark suit. 'He's relaxed!' Omar exclaims. 'He smiled!' adds Warda.

Saddam stands facing the judge, buttons his jacket, speaks in that unmistakable voice: 'Those who fought in God's cause will be victorious . . . . I am at the mercy of God, the most powerful.'

'He's quoting the Holy Koran!' cries Marwa.

To keep in touch with his country, Saddam used to maintain a rotating schedule of visits with carefully screened 'ordinary' Iraqis, whom he would then talk about on television. Marwa, the pretty medical secretary, obviously pleased him, for she met Saddam eleven times between 2001 and 2003. Her sister Warda, who has just completed a degree in tourism, met him five times.

The family are glued to Saddam's profile on the television screen. The judge interrupts the Koranic recitation: 'You are to give your full name to establish your identity to the court.'

'You know me,' Saddam sneers. 'You are an Iraqi and you know who I am. I won't answer to this so-called court . . . . Who are you? What are you? I retain my constitutional rights as president of Iraq.'

In background briefings, journalists were told that Saddam would not be allowed to speak yesterday, yet he challenged the legitimacy of the court from the outset. Even Iraqis who hate Saddam told me they found Saddam strong, the court weak.

Judge Ameen makes a brief attempt to put Saddam in his place. 'You are Saddam Hussein al Majid . . . *former* president of Iraq,' he corrects the defendant.

'I did not say "former" president,' Saddam snaps back, shaking a finger.

This is the show the world was waiting for: an unrepentant Saddam, belittling the men who would bring him to justice.

The mere thought of Saddam still strikes fear into the hearts of many Iraqis – so much so that dozens of appointed witnesses did not show up for the trial yesterday, the ostensible reason for its adjournment until 28 November.

'I've been up and dressed since 2.30 this morning,' Saddam complains.

I recall how Iraqis were allowed to doze a few minutes between torture sessions, while my Sunni hosts are outraged at the treatment accorded their leader. 'But Iraqis know that I do not get tired,' he adds.

The trial takes an even more farcical turn when Saddam's co-defendants complain that guards have removed their Arab headdresses – an insult to a man's dignity. Judge Ameen relents. The headdresses are donned, on camera, and the trial continues.

'He looks strong!' says young Omar.

'It makes us so happy,' says Marwa.

'Like every time,' Omar continues, referring to Saddam's three previous post-capture television appearances, in July 2004, and June and July 2005. 'Except the first time, when they caught him,' Omar reflects.

'He was drugged,' says Marwa.

'I don't believe he was really in that hole when they captured him,' says her mother, Nadia, before adding: 'He is a brave man; they faked that.'

Marwa sings a few lines of *Al-Hamiya*, an Arab nationalist song about shedding blood which became famous during the Palestinian Intifada. She wears stylish Western clothes, a black fishnet cardigan over a yellow T-shirt, and rhinestone-studded jeans. Her favourite television programme is *Oprah Winfrey*. And she adores Saddam Hussein.

'I feel so proud of him,' Marwa says.

'Saddam Hussein is controlling the scene,' pipes in Warda.

'As always,' says Omar.

The trial is blacked out again.

Saddam's closing act of bravado, witnessed by only a few 'pool' journalists, will not be shown.

At the end of the three-hour session, guards tried to lead him out by the arms. 'Don't touch me! Take your hands off me!' Saddam said. The guards too relented, and allowed him to walk out alone.

Earlier, while we'd waited for the televised pictures, the cousins had shown me their watches – all the rage in Sunni circles. 'They cost $100 now in [the Sunni neighbourhood of] Aadamiya,' Omar said, showing me the photo of Saddam Hussein on his watch face. Warda arrives with two narrow boxes holding Swiss ladies' watches.

'I would like to give it to you,' Marwa says, 'but it was given to me by the dearest person in my life.' The ladies' watches show the Ba'athist eagle on the face and, in Arabic, the words 'Made from martyrs' weapons of Saddam's Qadissiya war [the 1980–88 war against Iran]'.

Omar's mobile phone rings: a friend of his in Falluja. 'There's a big demonstration,' he tells me enthusiastically. 'They're carrying Saddam's picture and wearing Saddam T-shirts. They're burning the police station.' Omar has just returned from Amman, where he saw photographs of Saddam Hussein posted all over the marketplace.

'He will be a hero to all Arabs,' Marwa predicts.

But much as they love Saddam, the cousins admit he will not return to power. 'The trial will not be fair, so history will not be fair to Saddam,' says Omar, and Marwa agrees. In the meantime, Iraq's Sunnis nurse their monumental grievance.

And look for a new leader.

20 October 2005

Misery of Life Beyond the Green Zone

Everyone in Iraq is afraid of being kidnapped: civilians, journalists, military, Iraqis, foreigners. The hostage-taking epidemic strikes men, women, children, young and old, rich and poor. It's hard to find an Iraqi who doesn't know someone who's been kidnapped, usually for ransom.

Like the Irish journalist Rory Carroll, eighteen year-old Faed Khasraji was freed very quickly. The motives for Carroll's brief abduction now appear to have been political. Khasraji spent three days in the hands of a whisky-drinking, pill-popping criminal gang that drugged its captives and used prostitutes to lure victims to their hideout.

When he woke up in a large tiled room with six other hostages on the afternoon of 15 June, Faed remembered the fond look his mother gave him as he left for school that morning. He was going to sit his final secondary school examinations, after which he hoped to enrol in university in Germany. 'I was so proud of him,' says Faed's mother Faiza, 45, sitting on the sofa next to her son. 'I realised my little boy was a man.' As he begins his story, she weeps softly.

While the students entered the examination building, Faed hung back to do some last-minute cramming. A van pulled up beside him, and a middle-aged man asked for directions to An-Nahda neighbourhood. 'That's the last thing I remember,' Faed says. 'When I woke up, I was on a dirty floor, and my arms and legs were tingling. I thought I was dreaming. A man asked for my father's phone number. I couldn't remember it, so I gave him my brother Ahmad's. He called Ahmad and said, "Faed is our guest. We will contact you in a few days."'

In his fury at having been kidnapped, Faed lunged at the guard. The guard called in several men, who beat Faed unconscious. Then his hands and feet were bound. The other hostages were only handcuffed. They were forbidden to talk to one another.

The following day two more hostages were brought to the room. The gang's leader burst in, addressing a man lying on the ground a metre from Faed as Othman Azawi. 'The leader was tall, with a goatee and a long, dirty moustache that hung over his mouth. He was very ugly,' Faed recalls. 'He shouted at Azawi: "I have come to this dirty place because of you. We were working together, and you took our money. Where is it? Is the building in Karrada [neighbourhood] from our money? Is the factory imported from Syria from our money?"'

The gang leader aimed a Kalashnikov at Azawi and fired at his knees. Azawi lost consciousness, but the leader continued insulting him. 'I will make you feel the pain the way we feel the pain of losing our money,' the gang leader said. 'You son of a bitch, you deserve to die.' When he fired into Azawi's forehead, 'I saw smoke come out of the hole before the blood spurted,' Faed recounts with horror.

'They were all drinking whisky and popping pills. I saw two women who worked with them; one of them wore *hijab*, but the other walked by the steel gate in her underwear. I heard the guards say: "She was very good; she brought a man with a BMW." One of the guards said "I'll sleep with her tonight" and the other said "No, I will."'

'They got very angry, and one of them broke a whisky bottle and plunged it into the other's stomach. He twisted the broken glass, as if he was digging. I fainted.'

On the last day of Faed's captivity, a relative of the man who was gored with the broken bottle entered the tiled room and opened fire on the guards, killing two. A third played dead on the floor. After the gunman walked out, the guard pursued him into the corridor, and Faed heard more shooting and screaming.

'Later, I heard them talking about us,' Faed continues. 'They said: "We should release them."'

The hostages were blindfolded and piled into a van. Faed was dropped about five minutes from his home in north Baghdad.

The teenager was given a second opportunity to sit his examinations, but was too frightened to leave the house. 'I hate all human beings now,' he says. He has lost a year's study, and the motivation to go to Germany.

Faed's mother Faiza says there are many days when she feels she cannot bear life any longer. 'I feel completely depleted,' she says. 'My sons give me the strength to carry on.'

Her husband Jabar's travel agency was destroyed when a suicide bomber attacked the Baghdad Hotel, CIA headquarters in the capital, in 2003. On 29 April of this year, Faiza's favourite nephew Nashat, a newly married twenty-six-year-old policeman, was killed by a suicide bomber in Aadamiya. Her husband Jabar identified the body.

'He was a big fellow,' Jabar says. 'I couldn't believe how a person looks when they have been burned; like shrunken charcoal. I recognised only a part of his shoe.'

Compared to many Iraqi families, the Khasrajis' losses are small. But their daily life is hard. 'We try to adapt,' says Faiza. 'We bought a generator because there is no electricity. At the beginning of this month the cesspool in our neighbourhood overflowed. We were lucky, because our house is on higher ground; the neighbours had sewage flowing into their houses.

'But we couldn't use the bathroom. I had to carry the dishes to the side of the road to wash them and throw the water in the street. I'm afraid the cesspool will overflow again, as soon as the rain starts.

'The Americans and the [Iraqi] government have done nothing for us,' Faiza continues. 'Do you think the Americans cannot fix sewers? Do you think they cannot prevent bombings? It is painful to say, but I want to leave Iraq, for the safety of my husband and sons.'

While Mrs Khasraji was talking, I remembered the engineer from Halliburton whom I'd met at the baggage carousel at Baghdad Airport. He told me he was working on electricity and sewers. 'For Iraqis?' I asked hopefully. 'No, for American bases,' he replied, complaining that his German sewage technician refused to travel to Iraq because it was too dangerous.

If the denizens of the 'Green Zone' – US military, embassy personnel and the entire Iraqi government and parliament – had to live in the real Iraq of the Khasrajis, they might stop spouting optimistic tripe about the 'march of democracy' in Iraq,

Post-invasion Iraq is an apartheid system in which foreigners and America's Iraqi allies enjoy water, food, electricity and above all security, behind the ten-metre walls of the Green Zone, a vast enclave that used to hold Saddam Hussein's palaces, swimming pools, parks, a convention centre, office buildings and the al-Rasheed Hotel.

Although a few bombs, rockets and mortars find their way into the Green Zone, it is infinitely safer than the dirty, impoverished and extremely violent

Iraq outside. The US publications *Newsweek* and the *Wall Street Journal* rent houses inside the Zone.

Some journalists stay at the al-Rasheed Hotel. Many foreign visitors to Iraq are helicoptered into the Zone and never see beyond its sprinkler-watered lawns and endless checkpoints. These are manned (in order of nationality as you enter) by the Iraqi army, Georgians (from the former Soviet Union – not the American South), Zimbabweans with Alsatian dogs, and Nepalese.

To enter, one is frisked repeatedly and passes through half a dozen metal detectors. Iraqi employees pass explosives swipes over all cell phones, equipment and cameras.

It takes a mind-boggling assortment of badges and security clearances to move within the Green Zone. Mere journalists are entitled only to the CPIC (Combined Press Information Centre) card, which grants admission to the convention-centre-cum-parliament. The Iraqi journalists who do most of the ground work for the Western media hang around the convention centre all day, waiting for Iraqi politicians, diplomats or the US military to give briefings, which are not announced in advance for security reasons. It's rarefied and claustrophobic; a test tube experiment in democracy under siege.

The Green Zone has spawned a series of imitations across Baghdad, with far less spectacular means. The Palestine and Sheraton Hotels form one security area. A few streets away a miniature Green Zone houses the French embassy, Reuters, the BBC and the *New York Times*. Most of the English-language press stay several miles from the Green Zone, in a small cluster of hotels and houses whose approaches are blocked by concrete barriers, steel gates and guards with Kalashnikovs.

Because the traffic is so bad, it takes an hour to reach the Green Zone from the hotel complex. Likewise, many neighbourboods have taken security into their own hands. Residents of a street or building chip in to set up barriers and hire security guards.

Most of the violence occurs outside these 'secure' islands. People are kidnapped every day, like Saadoun Jennabi, the lawyer for one of Saddam Hussein's co-defendants, who was taken from his office by gunmen about an hour before Rory Carroll was released on Thursday night.

Jennabi's body was found yesterday, shot in the head and chest. On Wednesday Mohamed Haroon, the head of the journalists' union, was gunned down in his car on the motorway.

Moving from the Green Zone to the real Iraq is especially dangerous for Iraqis who work for occupation forces. Marwa, 24, is a Sunni Muslim medical secretary who has several friends working inside the Zone. There are almost no jobs in Iraq's paralysed economy, but she has repeatedly turned down offers of work inside the Zone.

'I consider this money is not clean,' Marwa says. 'I could not eat from it. These Americans kill my Iraqi brothers. Second, I am sure the resistance would kill me.' One of Marwa's friends, named Raghad, was shot because she worked in the Green Zone.

'Three of her colleagues were killed,' Marwa recounts. 'The Americans sent them home in a minibus after work every day, wearing flak jackets. She said she felt the heat entering her body; she was hit by three or four bullets. She survived, but she stopped working for the Americans.'

Whole professional categories are being wiped out. After medical doctors were targeted for assassination, thousands of doctors fled abroad with their families. Then the killers went after pilots who bombed Iran in the 1980-88 war.

'My uncle was a pilot and he will not leave his house,' says Marwa. 'He couldn't attend my sister's engagement party. He has a gun at home – we all do – but bodyguards are too expensive. No one can lead a normal life.'

There was a telling moment when I went into the US military press office in the Green Zone to request to go on patrol with US troops. I asked for Aadamiya or Amariya, areas where the insurgency is active.

But the sergeant who deals with the media couldn't help me. 'We don't know their names for these places, Ma'am,' he said. So how do Americans identify Baghdad neighbourhoods?

'By the names of our headquarters,' he explained. For the US military, Baghdad is divided into Operating Bases Courage, Liberty, Honour, Prosperity and Justice.

22 October 2005

Kill the Dictator

What do you do when death squads roam the streets of Baghdad, when the security forces you've armed and trained systematically torture and murder detainees, when you've squandered three thousand American lives and hundreds of thousands of Iraqis in an ill-conceived military venture that sparked a civil war? Kill the dictator.

The execution of Saddam Hussein on 30 December betrayed the impotence that underlies US power. It took George Bush nearly four years to overthrow, apprehend and execute the 'butcher of Baghdad'.

But what an empty victory; nearly a month after the Hamilton-Baker report provided a rational basis for making the best of a bad job, Bush shows no sign of comprehending the catastrophe he has created. His comment on the execution of Saddam was a partial admission of the futility of the act which, Bush admitted, 'will not end the violence in Iraq', and an exercise in the same empty rhetoric that has characterised his conduct of the war.

Saddam's death was 'an important milestone on Iraq's course to becoming a democracy that can govern, sustain and defend itself and be an ally in the war on terror,' Bush said. Really? How? Why does the US president get away with such meaningless palaver? Yet again, the US has blithely committed an act of unforeseeable, far-reaching consequences. When I called friends in California to wish them a happy new year, they told me Americans were far more interested in the death of ninety-three-year-old former president Gerald Ford than in Saddam's execution. US media took the line that by pardoning the felonious Richard Nixon, the dim-witted Ford 'healed the nation'.

Saddam was executed at the beginning of the Muslim Eid al-Adha, the feast of the sacrifice, a time of forgiveness, when even the tyrant Saddam used to free prisoners. For the Shia, who were Saddam's main victims, and whom the US has now brought to power, the execution was a cause for celebration.

But for the Sunnis, who comprise the vast majority of Arabs and Muslims in the world, the choice of day was yet another provocation. In the West, the coincidence with New Year's Eve added a grotesque, Roman circus feel to an already barbaric act. One couldn't help wondering if the execution was meant to distract attention from the real milestone of the weekend – the three-thousandth US soldier to die in Iraq.

Saddam's last words, as recounted by Judge Munir Haddad, one of the official witnesses, were: 'I hope that you will remain united and I warn you: do not trust the Iranian coalition; these people are dangerous.' The former dictator's words sounded like a harbinger of the breakup of Iraq, the 'solution' which some US commentators have long advocated. Iraqi Sunnis, with some reason, consider the SCIRI and Dawa parties now nominally in power to be tools of Iran. Saddam's words point towards the danger of a region-wide Sunni-Shia conflagration. Last month an adviser to the Saudi ambassador in Washington caused alarm by saying that Riyadh could not stand idly by while Iran extends its influence.

Until his hands were bound behind his back, Saddam held a Koran, which, according to the Agence France Presse, 'he wanted sent to a person'.

To whom? To his widow, Sajida, or his daughters, Raghad and Rana? To a Sunni cleric for safe keeping? Such is the stuff of holy relics. My neighbour in Ireland, who attended the Jesuit school at Stonyhurst, told me how four hundred years after the execution of Mary Stuart, the school treasures the prayer book she held through the night preceding her decapitation.

I've often thought of the US magazine editor who told me how impressed he'd been by Saddam's Iraq. Compared to other Arab countries, it was modern, secular and progressive, especially in its treatment of women, he said.

Millions of Arabs now feel that 'the US has done one of ours'. Resentment of the US is strengthened, and I suspect that when Arab history books come to be written, Saddam's torture chambers and crimes against humanity will be forgotten. The memory of an enlightened leader who dared to stand up to the US will prevail.

Did Saddam's erstwhile friends in Europe and America, the Jacques Chiracs and Donald Rumsfelds of this world, feel a tinge of remorse, or relief, to learn he was dead? It is scandalous that the US boasted of organising a 'public' trial for Saddam, when the procedure was carefully devised to prevent the former dictator from dragging down his former allies with him.

Judges in the US-built courtroom disposed of two buttons, one to cut the sound when Saddam spoke, and another to draw a curtain across the dock when he misbehaved. Journalists and observers in the glassed-in gallery heard and saw only what they were permitted to. Excerpts were released for broadcast with a twenty- to thirty-minute delay, ensuring that any revelations by Saddam could be censored.

The Islamic Republic of Iran praised the execution. One might have expected Iran to demand a full account by Saddam of the weapons and intelligence that the US and European powers provided for his illegal invasion of Iran in 1980. When Saddam used chemical weapons – again provided by the West – to massacre thousands of Kurds at Halabja, the US State Department instructed diplomats to blame the atrocity on Tehran.

The statement by the British Foreign Secretary, Margaret Beckett, to which Prime Minister Tony Blair subscribed, at the same time welcomed Saddam's execution and condemned the death penalty. Could anything be more absurd? If capital punishment is immoral, it is in all cases, 'even if it deals with a person who was guilty of grave crimes', the Vatican noted.

It was chilling to see Saddam's executioners in their medieval black hoods. But television networks stopped short of showing us the snapped neck and twisting corpse. Time and again, we are spared the worst images of war in Iraq, Lebanon and the Israeli-occupied territories on the grounds of 'taste'. If we had to watch it all – dead children, mangled bodies, and yes, Saddam's execution – perhaps the citizens of Western democracies might hold their own leaders to account.

1 January 2007

Old Grievances

A suicide bomber struck my hotel in November 2005. One wing is closed, and in my room plastic sheeting is still taped to the window frames, which are devoid of glass. Sewage bubbles up from the drain in the bathroom floor. All this is secondary to the tragic smile of the night receptionist, whose son was killed in the bombing.

One hovers between indignation and pity for the desperate Iraqis who try to gouge you to the last dinar.

I couldn't help smiling at this echo of rip-off Iraq in retired US General William Odom's assessment of the Sons of Iraq militia. 'Let me emphasise that our new Sunni friends insist on being paid for their loyalty,' Odom told a Senate committee. 'I've heard, for example, the cost in one area of about a hundred square kilometres is $250,000 per day. And periodically, they threaten to defect unless their fees are increased.' With the occupation costing $411 million daily, who's counting?

There's only an hour of mains electricity each day now. Yet despite increasing hardship, most of the people I meet tell me life is improving. The explanation is simple: at the height of the Sunni-Shia civil war in 2006–07, some eighty bodies were found on the streets of Baghdad each morning. Now there are 'only' three or four. There is still car-bombing and kidnapping on a scale that would shut down any normal country, but in Baghdad people are almost cheerful.

The Sunnis feel the Americans are at last protecting them, and Prime Minister Nuri al-Maliki's repression of the Shia militia, Jaish al-Mehdi, and the Sunni al-Qaeda strikes civilians on all sides as non-partisan and long overdue.

There are light moments: I saw US and Iraqi soldiers eating melting ice cream at a joint checkpoint on Jadriya Bridge. There are symbolic moments: I saw a Humvee gunner train his fifty-calibre machine gun on an Iraqi boy who pointed his middle finger at him. The child dropped his hand and scowled impotently.

Grievances resurface quickly. A US army officer yesterday reminded me that his unit, Alpha Company 4-64, was the one that fired a tank shell at the Palestine Hotel on 8 April 2003, killing two journalists. I saw them carried out, dying.

The officer was still at military academy when it happened. The case is now taught in army courses, he said. He claimed it was an honest mistake. But nothing he said lifted the chill that fell over our meeting.

What then must it be like for Sunni and Shia?

20 May 2008

VII
ISRAEL &
PALESTINE

'We are living in cages'

'When He Walks Away'

The enemy who takes tea in our shack has a mare in the smoke
And a daughter with thick eyebrows, hazel eyes, and hair as long as the
*   night of songs on her shoulders*
And her image never leaves him when he comes to our home to ask for
*   tea . . .*

In our shack, the enemy takes a rest from his rifle
He leaves it on my grandfather's chair, and eats our bread
Like any guest
He dozes for a while on the wicker chair, strokes our cat's fur and says to
*   us always:*
Do not blame the victim
We ask: Who is the victim?
He answers: Blood that the night never dries.

The buttons of his uniform shine when he walks away
Goodnight! Say hello to our well and the patch of fig trees
Walk softly on our shadow in the oat fields
Say hello to our cypress trees overhead
And don't forget to close the gate at night
Remember that the horse is afraid of aircraft
And say hello to us over there, if you find the time.

He is the voice of a stateless people, the man widely regarded as the finest living Arab poet. But each time journalists knock on Mahmoud Darwish's door to ask about recurring rumours that he will win the Nobel Prize for literature, he tells them: 'Go home. I know I am not going to get it. I don't deserve it. I've achieved nothing until now.'

Over the past four decades, Darwish has published twenty books that gave expression to the despair and dispossession of the Palestinians. Longing for the lost fig and olive trees of his native Galilee is the leitmotif of Darwish's *oeuvre*. But his is a sensitive, wounded narrative, never a tirade. 'Against barbarity,' he has written, 'poetry can resist only by conforming its attachment to human fragility, like a blade of grass growing on a wall while armies march by.'

It is a message that interests French, Spanish and even Israeli readers more than the English-speaking world. Most of Darwish's books have been translated into Hebrew, far fewer into English. He was recently invited to Paris by the French culture ministry for its 'Springtime of Poets', and to launch a new collection of his work published by Gallimard.

A frail-looking, ascetic fifty-nine-year-old whose work includes as many love poems as it does odes of exile, Darwish wrote the 1988 Palestinian declaration of independence. Five years later, he resigned from the PLO's Executive Council because of what he saw as the sloppy, hurried way in which the 1993 Oslo accords were being negotiated. 'I am very sorry to see I was right,' he says. 'After seven years, the accords have not been implemented.' But his mood lightens when our conversation turns to the poets he admires: the tenth century Arab wanderer Al-Moutanabbi, Derek Walcott, Joseph Brodsky and Seamus Heaney.

Darwish's life changed one summer night in 1948, when his mother woke him in a panic. His family ran through the forest, along with hundred of inhabitants of his village, El Birwa. 'Bullets were whistling over our heads, and I didn't understand what was happening. After walking all night, we arrived in a foreign village with children I didn't know. I asked innocently "Where am I?" and I heard the word "Lebanon" for the first time.'

After a miserable year in a refugee camp, Darwish's parents decided to sneak back into northern Israel – something forbidden by the Israelis. They returned to El Birwa to find it had been razed. Darwish grew up in Israel, and was imprisoned for political activities five times between 1961 and 1967, before being banished in 1970. A long period of wandering then began, from Beirut to Damascus, Paris, Tunis and Cairo.

In 1995, after twenty-five years of exile, Israeli authorities allowed Darwish to return for the funeral of his friend, the writer Emile Habibi. He now lives in the West Bank town of Ramallah. The Israelis renew his multiple reentry visa twice a year, enabling him to visit his mother and family in Galilee.

It was in Ramallah that Darwish recently watched five hours of Israeli Knesset debates, broadcast live on television. The education minister, Yossi Sarid, had requested that three Darwish poems written in Israeli jails become optional texts in Israeli schools. 'To My Mother', about the young poet's longing for his mother's bread, coffee and tenderness, is an Arab classic, made famous by the Lebanese singer Marcel Khalife. Although the poems were written thirty-four years ago, Sarid's suggestion nearly brought the Israeli government down – and prompted an Orthodox rabbi to call the education minister a 'satan whose memory must be erased'.

Darwish says he was indifferent to the internal Israeli dispute over his texts, but he was obviously amused by it. 'They were all carrying poems in their hands!' he laughs. 'A woman from the Labour Party read my poem "I am a woman, not more not less . . . " to prove that I wasn't a misogynist. It took them two sessions – two hours plus three hours. Did this ever happen in history? Five hours of parliamentary debate about poetry!'

Although he is a former communist who considers the Bible to be mythology, Darwish said that Pope John Paul II's March 2000 visit to Israel and the occupied territories gave Palestinians great moral encouragement. 'He mentioned our fifty years of suffering, which means he named the victim. The Israelis are obsessed about monopolising the status of victims. They don't want anyone else to be victims. What the Pope said changed the way people see history. It recognised that we were here before the state of Israel.'

Palestinian leaders, Darwish says, are wondering if now, fifty-two years after what they call 'the catastrophe', they are any closer to a solution. 'What is clear is that the period of dreams and illusions is over. We are more realistic now. We know that it will be impossible to obtain justice, that history does not dictate just solutions. But even the possible peace we are trying to achieve is ambiguous for us, because of the conditions that the Israelis are imposing.'

Those conditions, Darwish says, are the refusal to consider allowing Palestinians to return to the land they left in 1948 – the sacrosanct 'right of return' enshrined in UN General Assembly resolution 194, the continued building of Israeli settlements in the occupied territories, and the insistence that 'united' Jerusalem remain Israel's capital alone.

Of the three, the settlements are the most palpable. 'When I was outside Palestine and Israel and I heard about settlements, I thought they were like army camps that could be dismantled,' Darwish explains. 'But when I went to live in Ramallah in 1996, I was deeply shocked. We have small ghettos separated by settlements that are actually towns – and I don't think the Israelis will remove them. These three obstacles make our dream of independence very humble.'

Darwish fears that a final accord on Israel's terms will fail. 'Peace between Israel and any other Arab country is possible, because they are neighbours,' he continues. 'But Israel and Palestine are not neighbours; Israel is built not next to Palestine but *on top of* Palestine.' Ideally, he would like to see a single, secular democracy for Palestinians and Israelis alike. 'But this will be very difficult to realise because the Israelis are obsessed by the purity of their identity,' he says. 'There is a contradiction between their claim to be democratic and their identity as the Jewish state. If they want a pure Jewish state, they should have no Arabs, yet from the beginning there were Arabs in Israel. If they want to be democratic, then they must have Arabs.'

A less satisfactory solution, Darwish says, is for Israel to withdraw from the entire West Bank and Gaza Strip. 'If we don't get that much, it cannot work. What Likud and Labour have offered us is less than 50 percent of the occupied territories.' He explains how the Israeli-occupied land is divided up into zones A, B and C. Zone A represents the centre of towns and villages under the control of the Palestinian Authority. Zone B, under joint Israeli-Palestinian control, comprises the suburbs, including the main Palestinian university at Bir Zeit. Zone C applies to the connecting roads, which are under complete Israeli control.

'We are living in cages, and all around the cages is Israel,' he says. 'Every time they make a closure, all life stops; we cannot move. How can you call this a state?'

Ramallah is a hot, lacklustre town; I ask Darwish if he is happy living there. 'I am unhappy everywhere,' he says, before revising his answer. 'I feel happy rarely, but really happy when I finish a new work. I feel useful. But these moments are very unusual.' Many of Darwish's poems are about the women he has loved, whose names are Hebrew as well as Arabic. 'I'm not interested in whether a woman is Jewish or Muslim or Christian,' he says. 'I loved many Israeli girls. It is the person, not the nationality, that interests me.'

Darwish says he has not abandoned the theme of dispossession. 'But there is a change of focus. I am trying to normalise my life, not to be jailed by what the [Israeli] occupation decides for me by writing only about Palestinian land.

I am liberating myself through language, because the most dangerous thing is to stay where others decide to put you.'

4 April 2000

When Mahmoud Darwish died on 9 August 2008, Palestinian President Mahmoud Abbas declared three days of mourning. Darwish was given the equivalent of a state funeral in Ramallah, where he is buried on a hilltop overlooking Jerusalem.

France Puts on Ceremony Worthy of a Head of State

Yasser Arafat died not in Palestine but in a soulless French army training hospital in a suburb of Paris, at 3.30 AM yesterday. Later in the day, his casket, accompanied by his widow Suha and his foreign minister, Nabil Shaath, began a last journey, reversing the steps made two weeks ago in a desperate bid to save his life.

France gave the Palestinian leader a send-off worthy of a head of state. The French prime minister, foreign minister, speaker of parliament and at least four former prime ministers and foreign ministers were among the four hundred guests who assembled at Villacoublay Military Airport.

They watched as Arafat's flag-draped casket was carried by white-gloved Republican Guards from a helicopter to an Airbus emblazoned with the words 'République Française'.

Suha Arafat stood beside French prime minister Jean-Pierre Raffarin, her long blonde hair pulled back from her face. At the end of the runway, beyond the security fence, some three hundred French people, many of them families with children, chanted 'Farewell, Arafat'.

The Israeli journalist and Arafat biographer Amnon Kapeliouk told LCI television the French ceremony made up for some of the indignities the Palestinian leader suffered. 'If only Arafat could see the honours bestowed upon him after three years locked up in the Muqata,' he said.

President Jacques Chirac issued a statement at 6 AM, offering condolences to Arafat's family. 'With him disappears the man of courage and conviction who embodied, for forty years, the struggle of the Palestinians for their national rights,' Chirac said, promising that France and the European Union would continue to work for two states 'living side by side, in peace and security'.

At midday, Chirac went to the military hospital 'to pay a last homage' to Arafat. He reportedly embraced Mrs Arafat before leaving. Former President

Valéry Giscard d'Estaing boasted on France Info radio that he was the first Western leader to reach out to Arafat, sending his foreign minister to Beirut in 1974, then allowing the PLO to open an office in Paris. Hubert Védrine, a former foreign minister, noted that François Mitterrand was the first to use the words 'Palestinian state', before the Israeli Knesset in 1982.

It seemed appropriate that a man who spent so much of his life in airplanes should go through three airports in two days on the way to his burial. Even the military funeral today is to be held in Cairo Airport. The Palestinians had hoped for the grander Arab League headquarters, but president Hosni Mubarak apparently feared that a large gathering in downtown Cairo could turn into a protest against his rule.

The French allowed the Palestinians to announce Arafat's death first in Ramallah. 'He closed his eyes and his big heart stopped,' Tayeb Abdel Rahim, the secretary of the presidency of the Palestinian Authority, said, weeping. 'He left for God but is still among this great people.'

Dr Christian Estripeau's laconic statement to the cameramen waiting outside the hospital was far less poetic: 'Monsieur Yasser Arafat, President of the Palestinian Authority, died at Percy Army Training Hospital on November 11th, 2004, at 3.30.'

There was not a word of explanation about the cause of death, perhaps because Mrs Arafat wants to keep it secret. According to a report in *Le Canard Enchaîné*, Mrs Arafat, accompanied by three lawyers, haggled over every word of every communiqué issued by the hospital. No autopsy was performed.

Though he was one of the most instantly recognisable figures of the late twentieth century, Arafat's birth and death were shrouded in secrecy. The Israelis claim he was born in Cairo; he said he was born in Jerusalem. We may never know what he died of.

Despite denials by French doctors and Palestinian leaders, many Palestinians believe the Israelis poisoned Arafat – a suspicion deepened by TV images of Israeli prime minister Ariel Sharon grinning through the final stages of Arafat's coma. The fact that Arafat died on the Night of Destiny, between the twenty-sixth and twenty-seventh days of the holy month of Ramadan, strengthened rumours that his entourage 'programmed' his death for maximum effect.

During the Night of Destiny, God is said to have dictated the Koran to the Prophet Mohammed. The timing of Arafat's death made it possible for him to be buried on the most propitious day, the last Friday in Ramadan.

12 November 2004

Massacre in Munich

When the terrible dénouement of the hostage crisis in Munich was broadcast on television screens around the world on the morning of 6 September 1972, Palestinian refugee camps across the Middle East resounded with cries of joy. Eleven Israeli athletes, five Palestinian gunmen, a German policeman and a helicopter pilot were dead, but the Palestinians considered it victory. The attackers, from refugee camps in Lebanon and Syria, had not given up, had not surrendered.

Within weeks, on orders from the then Prime Minister of Israel, Golda Meir, the Israeli intelligence agency Mossad began assassinating PLO figures. The story of the Israelis' revenge is recounted in Steven Spielberg's film *Munich*.

Two years before the Munich massacre, King Hussein's army had driven Yasser Arafat's Fatah out of Jordan. In the hope of lifting Palestinian spirits, Abu Iyad and Abu Daoud (whose real name is Mohamed Daoud Oudeh) transformed the name of their defeat, Black September, into that of an avenging armed group which for three years struck at Israelis in Europe.

Abu Iyad and Abu Daoud planned the Munich hostage-taking. Abu Iyad was murdered in Tunis in 1991. Although Abu Daoud was second on the hit list drawn up by Golda Meir, he survived an assassination attempt and has reached the age of sixty-nine. He lives in Damascus, where he told *The Irish Times* his version of what happened in Munich.

In Israel and much of the West, Abu Daoud is regarded as a 'terrorist mastermind'. In the Arab world, he is a hero. When his autobiography, *Palestine: from Jerusalem to Munich*, was published in French in 1999, the Arab satellite television network al-Jazeera recorded a nine-hour interview with Abu Daoud. It has been re-broadcast twice, in its entirety.

Heads turn when Abu Daoud, who is nearly two metres tall, lumbers into the lobby of a Damascus hotel. You might mistake him for an ageing professor or a retired lawyer – the profession for which he trained.

'I don't like it,' he says of the resuscitated 'terrorist' label. 'I am not a terrorist. I am a nationalist fighting for my rights.'

Abu Daoud does not hesitate to wade into the moral swamp in which Spielberg's characters flail about. But unlike the semi-fictional Mossad agents, Abu Daoud is not one for soul-searching and anguish. More than thirty-three years after Munich, he quotes the old Arab saying that 'blood brings blood'. He wants justice, he says. Not revenge. Though he professes admiration for the two Israeli athletes who died at the outset, fighting the hostage-takers, and says he is sorry for Israeli and Palestinian deaths alike, he does not regret his own actions.

'We cannot fight a "clean" war, targeting only Mossad or Israeli military, when they don't distinguish between civilians and military among us,' Abu Daoud argued in the summer of 1972.

The Israelis had just assassinated Ghassan Khanafani, the editor of a magazine published by the radical Popular Front for the Liberation of Palestine (PFLP), along with his young niece, in retaliation for the group's attack on Lod Airport in Tel Aviv. Two other Palestinian intellectuals were maimed by letter bombs. The eye-for-an-eye, tooth-for-a-tooth reciprocal bloodletting recounted in *Munich* was well under way before the Munich Olympics.

The Palestinians were demoralised after their retreat from Jordan to Lebanon. The Israelis retaliated for cross-border raids by bombing refugee camps in Lebanon where they said the fighters lived with their families. The world was indifferent to the attacks on refugees.

'People were more interested in sports than in the plight of the Palestinians,' Abu Daoud says. 'In one sense, we succeeded in Munich: we forced our cause on to the television screens of 500 million households.'

Abu Daoud rejects the widespread perception that Palestinians perpetrated a massacre in Munich, preferring to blame Golda Meir for refusing to consider a prisoner exchange, and the German security forces who negotiated a departure, then opened fire on the hostage-takers. But surely, I say, ultimate responsibility lies with the Palestinians who burst into the sleeping Israeli athletes' quarters at 4 AM on 5 September 1972?

'We gave strict orders to our people not to kill anyone except in self-defence,' Abu Daoud says. 'If after twenty-four hours the Israelis did not accept our demands [for the release of 234 mostly Palestinian prisoners], they were to ask for aircraft and take the athletes to an Arab country. If the Germans hadn't given in to Golda Meir, the Israelis and our people would still be alive today.' It is not clear if the nine remaining Israeli hostages were killed by their Palestinian captors or by German gunfire. Abu Daoud wants to believe it was the Germans.

Abu Daoud claims the Israeli athletes were military reservists and hence 'legitimate targets', while Palestinians killed in revenge by Mossad were innocent. The first two hit squad victims, Wael Zwaiter and Mahmoud Hamshari, were the representatives of the Palestine Liberation Organisation (PLO) in Rome and Paris.

'I knew Zwaiter,' Abu Daoud says. 'He was a philosopher who always had a book under his arm. He never held a gun in his life.' Hamshari, who was killed by a booby-trapped phone in his apartment, is also portrayed in *Munich* as a man of culture, with a beautiful wife and daughter.

'The Israelis wanted to eliminate anyone who conveyed a positive image of Palestinians,' says Abu Daoud. At the end of *Munich*, the assassination squad leader, 'Avner', demands proof that the people he murdered had anything to do with the attack on the athletes.

The carnage on the tarmac at Munich's Fürstenfeldbruck Airport at dawn on 6 September 1972 was in complete contrast to the sunny afternoon some six weeks earlier when Abu Daoud, Abu Iyad and his assistant Fakri al-Omari (who would later die with him) sat at an outdoor café on the Piazza della Rotonda in central Rome. They were enraged by a newspaper article saying the International Olympic Committee had refused a Palestinian request to send a delegation to the Munich Olympics.

'So, since they won't let the Palestinians participate in the Games, why don't we enter the Olympics in our own way?' Fakri asked. 'What would we do there?' Abu Iyad asked.

'We'd seize Israeli athletes,' Fakri replied.

From Rome, Abu Daoud flew to Munich on the first of several reconnaissance missions. Claiming to be Brazilian, he and the two lead Palestinian gunmen approached an Israeli woman outside the athletes' quarters, six days before the attack.

'I dream of visiting Israel,' Abu Daoud told her. 'My friends also dream of a vacation in Israel. We'd like some brochures about your country. Perhaps you could give us some little Israeli flags, for our children?' The athletes were out training or in competition, so the young woman gave the three Palestinians a guided tour of their quarters. 'She tried to make me look at her as a woman; at the time, I was rather handsome,' Abu Daoud laughs.

One of the Mossad agents in Spielberg's film is lured to his death by an attractive Dutch prostitute. In real life, an Israeli woman unwittingly assisted in the killing of her colleagues because she fell for Abu Daoud's 'Brazilian' charm and good looks.

'She wasn't bad,' Abu Daoud recalls. 'But I was on a mission. When I am on a mission, I set all my emotions aside.'

Abu Daoud bought eight identical tracksuits and Adidas sports bags for the gunmen. On the day before the attack, he filled each bag with a ski mask, rope for tying the hostages, a knife, tinned food, processed cheese, sandwiches and biscuits. Each Palestinian was given an assault rifle, spare cartridges, and one or two hand grenades.

To protect Abu Daoud's identity, even the Palestinians, apart from the two commando leaders, were meant to believe he was a Brazilian sympathiser of the PLO. As he helped the last of the gunmen scale the fence of the Olympic village, he was appalled to hear the young man say: 'Thanks, Abu Daoud.'

Spielberg's critics claim he establishes a 'moral equivalence' between Palestinian hostage-takers and Israeli assassins. Both sides hate being compared to each other, but there are parallels.

'The Israelis want to drive us off our land,' Abu Daoud says, echoing the Israeli refrain of the Arabs wanting to drive *them* into the sea.

In the film, the Israeli hit squad leader 'Avner' must account to his case officer for the hundreds of thousands of dollars he spends tracking down Palestinians. In real life, Abu Daoud returned $500 and thirty-seven marks left over from the Munich attack to the PLO's finance department. He estimates that the entire Munich operation cost $4,000, not including the weapons supplied by Abu Iyad.

Abu Daoud is annoyed that Spielberg's film credits Ali Hassan Salameh, a flamboyant figure who was assassinated by Mossad in 1979, with planning Munich. Known as 'the red baron', Salameh married Georgina Rizk, then the Lebanese Miss World.

Spielberg's film insinuates that Salameh worked for the CIA – an allegation made in Abu Daoud's book. 'What you did in Munich will go down in history.

At every Olympic games they'll talk about it,' Abu Daoud quoted Salameh in his book. Salameh led others to believe *he* planned the attack.

It is a measure of the prestige attached to Munich in Palestinian circles that the PFLP leader, Wadiya Haddad, who specialised in airline hijackings, approached Abu Daoud in October 1972, saying: 'I'm proud to shake the hand of the man who did Munich!'

Aside from the fact that Spielberg consulted no Palestinians who were involved, Abu Daoud's other grievance with the film is the omission of the story of Ahmed Bouchiki, the Moroccan waiter in Lillehammer, Norway, whom the Israelis gunned down as he walked home from the cinema with his pregnant wife. Mossad had mistaken Bouchiki for Ali Hassan Salameh.

'It proves the Israelis were not professional,' Abu Daoud sniffs.

Asked how he survived Golda Meir's death sentence against him, Abu Daoud grins. 'Because I am more professional than they are,' he replies.

In a hotel coffee shop in Warsaw, in August 1981, a gunman fired a 9mm Glock pistol into Abu Daoud's left wrist, followed by a shot to his jaw, which still causes his lower lip to hang sideways. Five more bullets to his chest, stomach and side followed, but Abu Daoud pursued the gunman to the hotel door.

'I could have broken him in two, but I didn't go outside because I thought it might be an ambush. I came back to the lobby and sat bleeding until the ambulance came.'

The PLO caught the gunman ten years later, then interrogated, tried and executed him. He was a Palestinian named Khaled and was in his early twenties when he tried to kill Abu Daoud and murdered his close friend Issam Sartawi in Lisbon. 'He was a Palestinian looking for money, recruited by Mossad,' explains Abu Daoud.

That Khaled also worked for the renegade Palestinian extremist Abu Nidal was symptomatic of the netherworld of Middle East intelligence services and terrorist groups, where it is impossible to know with certainty who works for whom, who kills, and why. Spielberg shows this dark confusion, when 'Avner' fears that his former Mossad colleagues may want to harm him.

Today, Abu Daoud is still stateless. He accepted the 1993 Oslo Accords and moved to Ramallah in the West Bank. But after his book came out, the Israelis did not allow him to return from a trip to Jordan. The Jordanians refused to renew his expired passport in 2001. So he lives in Damascus, a Syrian driver's licence his only proof of identity.

Nearly three and a half decades after Munich, does Abu Daoud fear Israeli revenge? 'I don't care,' he shrugs. 'Although I drink whisky [which is against Islam], I think God will take the decision.'

The architect of Munich shakes the ice cubes in his double Black Label on the rocks. 'If I were the Israelis, I'd stop thinking about what Abu Daoud did thirty-four years ago,' he muses. 'The young people want to fight them. They should put Abu Daoud beside them. They need influential people who say peace is good. I would do it; believe in it. If they give us our rights.'

21 January 2006

Abu Daoud died of kidney failure in Damascus on 2 July 2010, at the age of seventy-three.

Palestinians Being Punished for Choosing Hamas

So the gutless European Commission has cut aid to the Palestinian Authority. What sin did the Palestinians commit to deserve being rejected by their main donor? They held a free and fair election that was regarded as exemplary throughout the Arab world. But the wrong people won: the Islamic party Hamas. The Palestinians have to be punished.

The EU once showed a modicum of courage in attempting to counterbalance Washington's unconditional support for Israel. Even Tony Blair, when he was being sucked into George W. Bush's Iraq disaster, sought assurances that, once it was over, the US would seek justice for the Palestinians.

Now the EU slavishly follows Washington's cue. The Hamas-led government must jump through the hoops, submit completely, or we'll boycott them, starve them and impose a take-it-or-leave-it 'unilateral peace'.

Yes, Hamas carried out horrific suicide bombings. Dare one even mention the disproportion in casualties: that more than three thousand Palestinians have been killed since the second Intifada started in September 2000, compared to some one thousand Israelis? Hamas has maintained a unilateral ceasefire for nearly a year and a half, with no encouragement from the West.

The US and EU demand that Hamas recognise Israel, renounce violence and observe past peace agreements. When did Israel recognise Palestine, renounce violence against Palestinians or observe past peace agreements? Ariel Sharon, hailed by Bush as 'a man of peace', renounced the Oslo agreement and violated the 'road map'. Our double standards have never been so blatant.

Diplomats in Israel compare Hamas to Sinn Féin during the twilight zone before peace and decommissioning. Hamas officials keep making conciliatory statements – trial balloons that they often pull back. Twice this week, the

Palestinian foreign minister, Mahmoud Zahar, a Hamas member, spoke of a 'two-state solution', once in a letter to the UN Secretary General, Kofi Annan.

In a recent interview with *Le Figaro*, Khaled Meshaal, the head of Hamas's political bureau, whom the Israelis tried to assassinate, said Hamas is 'reaching out' to Israel. 'If Israel evacuates the West Bank and East Jerusalem, and recognises the right of return for refugees and dismantles the new wall, I can guarantee you that Hamas, and with it all Palestinians, will be ready for serious steps, founded on justice and equity, in view of a permanent peace with the Israelis,' Meshaal said. All Meshaal's demands are grounded in international law.

Since Hamas won the election, Israel has kept $50 million per month in customs duties which it collects at crossings into the Palestinian territories. This money belongs to the Palestinians.

Without it, the Authority cannot meet its 150,000-strong payroll. Nearly half the Authority's employees are policemen. 'Imagine 73,000 unpaid, armed men in the streets of Gaza and the West Bank,' a UN official told *Le Monde*.

The EU cut another €30 million in direct aid to the Authority yesterday. The US and EU say they'll funnel humanitarian aid through the UN agency UNWRA and non-governmental organisations. But aid workers are neither able nor willing to circumvent the role of the Authority. By dividing Palestinian officials into 'good guys' and 'bad guys', Washington and Brussels are destroying the administration that was to have served as the foundation for an independent Palestinian state.

On a trip to Jerusalem at the beginning of this month to participate in a TV5 *Monde* programme, I was struck by the deep pessimism of Israeli and Arab colleagues. Conditions in the Palestinian territories have never been worse. The contrast between the Pharaonic grandeur of Tel Aviv's new Ben Gurion Airport and the Gaza Strip, just a few miles away, is shocking.

Two-thirds of Palestinians now live on less than €55 per month; the average monthly salary in Israel is €1,268. Since January, there have been shortages of milk and flour in Gaza, where children are suffering from malnutrition.

Yesterday's EU slap in the face for the Authority occurred one day after Ehud Olmert was asked to form the new Israeli government. Olmert repeated his intention to work towards setting 'a permanent borderline, even without an agreement', along the eight-metre-high wall which Israel is building along the length of the West Bank. If Israel can't get the Palestinians to go along with the plan (why would they?), Olmert says he'll seek 'an understanding with the international community, particularly the US and President George W. Bush'.

Olmert intends to annex all land east of the wall. Remember: when the wall was started, the Sharon government swore it was temporary. 'We have already lost 78 percent of British Mandate Palestine,' Awad Duaibes, a journalist with the Voice of Palestine radio station in Ramallah, told me. 'Now we're expected to give up another 10 percent of the 22 percent that's left.'

The new Palestinian government was sworn in by videoconference because Israel will not allow Hamas officials to travel from Gaza to the West Bank. The Israelis are considering a Gaza-West Bank tunnel, probably for rail traffic only.

The large settlement blocs Olmert intends to annex, and the Israeli 'military zone' in the Jordan river valley would break the West Bank into at least five pieces. Olmert will also keep aquifers and the holy sites in Arab East Jerusalem, Hebron and near Bethlehem.

Israel does not allow the Palestinians to have a port or an airport. All merchandise enters Gaza through the Israeli-controlled Erez crossing. Olmert would maintain a similar stranglehold on the West Bank, with Israel controlling the Jordanian border.

Olmert's objective is to keep as much land as possible, with as few Arabs as possible. 'The most painful moment of my life was the day I discovered that accounting was stronger than the history and geography of Israel,' he said recently. 'I realised with alarm that if we hung on to everything, in 2020 there would be 60 percent Arabs and 40 percent Jews.' This is the Palestinian state that Israel and the US are concocting: famished and thirsty, shrunken and chopped into pieces. It doesn't take a Middle East expert to see there's no peace for Palestine down this road. Surely the EU can do better.

8 April 2006

Israel's Calling Card

Broken glass crunched under my shoes as I stepped out of the taxi. The shattered pieces glimmered in the dark, and a line from a Second World War song about the Blitz in London went through my head: 'The streets of town were paved with stars . . . .'

But there is nothing romantic about Gaza in 2009. The hotel lobby was dank and cold.

Perhaps to prepare me for the plastic sheeting that has replaced my bedroom window, the receptionist complained that the price of glass had multiplied tenfold, from fifty Israeli shekels per square metre before the three-week war to five hundred Israeli shekels since hostilities stopped last Sunday. But is it really over? I woke before dawn to a loud, hammering noise. From the street outside, I could see an Israeli gunboat lobbing artillery shells along the coastline.

The practice may prevent Hamas receiving weapons, but Gazans see it as a wicked way to stop them from fishing and eating. Several people were hospitalised as a result of yesterday's shelling.

In central Gaza, the bomb sites were purposefully chosen, as in Baghdad in 2003. Like the Americans in Baghdad, the Israelis took a swipe at the press building, wounding two journalists.

Cheerful, uniformed policemen lined the pavement opposite the bombed-out central police station. 'We're back at work. This is our office now,' they told me.

The Palestine Legislative Council, once the finest building in Gaza, was flattened: so much for promoting Arab democracy. Flattened too was the government palace overlooking the sea, where Yasser Arafat received world dignitaries.

The former home of Nizar Rayan, a Hamas leader who was killed by a one-tonne bomb with two of his four wives and twelve of his children on 1 January, has become a shrine. The targeting of Rayan's building was not precise. Most of a city block was chopped into debris, with brocade curtains and living room furniture dangling from uprooted girders.

Men, women and children strolled past Rayan's house, pointing and staring at the home of the 'martyr'. A Hamas youth group arrived on motorcycles.

The farther one advances towards Gaza's northern border, the more extreme the destruction. Beyond the crest of a hill in the Abed Rabbo residential district lies a vista of devastation which again reminds one of the Second World War or, more recently, the villages of southern Lebanon.

At twilight, donkey carts rattled down the hillside towards Jabalya. Orange campfires burned brightly in the rubble, where refugees brewed pots of tea.

The Israelis destroyed some 4,300 Gazan houses in three weeks, a good proportion of them on the high ground to the north of the enclave. These fields of ruined homes and ruined lives have become a calling card that says: Israel passed here.

23 January 2009

Inside the World's Biggest Prison

There were many ways to die during the Israeli offensive against Gaza. From their hospital beds at Gaza's Shifa Hospital, Atallah Saad, 13, and Yussef Salem, 17, told me how 'zananas' – remotely piloted drones that fire missiles – wounded them and killed Atallah's mother and pregnant sister-in-law, and two of Yussef's school friends. The drones were given the nickname because they make a loud 'z-z-z-z-z' sound. But the most shocking thing about them is that an Israeli operator watches his target – in these cases, all civilians – through a surveillance camera before launching the missile. Death by remote control.

White phosphorus was another, much-publicised means of death. Each M82581 artillery shell, manufactured by General Dynamics in Pine Bluff, Arkansas, bears the initials 'PB'. And each of the 155mm shells contains 116 felt wafers soaked in phosphorus, which ignites on contact with oxygen. The phosphorus makes the white jellyfish-shaped clouds seen on television during the 27 December–17 January Israeli offensive. It provides cover for advancing troops, but it also burns houses and people. If one of the felt pads lands on your skin, it burns until all the fuel is consumed, creating deep, wide, chemical burns, often to the bone.

Dr Nafiz Abu Shabaan pulls a plastic bag from under his desk. It is filled with white phosphorus, buried in sand. The brown pieces look like dog dirt, and reignite if broken open. Mahmoud al Jamal, 18, sits in the doctor's office, his right ear congealed, his fingers and part of his chest eaten away by white phosphorus. The unsightly wounds make him look like a leper.

Al Jamal was walking at dawn when he saw the white jellyfish in the sky. 'Everything was set on fire around me. I felt my body burning. I fell down and I asked the man lying next to me to help me, but he was dead. Then I lost consciousness.' Al Jamal's brother later told him how smoke poured from his body in the ambulance on the way to the hospital.

The Israelis' use of white phosphorus is amply documented. Israel says it is legal, but human rights groups say its use in civilian areas might constitute a war crime. Dr Abu Shabaan is more concerned by evidence of new, mysterious weapons, and appeals for an impartial international investigation into Israel's use of new weapons. 'We've seen many, many cases of amputation – like a cauterised wound, with no bleeding,' he recounts. 'Some have minor chest injuries, but the X-rays show nothing, and they die suddenly, without explanation.'

Palestinian and foreign doctors who have treated the war-wounded at Shifa suspect that the injuries may be caused by Dense Inert Metal Explosive, also known as Focus Lethality Munition, a weapon invented through Israeli-American cooperation. 'We are guinea pigs to the Americans and Israelis,' says Dr Abu Shabaan. 'The Americans give the Israelis new weapons, and they try them out on us.'

'They are definitely testing weapons on us,' says Dr Sobhi Skaik, a member of the Royal College of Surgeons in Edinburgh, and the head of the surgery department at Shifa. 'The amount of damage done by these weapons is not commensurate with the wounds. We found computer chips, magnetic pieces and transistors in wounds. Sometimes there are only minute pinpoint punctures to the abdomen and chest, but you see huge damage to internal organs. One patient had his liver burned black, as if it had been grilled. We think there must be something embedded in the human body that is releasing poison and killing.'

Yet for all the high-tech and Frankenstein weaponry, perhaps Israel's most vicious arm against the Palestinians has been *al-hissar*, the siege, imposed in the Gaza Strip nineteen months ago when Hamas, after winning a democratic election that the world refused to recognise, seized power from the Fatah Palestinian Authority.

The 'international community' turned a blind eye as Gazans languished in the world's biggest prison, unable to travel, import, export or interact with anyone or anything beyond their borders. And the world largely ignored the rockets Hamas fired in anger and frustration from within the siege. As a result of this dual negligence, the conflict exploded, killing thirteen Israelis and 1,434 Palestinians.

The siege was one reason casualties were so high in the three-week war, says Fred Abrahams of Human Rights Watch. With the Israeli and Egyptian borders closed, 'It wasn't possible for Gazans to escape. The only way to get out was on a stretcher.'

For nineteen months, Gaza has endured shortages of fuel, food, medicine and building materials. The Palestinians suffer the additional humiliation of using their tormentors' currency, but two months ago the Israeli government cut the supply of shekels, creating a severe cash shortage. Fayad Salam, the prime minister of the Palestinian Authority in Ramallah, was forced to plead with Israeli prime minister Ehud Olmert.

There were long queues at ATMs in Gaza City this week, but no matter how much they have in salary or savings, cash is rationed and Palestinians can withdraw only one thousand Israeli shekels per month. 'If the Israelis could deprive us of air, they would do it,' says a Palestinian doctor.

The siege of Gaza lies at the heart of the conflict. 'If the Israelis want the war to end, they must open all the borders and end the siege,' says Hamas government spokesman Tahir al-Nounou. 'Because the siege is war; the siege is killing our people.'

The 1,300 tunnels beneath the Gaza-Egyptian border are the only lifeline for Gaza. It costs $10,000 (€7,800) to dig a tunnel. The best tunnels are bored with sophisticated machines that compress earthen walls, so no give-away sand appears outside. Some tunnels have railway tracks and electricity, and they are a lucrative business for Gazans and Egyptians. Because Hamas is believed to import weapons through the tunnels, Israel carpet-bombed them during the offensive. Yet only an estimated four hundred were destroyed, and by midweek they were again open. Huge plastic cubes in metal frames, holding petrol, appeared on the pavements of Gaza City.

But the return to a semblance of normality cannot efface the three-week nightmare. Whole families were wiped out. Abu Mohamed Balousha, who lost five daughters, and the Samounis of Zeitoun, where a four-year-old boy was the only survivor in a family of thirty, have become *causes célèbres*.

Everyone has a worst memory. For ambulance driver Hathem Saleh, it was desperate telephone calls from the wounded. 'When you have been talking to him on the phone and you cannot reach him because the Israeli tank will hit you – it happened to me many times . . . . I could hear cries and the Israelis were shooting at us.'

Dr Mahmoud al Khozendar, a chest physician, tells of a colleague whose Russian wife was cut in half when an Israeli missile hit their home. It also killed their six-month-old child. 'He took the two parts of his wife and put her on the bed with the baby. He escaped with a wounded son and daughter, and asked the Red Crescent to go back for the bodies.'

At Shifa, al Khozendar had a room full of limbs he could not match with bodies, and a head with no body. 'Most of the bodies were buried without names,' he says.

There were many ways to die during the Israeli offensive on Gaza. Perhaps the greatest number killed were crushed to death when the Israelis fired heavy artillery at their houses. Halima Radwan, 60, seemed particularly symbolic to me. Radwan was a young woman when she and her family fled from Israel in the 1967 war. She spent her life as a wandering Palestinian, moving to Gaza, Jordan, Lebanon, Egypt. In 1996, in the glory days when Gaza had an airport and Palestinians carried passports, she and her husband Ahmad, a PLO official, decided to move back to 'Palestine'. They built a five-bedroom villa in the Abed Rabbo district of Gaza. A month before the offensive, they paid off their debts and celebrated.

Maher Radwan, 36, Halima and Ahmad's only son, is a mechanical engineer with the Palestinian Authority. He, his wife and children lived with his parents. 'Before the ground offensive started, I decided to take my wife and children farther from the border,' Maher recounts in front of the ruined villa. 'I begged my parents to come with us, but they said "No, we are old. The Israelis won't harm us."'

On 6 January, an Israeli tank fired a shell at the Radwans' house. Ahmad was wounded in the head and walked out with a white flag. He begged the Israelis to allow the Red Crescent to rescue his wife Halima, who was buried alive in her kitchen. The Israelis said no. Halima lived for four days under the debris of her house, which the Israelis then dynamited.

'They knew she was there and they saw her, because they searched the house before they destroyed it,' says Maher.

As soon as the ceasefire took effect last Sunday, he went with friends and relatives to dig out his mother. 'I had the tiniest hope she might still be alive,' But Halima's legs, shoulder and head had been crushed by concrete.

Broken porcelain, a framed verse from the Koran and a piece of plaster with Hebrew writing by the Israeli soldiers are scattered in the ruins of the Radwan family home. The pigeons they raised have returned to roost on the broken roof. Maher Radwan's neighbours say there can be no peace with the Israelis who did this. But Maher is more sad than angry. Peace might still be possible, he says, 'if only there were wise Israeli people'.

24 January 2009

'We hope our sacrifice will be the last . . .'

The last act of Orith Shitrit's life was to dial her husband Herzel's mobile-phone number. 'I heard only screaming. I hung up and dialled back, and there was no answer,' the tall, thin construction company manager recalls, one month to the day after his wife was killed by a grad missile fired from the Gaza Strip.

It was 9 PM on 28 December. Herzel Shitrit drove to the gym where his wife had been working out with her sister, Eilelit. When he saw police cars with flashing lights, and his wife's car, he knew something terrible had happened.

'She was driving home when she heard the alarm siren,' explains Hen, 19, the eldest of the couple's four children. 'My aunt and mother ran into the bus station. It wasn't very safe, but it was the closest building. The grad hit them. Eilelit was slightly wounded. My mother's stomach was ripped open, and she was wounded in the neck and leg. She died half an hour later in hospital.'

Orith was the only Israeli woman to die in the three-week war with Hamas, and one of three Israeli civilians. Her death marks the first time Hamas has struck Ashdod, Israel's main port, forty kilometres north of the Gaza Strip. Missiles also reached the outskirts of Be'er Sheva, the same distance to the east.

The Shitrit family have until now refused to speak to journalists. When I ring the bell of an apartment in a high-rise block overlooking the harbour, Herzel, 41, opens the door, ashen-faced, with deep circles under his eyes. In the family's grief, Hen is looking after her father, sisters Gal, 17, and Eliya, 12, and brother Tal, 10.

A photograph of Orith with Tal is prominently displayed in the living room. While we talk, Herzel pulls a plastic bag filled with family photographs from a cabinet and begins looking through them. He thinks of Orith every moment, looks through the pictures several times a day, is unable to sleep without medication. From time to time a ghostly smile flickers across his face. 'They are happy memories,' he whispers. 'Here we are on holiday last summer. We went to Holland, Belgium, France. This was two years ago, in Thailand . . . .' There are photographs on Paris bridges, at Disney World with the children, beneath the Eiffel Tower, Orith and Herzel embracing. She was thirty-nine years old when she died; she spent more than half her life with Herzel. The couple met at summer school and married when she was eighteen, Herzel twenty.

'My mother was amazing,' says Hen. 'She worked as a secretary at Gal's high school, and she went back to college and had almost completed her Bachelor's. She took the two youngest kids to school and picked them up every day, cleaned the house . . . . She was happy, funny, full of life. She had . . . a lot of friends.' Ten thousand people attended her funeral.

A *Ner Neshama* ('soul candle') burns on the kitchen counter. 'Jews mourn for one year,' explains Hen. 'For a year we will wear dark clothes, attend no parties, listen to no music. We burn a candle for one month, then one day each month, then one day each year.'

Orith Shitrit was one Israeli civilian, compared with more than a thousand Palestinians killed in the three-week war. I broach the subject gently, for the Shitrits' grief is raw. 'The Palestinian families are suffering as we are,' says Herzel.

Hen, who is doing her military service, believes Israeli claims that most of those who died in Gaza were Hamas militants, despite substantial evidence to the contrary. 'You cannot not react for years and years,' she says, referring to Hamas rocket attacks. 'You have to hit them. This is the price.'

Was it worth her mother's death? The young woman pauses for a fraction of a second. 'No,' she says. 'Nothing was worth it.'

Then Herzel Shitrit speaks up, and the grieving widower's words provide more hope than anything I have heard in Israel or Gaza. 'Peace is the only solution,' he says. Yes, but how does one reach it? 'If each side will compromise a little, we can reach peace.' But Israeli politicians say it's impossible to deal with Hamas, that Hamas is the devil incarnate. 'They said that about Arafat too,' says Herzel. 'They said, "We cannot talk to Yasser Arafat. He's a terrorist and he wants to destroy Israel." Now they say the same about Hamas . . . . Orith thought the way I do. She wanted peace. There are many Israelis who feel this way . . . Our family made a huge sacrifice; we hope our sacrifice will be the last one.'

The pundits are not optimistic. 'There is no hope whatsoever as long as Hamas is in power,' says David Horovitz, editor-in-chief of the right-wing *Jerusalem Post* newspaper and a former correspondent for *The Irish Times*. The official line boils down to the idea that the Palestinians of Gaza must be punished for voting for Hamas in democratic elections three years ago. 'I don't know of a precedent of a terrorist organisation being voted into office,' says Horovitz. 'The Palestinians of Gaza chose to be led by people whose adamant platform is to destroy the people next door.'

Conciliatory statements by the Hamas leader Khaled Meshaal, who lives in Damascus, fall on deaf ears. 'The problem is not that there is an entity called Israel; the problem is that there is no Palestinian state,' Meshaal said two years ago. Last October, he added: 'The Muslim Arab world has always welcomed Jews and let them live in peace. Hamas has clearly given its accord for the foundation of a free and independent Palestinian state along the 1967 borders, on the territory of Gaza and the West Bank. It is up to the occupier [Israel] to respond to our legitimate demands.'

So why not take Hamas at its word? I ask Horovitz. Hamas has 'an ideology of suicide bombing and ending Israel's existence,' he insists. The Islamist movement has close ties to Iran, and in 2007, a few months after creating a unity government with Fatah, Hamas overthrew Arafat's old movement in street fighting in Gaza. 'If that's what [Meshaal] does to his own people, why on Earth would we trust him?' says Horovitz. 'There is no way that Israel is going to risk national suicide by taking Hamas at its word.'

Nomika Zion, the director of the Centre for Social Justice at the Van Leer Jerusalem Institute and the founder of an urban kibbutz in the frontline town of Sderot, opposed the Gaza war from the outset. 'I am a mute voice, silenced by Israeli media and a monolithic, violent, public discourse,' she says. 'I heard an Israeli say on television: "The bombing of Gaza is the most beautiful music I have heard in my life." The euphoria and glorification of the war were frightening. It was very difficult to ask critical questions like: is this really necessary? How far can we go?'

Any solution to the Gaza problem must include the opening of crossing points, so that Gaza can interact with the outside world, and an international force, says Zion. 'When you suggest only brutal, violent options to people, it narrows their minds and they can no longer think clearly. That's how they created the myth that there was no choice but to wage this war.'

I talked to Maayan Sabton while she waited for a lift outside Sapir College in Sderot. The twenty-four-year-old woman left Israel in 2005, after her best friend, Dana Galkowicz, a pretty redhead with freckles, was killed by a Kassam rocket while she sat on a balcony with her boyfriend. 'I would have gone abroad anyway, but Dana's death was the trigger,' Sabton told me. She spent three years in Australia, India and South Africa.

'I came back three months ago, and the war started again. It's never-ending,' Sabton sighed. 'When I was in South Africa, I realised it's not normal to live with bombs falling on top of you. It's not normal to have to go into the army when you're eighteen, two years if you're a woman, three years if you're a man.' Though she loves her country, Sabton intends to leave it. The numbers of Jews who 'make Aliya' – immigrate to Israel – has fallen by 80 percent in the past nine years.

Sabton lives in a kibbutz next to the Erez crossing into the Gaza Strip. When the war started on 27 December, 'I thought, "Cool. It's about time." But when I saw how many civilians were being killed, I changed my mind.'

Two stories marked her most: the deaths on 28 December, the day Orith Shitrit was killed, of five daughters from the Balousha family while they were sleeping, and the grief of Ezzedine Abu' al-Aish, a Palestinian doctor whose three daughters were killed by a tank shell on 16 January. 'Last week, my friend Hadassah and I collected seven lorry loads of food, clothing, blankets and baby products for Gaza,' says Sabton.

Before Israel and Hamas can even begin to work towards Herzel Shitrit's dream of peace, they must establish a modicum of mutual trust. While she was living in South Africa, Sabton heard Nelson Mandela speak. 'He was asked how he forgave the Afrikaners, who killed his eldest son, and he said: "As soon as I decided to trust them, everything became possible. I realised that if I wanted to make peace with them, I had to trust them."'

31 January 2009

US and EU Must Impose Solution to Israeli-Palestinian Conflict

Israel used to react angrily when accused of disproportionate attacks on enemies. But when a group allied with the Palestinian president Mahmoud Abbas claimed responsibility for firing two rockets into southern Israel on Sunday, Israeli Prime Minister Ehud Olmert used the term defiantly, promising a 'disproportionate response' and adding that Israel 'will act according to new rules'.

Disproportion is a thread that runs through the entire Israeli-Palestinian conflict. Thirteen Israelis were killed in the three-week assault on Gaza, compared to 1,434 Palestinians. Hoardings on the motorway to Tel Aviv demand the liberation of the Franco-Israeli soldier Gilad Shalit, who was captured by Hamas in 2006. But I didn't find a single Israeli who could tell me how many Palestinians are illegally held in Israel. (There are eleven thousand.)

A few days ago, I travelled from Gaza City to Jerusalem, via Rafah, Taba, Eilat and Tel Aviv. In a peaceful world, the journey would have taken less than two hours, but because Israel's border with the Gaza Strip is closed, it took fourteen. In Gaza, whole neighbourhoods were flattened by bombardment. Comparisons to an earthquake or tsunami are not an exaggeration. It was a visual shock to arrive in the Israeli Red Sea resort of Eilat, with its glitzy opulence, cruise liners and airport. Israel long ago destroyed Gaza's port and airport.

Two memories came back to me: an ancient, wizened Palestinian who, during an earlier assault on Gaza, in December 2001, took my hands in his and pleaded: 'Please, lady, tell the world: they have everything; we have nothing.'

Ten days ago, at Shifa Hospital in Gaza City, a surgeon said to me: 'We are all sons of Abraham. Okay. Let my Jewish cousins have 99 percent. But give us just 1 percent. The world treats us like stray cats and dogs.'

The recent war rendered tens of thousands of Palestinians homeless. Israel now refuses to allow building materials into the Gaza Strip to enable people to rebuild. To survive, the Palestinians are forced to become human moles, risking their lives to burrow under Rafah.

There has got to be a more efficient, less cruel way of depriving Hamas of weapons. The EU and US have promised to help Israel curb arms transfers. In view of the disproportion in casualties and damage, perhaps they ought to think about cutting the flow of weapons to Israel too. One-tonne bombs and heavy artillery shells are also weapons of terror.

When is murder not murder? The foreign minister and prime ministerial candidate Tzipi Livni told *Ha'aretz* magazine at the weekend: 'In law a distinction is made between a murderer and someone who kills accidentally. The terrorists are murderers. They are out to kill children. In contrast, we are out to kill terrorists.'

So it's all right then?

Rhetoric during the war was particularly ugly. Avigdor Lieberman, the leader of the Yisrael Beiteinu Party (and subsequently Israel's foreign minister and deputy prime minister), said his country should 'fight Hamas the way the Americans fought the Japanese in the Second World War' (i.e. nuke them). The deputy prime minister, Eli Yishai, suggested Israel should 'raze Gaza; then they won't bother us any more'. Ms Livni said Israel had responded to Hamas rockets 'by going wild – and this is a good thing'.

Israelis I talked to believe that Gazans are oppressed and terrorised by Hamas. (Some Fatah supporters are terrorised by Hamas; Fatah reciprocates in the West Bank, where it is in control.) But most of the Gazans I met supported the self-styled Islamic Resistance Movement, just as Lebanese Shia in southern Lebanon genuinely support Hizballah. Israel should have learned by now that collective punishment never turns civilian populations against such movements, who are comprised of their sons and brothers.

In the Gaza Strip, I interviewed dozens of people who had lost their homes, or family members, or both. Not one expressed self pity. In Sderot, the Israeli town which has suffered the brunt of Hamas rocket attacks, a government employee told me she was traumatised because one rocket exploded in her parking lot last year. Even opponents of the war saw the conflict through the prism of their own emotion. 'Everybody [in Sderot] is emotionally damaged,' a left-wing activist told me. 'I define myself now as a victim of shock and anxiety.'

A study by the Israeli political psychologist Daniel Bar-Tal and Rafi

Nets-Zehngur, a doctoral student, strengthened my impressions: 'Israeli Jews' consciousness is characterised by a sense of victimisation, a siege mentality, blind patriotism, belligerence, self-righteousness, dehumanisation of the Palestinians and insensitivity to their suffering,' *Ha'aretz* reported in its summary of the study. If Israel wants peace, why have successive governments continued to steal Palestinian land on the West Bank, in defiance of international law, increasing the number of settlers from 80,000 at the time of the Oslo accords in 1993 to 285,000 last year?

The Saudi King Abdullah, in 2002, the Geneva Accord, in 2003, and former US president Jimmy Carter, in books published in 2006 and 2009, have all offered sensible peace plans. With slight variations, all propose a two-state solution whereby Israel would relinquish control of the lands it occupied in 1967. Jerusalem would be the capital for both countries, and Palestinian refugees would renounce their right of return to what is now Israel in exchange for compensation, or the right to emigrate to the new Palestinian state.

The most maddening thing about the conflict is that there is such an obvious solution, as there was in Northern Ireland for the quarter century before the Belfast Agreement.

Benjamin Netanyahu, the Likud leader who did much to destroy the Oslo Accords in the 1990s, looks set to become Israel's prime minister following the 10 February election. Netanyahu refuses to dismantle settlements or compromise on Jerusalem. With Netanyahu likely to return to power and the Palestinians divided between Hamas and Fatah, prospects for a peaceful settlement are bleak.

'We want to live' was the one sentence I heard repeatedly in the Gaza Strip and in Israel – perhaps the only thing Palestinians and Israelis agree on.

Why don't the US and EU take a brave, bold step and impose a solution on both parties, based on existing peace plans? The UN should flood the Gaza Strip with blue helmets, who would prevent Hamas firing rockets, and Israel from carrying out assassinations and bombing raids.

Israelis and Palestinians have shown they will not make peace if left to their own devices. There is a point beyond which hand-wringing before so much slaughter veers from criminal negligence into complicity. By shepherding Palestine to independence, the way it helped the former Yugoslav republics, the much-discredited international community could re-establish its own reputation, and put a halt to the self-destruction of two peoples.

3 February 2009

VIII
THE UNITED STATES

America's Irrational Streak Runs Deep

Sergeant Luke Wilson, who survived the ambush of his convoy in Baghdad five months ago, is a brave young man. His left leg dangled by a tendon after he was hit by an RPG. Before it was amputated, the twenty-four-year-old from Oregon told his comrades how to put a tourniquet on his thigh so he wouldn't bleed to death, joked with doctors, sent the army chaplain packing.

But is bravery in the pursuit of an illusion heroism? Or folly? Sergeant Wilson, whom I met at the Walter Reed Army Hospital, said he wished he could give his other leg for 'freedom and democracy' in Iraq. As I travelled across America these past two weeks, I thought of Sergeant Wilson often. He came to symbolise for me the self-deluding, logic-defying streak that runs through tens of millions of Americans who look likely to re-elect George W. Bush in November.

From Luke Wilson, the hyper-patriotic residents of a small Appalachian town and the born-again Christians of Colorado Springs, I heard the same broken record. Not only do Bush supporters not care that the president has repeatedly lied to them, they make excuses for him.

It doesn't matter that Saddam Hussein had no weapons of mass destruction, I heard over and over. He *wanted* to have them. And he used them against his own people. That was fifteen years before the 2003 invasion, I protested. The US sold him chemicals, and the State Department instructed diplomats to say that Iran, not Saddam, had gassed the Kurds at Halabja. My objections met with a shrug.

Nor did it matter that the 9/11 Commission found no links between Saddam Hussein and al-Qaeda – another lie of the Bush administration. The bad guys would have linked up sooner or later, Bush supporters told me.

Perhaps the biggest Bush administration lie is that Iraq is improving; that, as Bush said on Thursday, 'this country is headed towards democracy'. The President contradicted a pessimistic intelligence report revealed by the *New York Times* the same day. But Bush supporters believe the 'progress in Iraq' lie too, despite the fact that much of the country lies outside US control and dozens of Iraqis are being killed daily.

The half of America that supports Bush feeds on clichés that are simple and easy to understand. The US is in Iraq 'because of 9/11', 'to defend freedom' and 'because it's better to fight them there than here'. But freedom means only freedom to agree with the Bush administration: when I raised questions about the Iraq war, I was accused of being a 1930s-style appeaser.

The majority of Iraqis want the US there; an opinion poll proved it, Sergeant Wilson insisted. Mrs Simpson in her pizza parlour said the same thing. So did Pastor Ted in Colorado.

The problem in Iraq is not the US presence, but the insurgents, supporters of the war told me with absolute conviction. But if the Iraqis love America so much, why are there so many insurgents? The insurgents are 'foreign Arabs', not Iraqis, I was told. Okay, setting aside all the evidence to the contrary, why do 'foreign Arabs' or even al-Qaeda, want to kill Americans? Except for Pastor Ted, who thought it was 'because they think we're infidels', no one had a clue.

For days before and after the anniversary of September 11th, there was non-stop coverage of commemoration ceremonies for the 2,752 victims in the World Trade Center. Not once in two weeks did anyone mention the Iraqi civilians – between 12,721 and 14,751 killed since the US invasion.

I asked Michael Ratner of the Centre for Constitutional Rights in New York why Americans were so indifferent to the people their armed forces arrest, torture and kill. 'Because it's not us,' he replied.

When it came to wilful self-delusion, Sheriff Larry Stewart of Tulia, Texas, took the cake. He asked me what I thought of Iraq, since I'd been there. I answered truthfully that the war was a catastrophe. Rubbish, the Sheriff sniffed. The bad news from Iraq is 'a complete media fabrication', just like allegations of racism against his dear little town, which charged more than 10 per cent of its black population with selling cocaine.

There is none so blind as he who will not see. How else can you explain that millions of Americans vote against their own interest, from the lower middle class affected by slashed government programmes to soldiers whose tours of duty have been repeatedly extended by the Pentagon's 'Stop Loss' programme?

This irrational behaviour was summed up by a cartoon in the *Kansas City Star*. '1,000 War Dead . . . 8 Million Americans Out of Work . . . A $422 Billion Deficit . . . AND an 11-point Lead,' said the headline, above a caricature of Bush. 'Just what do you have to do to get thrown out of office in this country?'

Americans passively accept that the government lies to them. Take the casualty figures in Iraq. The Pentagon says seven thousand soldiers have been wounded. But Stephen Robinson, the veteran and former Pentagon analyst who runs the National Gulf War Resource Centre in Washington, says Transport Command has recorded the medical evacuation of nineteen thousand soldiers from Iraq. 'Someone's not telling the truth,' Robinson adds.

Members of Bush's own party are getting wise. The Republican Senator Richard Lugar, chairman of the Senate Foreign Relations Committee, this week criticised the 'dancing-in-the-street crowd', who wrongly predicted that Iraqis would welcome US soldiers. The 'nonsense' of the predictions and lack of planning were obvious, Lugar said.

Another Republican senator, Chuck Hagel of Nebraska, suggested a hearing for 'these smart guys that got us in there and said "Don't worry."' But the average Bush supporter sticks blindly to his guns. With the exception of the main daily newspapers, which most people don't read, American media give lowest priority to foreign news.

For two weeks I zapped through television channels in hotel rooms every evening. I saw very little reporting about Iraq, not a single news story about Europe, but saturation coverage of the September 11th anniversary, Bill Clinton's heart surgery, and Hurricane Ivan.

It's enough to watch a White House press conference, where spokesman Scott McClellan is on chummy first name terms with reporters, to understand why ignorant nationalism is endemic. Dennis Bernstein of Pacifica Radio calls them 'the media stenographer crew'.

Under the guise of objectivity, there is no attempt to determine who tells the truth and who is lying. 'Self-censorship has sunk deep into the bones,' Bernstein said over coffee in New York. 'US journalists have lost their understanding of what it means to seek the truth.'

No wonder a West Coast peace activist was stunned to see Carole Coleman, RTÉ's Washington correspondent, challenge Bush in an interview. 'You would *never* see that here,' Susan Galleymore said. 'The journalists here have been neutered.'

On 7 September, Vice President Dick Cheney said it was 'absolutely essential' that US voters 'make the right choice' in the presidential election. 'Because if we make the wrong choice, then the danger is that we'll get hit again, and we'll be hit in a way that will be devastating.'

The following day, Jim Houx, a businessman in Kansas City, told me what he thought of the administration's fear mongering. 'If you get on a plane and the pilot runs up and down the aisle shouting, "Look out! Look out!" everybody is going to be terrified,' Houx said. 'That's what the Bush administration is doing. That's how he's going to win the election.'

Though Cheney later qualified his remarks, the 'vote Bush or the terrorists will get you' message seems to be working. Polls show that far more Americans trust Bush to protect them from terrorist attack than Kerry. The Bush campaign has deftly turned what should be John Kerry's greatest strength – his record as a Vietnam War hero – into his greatest weakness. Bush's blunders – ignoring evidence that al-Qaeda was about to strike America, the ill-conceived invasion of Iraq – are used to portray him as a strong commander-in-chief.

John Kerry is part of the problem. Though a substantial minority of the Americans I talked to said they would vote for him, not one expressed fervour comparable to that of Bush's supporters. 'The man is running such a pathetic campaign that it's embarrassing,' Susan Galleymore told me. 'George Bush plays dirty. He doesn't have many messages, but he stays on track. Kerry doesn't even stand up for himself.'

Only a few of the Americans I met expressed concern about the deteriorating image of the US abroad. 'We're hated all over the world because of Bush,' Pamela Ford, a black cardiac nurse, told me in Detroit. But others felt that the US had been betrayed by Europe.

The evangelical leader Pastor Ted Haggard was openly scornful. 'Europe thinks they're the light of the world,' he told me. 'Well, they're mistaken.'

Americans' deep-seated distrust of "big government" is not the least of the country's contradictions. They're happy to let Bush ride roughshod over the Middle East at a cost of hundreds of billions of dollars, but don't think Washington is capable of organising health care.

'Americans just don't trust the government to get involved in health care,' a doctor's wife in Maryland told me. As a result, 45 million Americans have no health insurance.

The ideological desire for government to wither and die has led to widespread deregulation, which in turn leads to chaos. Try changing planes at Chicago's O'Hare Airport. In the American Airlines terminal, it's impossible to find out where connecting flights on other airlines leave from. Each airline is a power unto itself. Some refuse to transfer each other's baggage, and to hell with the passenger.

The doctrine of free markets and individual responsibility means it's every man for himself. The upside is low taxation and the possibility of getting rich if you work very hard. The downside is a cruel world where there is no safety net for the weakest members of society.

In the trailer parks of the Appalachians, on Indian reservations in South Dakota, talking to homeless people in San Francisco, I remembered the lyrics of an old Bruce Springsteen song: *There's just winners and losers, and don't you get caught on the wrong side of that line.*

Some Democrats, like Bridget Nolan, an Irish-American journalist I met in the Appalachians, recognise the shamefulness of a rich country that fails to provide for its citizens. Haitham Mashalah, a Jordanian-American taxi driver in Detroit, said that in Amman you never see people ill and hungry in the street; it's a question of honour. Mashalah has spent twenty-one years in the US, and he still can't understand 'why the Americans don't care about their own people'.

Truly, America's irrational streak runs deep.

18 September 2004

Pastor Ted Haggard resigned from the leadership of the New Life Church in November 2006, after admitting to sex and drug use with a male prostitute.

Old Interview Gives New Insights into First Couple

It is like stepping back in time, to an afternoon in November 1996 when Barack and Michelle Obama were not famous, not President-elect and imminent First Lady, just an ordinary, up-and-coming young professional couple who agreed to meet the photographer Mariana Cook for her book, *Couples in America*.

Indeed, the Obamas were so 'ordinary' that Cook's publisher cut them out of the book. But Cook kept rolls of film and tape-recorded interviews until the French newspaper *Le Monde* published them at the weekend.

The impression given by *Le Monde*'s two-page exclusive is of two people wise beyond their years, certain of their love for each other and imbued with a powerful sense of public service. Nothing they have said or done has contradicted these separate interviews, given twelve years ago.

The Obamas had been married for four years when they talked to Cook. Their union seemed unshakeable. Michelle said they 'just built a friendship first, and then that grew from there'.

'She is at once completely familiar to me, so I can be myself, and she knows me very well and I trust her completely, but at the same time she is also a mystery to me,' Barack said.

In bed at night, he continued: 'I look over and sort of have a start, because I realise here is this other person who is separate and different and has different memories and backgrounds and thoughts and feelings, and I think it's that tension between familiarity and mystery that makes for something strong, because even as you build a life of trust and comfort and mutual support, you retain some sense of surprise or wonder about the other person, and I think that's important.'

Barack Obama's white American mother and black Kenyan father stayed together for just two years, when both were students in Hawaii. 'I think in some ways all my life I have been stitching together a family, through stories or memories or friends or ideas,' he said.

In his autobiography, *Dreams From My Father*, the US President-elect recounted how his father had eight children with four different women. Obama's interest in politics seems to be driven by a broader sense of family. Cook asked the former social worker, who was considering standing for a seat in the Illinois state senate, what he hoped to achieve in politics. As an African-American, Obama said, his greatest concern was children in the inner cities.

'My first priority is to restore a sense of public or collective values to the debate,' Obama said. 'And that means recognising that we have mutual obligations and mutual responsibilities. And that's maybe where the public and the private meet . . . that the overriding priority in all those associations is a sense of mutual responsibility and empathy, then being able to put yourself in another person's shoes. That's how the marriage between Michelle and me sustains itself. We can imagine the other person's hopes or pains or struggles, and we have to extend that beyond just the individual families to other people.'

Both alluded to tension between them over his hopes of embarking on a political career. 'When you are in politics, your life is an open book, and people who don't necessarily have good intent can come in,' Michelle said. 'I'm pretty private and like to surround myself with people that I trust and love. I want to have kids and travel and spend time with my family. That [political] lifestyle may lead us more away from that than towards it . . . . It'll be interesting to see what life has to offer.'

Michelle Obama said she initially hesitated to date Barack when they met at the Sidley and Austin law firm in Chicago. He was a student intern, she a first-year associate, and she'd been assigned to show him the ropes. 'It was funny, because when there was all this scuttlebutt about him, this sharp, handsome, smart, young first-year, you know everybody was oh, Barack, Barack, Barack. And I'm kind of sceptical. I thought yeah, well he's probably kind of a nerd. I always think when lawyers pump someone up they are probably lacking on the social side.'

The couple were attracted to each other 'because we didn't take the whole scene as seriously as a lot of people do,' Michelle said. 'He liked my dry sense of humour and my sarcasm.'

'It's not often that a girl from the south side of Chicago meets somebody who can speak Indonesian and has travelled and seen a lot of interesting things. That added a dimension to his character that I didn't see in the upper middle class professional work environment.'

The couple come across as interlocking parts of the same human puzzle, a microcosm of American society. His multiracial, unorthodox upbringing is complemented by her traditional, African-American, working class family. He is rootless and restless, she stable and secure. Contrary to their image during the campaign, she is the more cautious partner.

When Barack met Michelle, he thought she 'looked real good' and was impressed by her strength. 'But I also think in her eyes you can see a trace of vulnerability – or at least I do – that most people don't know, because when she's walking through the world she is this tall, beautiful, confident woman and extremely capable. But there is a part of her that is vulnerable and young and sometimes frightened, and I think seeing both of those things is what attracted me to her.'

12 January 2009

Following in Lincoln's Footsteps

Before he took office, America's new president wanted to share with his family the place he often went to for moral sustenance. On a freezing January night, Barack Obama took his wife Michelle and their daughters Sasha and Malia to the Lincoln Memorial. The Obama family climbed the steps to the twenty-foot statue of the president who abolished slavery, and stopped to read Lincoln's speeches engraved on the walls.

At the end of his political autobiography, *The Audacity of Hope*, Obama recounts how when he felt discouraged as a senator, he would jog to the memorial in the evening. 'Standing between marble columns, I read the Gettysburg Address and the Second Inaugural Address,' he wrote. 'I look out over the reflecting pool, imagining the crowd stilled by Dr King's mighty cadence [in August 1963], and then beyond that, to the floodlit obelisk and shining Capitol dome. And in that place, I think about America and those who built it.'

Lincoln is the president whom Obama most reads, quotes and admires. The two tall, thin men are the only US presidents from Illinois. Obama announced his candidacy in Lincoln's hometown of Springfield.

Neither Lincoln's log cabin nor Obama's childhood in Hawaii and Indonesia predisposed them to careers in politics. Lincoln opposed the 1847-48 Mexican war which annexed Texas, Obama the 2003 invasion of Iraq. Both were relatively inexperienced and considered long shots for the highest public office. Like Lincoln, Obama is extremely pragmatic and has an immense capacity for mastering detail. And like Lincoln, he is learned without appearing pedantic or intellectual.

The bicentenary of Lincoln's birth falls on 12 February, so Obama's inauguration was bound to be steeped in Lincoln allegory. It almost seemed as if the new president wanted to indulge in a last binge of Lincoln mania before setting out to govern the country. The festivities were entitled 'A New Birth of Freedom', a phrase from the Gettysburg Address. Sunday night's concert was held at the Lincoln Memorial. Like Lincoln, Obama took the train to Washington, and he took the oath of office over the Bible last used by Lincoln in 1861. The menu at the inaugural banquet was based on Lincoln's favourite dishes.

Why Lincoln? 'Because the 1860s were a period of great importance, not only to African-Americans, but to all Americans,' says Scott Lucas, professor of American studies at the University of Birmingham and creator of the *enduringamerica.com* website.

Some 620,000 Americans were killed in the 1861-65 Civil War – more than in either world war or Vietnam. Lincoln refused to punish the Confederates, demanding only that they return to the union. From this history, 'Obama has distilled the notion that from conflict can come unity – that's why you reach back to Lincoln,' Lucas explains.

Obama wants to be a great unifier, even if it involves a certain sleight of hand. 'In his book *Lincoln at Gettysburg*, Garry Wills says that Lincoln intellectually pickpocketed the Americans in the Gettysburg Address,' notes David Ryan, senior lecturer in US foreign relations at University College Cork.

The short, 272-word speech, doubtless the best known in America, does not mention division between Unionists and Confederates, but portrays all fifty thousand men who died at Gettysburg as heroes. 'Lincoln did what Obama is trying to do,' says Ryan. 'To provide Americans with a new past, to reunite the country.'

Obama has been influenced by the best-selling book *Team of Rivals* by historian Doris Kearns Goodwin. It recounts how Lincoln appointed New York senator William Seward, whom he had challenged for the Republican presidential nomination, as Secretary of State. Taking a cue from Lincoln, Obama made his defeated rival, New York Senator Hillary Clinton, his Secretary of State.

Lincoln may be Obama's spiritual father, but the circumstances in which Obama comes to office are more reminiscent of those faced by Franklin D. Roosevelt in 1933. In *The Audacity of Hope*, Obama praised Lincoln's and FDR's economic policies. 'We can be guided by Lincoln's simple maxim,' Obama wrote. 'We will do collectively, through our government, only those things that we cannot do as well or at all individually or privately.'

Obama said he hoped 'to modernise and rebuild the social contract that FDR first stitched together in the middle of the last century'. The current US recession is not as severe as the Great Depression. Up to a third of the US workforce was jobless then, compared to 7.2 percent at present. Millions of Americans became homeless and hungry, on a scale unimaginable today.

In his inaugural address, FDR told Americans they had nothing to fear but fear itself. Like Obama, FDR took office with a well defined plan and a 'brain trust' of expert advisers. In a hundred days, he pushed through fifteen pieces of New Deal legislation. FDR based his second New Deal, in 1935, on British economist John Maynard Keynes's principle of using budget deficits to relaunch the economy. Barack Obama has asked to be judged on his first thousand days – not one hundred, like FDR.

John F. Kennedy is the standard against which young politicians have been measured for nearly half a century. Until Obama, though, no one matched Kennedy's charisma and promise of generational renewal, hope and change. Never before did the Kennedy clan anoint a would-be successor.

As early as 2006, Ted Sorensen, Kennedy's speechwriter, said Obama reminded him of JFK. Kennedy's daughter Caroline published an enthusiastic endorsement of Obama in the *New York Times*, entitled 'A President Like My Father'. Like Kennedy, Obama has changed the way America sees itself and the way it is seen by the rest of the world.

With his attractive wife and young daughters, Obama is re-creating Camelot. JFK and Obama share a certain rock star quality, but these similarities seem superficial compared to Obama's deeper attachment to the ideas of Lincoln and Roosevelt.

Barack Obama has tapped into the US collective memory of its great presidents. Black America, though, has a different collective memory, cautions Peniel Joseph, professor of history at Tufts University and a leading scholar of African-American history. Although Lincoln abhorred slavery, he long regarded it as a matter of personal conscience and was a reluctant abolitionist.

'There's a feeling among African-American historians that we have to stop this hagiography of Lincoln,' says Joseph. 'Obama buys into the hagiographic vision. It's one of the things that made him palatable as a presidential candidate . . . . The people revered by African-Americans, the way white folks revere the founding fathers, are Martin Luther King, Jr and Malcolm X. And certainly Obama is going into the pantheon. There will be a hagiography about him as well.'

Historians are ambivalent towards Thomas Jefferson, a president who did not practise the democratic ideals he preached. Yet Jefferson's preamble to the Declaration of Independence: 'We hold these truths to be self evident, that all men are created equal . . .' was quoted by Lincoln at Gettysburg in 1863 and by Martin Luther King in his 'I have a dream' speech at the Lincoln Memorial a hundred years later.

In 1968, on the eve of his assassination, King added: 'All we say to America is, "Be true to what you said on paper".' With Barack Obama's inauguration, the presidential legacy has swung full circle, from the second president, who wrote those revolutionary words, to the forty-fourth president, who embodies them. Martin Luther King's prophecy has been fulfilled. America, at last, has proved true to what it said on paper.

21 January 2009

Edward Kennedy, 'the kind and tender hero', is Laid to Rest

Senator Edward Moore Kennedy made his last trip to Washington, where the patriarch of the Kennedy family was laid to rest near his assassinated brothers John and Robert in Arlington National Cemetery.

Accompanied by his widow, Vicki, Kennedy's flag-draped casket was flown to Andrews Air Force Base, then driven to the steps of the Capitol, where hundreds of members of Congress and staffers waited. They sang 'America the Beautiful', after which well-wishers burst into an impromptu rendition of 'When Irish Eyes are Smiling'.

The hearse drove down Constitution Avenue, past the Lincoln Memorial, across the Memorial Bridge into the cemetery as the sun was setting on Saturday. At the graveside, Cardinal Thomas McCarrick, the former archbishop of Washington, quoted Kennedy's recent letter to Pope Benedict XVI, in which the Senator said he'd been 'an imperfect being but with the help of my faith I have tried to right my path'.

It was the culmination of three days resembling a royal funeral. The morning started at the Kennedy Library in Boston, from where Kennedy's remains were transported under pelting rain to the Basilica of Our Lady of Perpetual Help. He had prayed there for his daughter, Kara, who recovered from lung cancer, and then for himself, when he was diagnosed with a fatal brain tumour. In his eulogy, President Barack Obama said: 'We do not weep for him today because of the prestige attached to his name or his office. We weep because we loved this kind and tender hero.'

Kennedy meant many things to many people. To the Irish politicians, north and south, who travelled to the wake and funeral services in Boston, he was a guarantor of the peace process.

Matt Reilly, an Irish emigrant and retired New York bus driver, drove to Boston to watch the cortège in the rain. 'Teddy Kennedy was the link that brought Ireland and the US together,' he explained.

Cinde Warmington, a lawyer from New Hampshire, loved Kennedy for his struggle to achieve universal health care, and held up a placard urging US senators to vote for President Obama's reforms. Rhoda Johnson, a black nurse, said Kennedy 'was just a regular person, like your neighbour'.

Down the street from the funeral Mass stood a lone trumpeter wearing a fedora and crumpled suit, looking for all the world like Louis Armstrong. He played 'Ave Maria', then, as the hearse rolled by, 'Taps'. He was Massillon Laporte, a Haitian emigrant who had taken the bus all night from Montreal to pay his respects to Kennedy. 'We have to appreciate good people, because there are so few of them,' he said.

31 August 2009

Homeless on the Capitol's Doorstep

Every evening they show up outside the AT&T offices at Fourteenth and H Streets, men and women clutching sleeping bags and small tents, staking out a few square metres to bed down for the night. The overhang of the building protects them from rain, and it is well lit. Warm air wafts up through the grates of the metro. By 10 PM, the pavement is carpeted with dozens of homeless people. It is exactly two blocks from the White House.

Scientists at Harvard University say forty-four thousand Americans, nearly fifteen times the number who died on 9/11, die every year for lack of health insurance. Yet passing health care legislation is requiring a Herculean effort.

A US Department of Agriculture report issued this week found that 49 million Americans, including 17 million children, lack reliable access to food – the highest number since the government began keeping records.

A few days ago, Vice President Joe Biden served lunch to homeless men at a shelter near the Capitol. 'You've got to remind yourself that there but for the grace of God go I,' Biden said. Despite such gestures, the plight of the homeless and hungry is largely ignored.

Whatever happened to the social contract in America?

With her print dress, worn leather jacket, boots and book-filled rucksack, Alyce McFarland, 32, looks like any other student at the University of the District of Columbia (UDC). But for more than a decade, McFarland was a walking statistic: a homeless, African-American single mother and drug addict.

The odds were against Alyce McFarland breaking out of the cycle of drugs, prostitution, jail and homelessness. 'I've been in near death situations. I've been beaten and raped. It's only by the grace of God I didn't get HIV,' McFarland says when we meet for coffee next to the Van Ness metro station.

Like many addicts, McFarland contracted hepatitis C. But she has been clean since June 2008. She lives in government housing in southeast Washington, just down the street from the place where she bought heroin and got high. 'Sometimes I see my old friends and they tear up,' she says. 'They ask me: "How do you do it?" '

McFarland came from what she calls 'a productive family'. Her parents stayed together until she was fourteen, and her father worked as a driver for PepsiCo. She did well in school.

But on McFarland's nineteenth birthday and high school graduation day, she snorted heroin for the first time, with a boyfriend who dealt drugs. She used the drug every day, and realised she was addicted only when the boyfriend was arrested. 'I stopped working. I slept with guys in exchange for drugs. I was not nice. I wanted what I wanted and I did whatever it took to get it. Unfortunately, I was always surrounded by people [who were] on drugs, and people who sold drugs.' McFarland switched to the heroin substitute methadone during her first pregnancy, with Malachi, now ten, but started taking heroin intravenously after his birth. 'I realised I was wrecking my life, but I didn't care,' she said. 'I thought I was rebelling. I lost a court battle with my mother for custody of Malachi.' The boy still lives with his grandmother during the week.

After Malachi was born, McFarland became homeless. 'You don't realise you're homeless, because you think you always have somewhere to go,' she says. 'I was always on the go, looking for drugs. The only time you realise you're homeless is when you want to sleep.' McFarland became pregnant by the boyfriend she did drugs with. 'We were sleeping in the hallway of the building where we bought our drugs. I paid for it by prostitution, robbing, any means. It felt normal. Everything changed when I got pregnant; nobody wants a pregnant woman around. I was depressed and I didn't like who I'd become.'

The couple argued, and McFarland's boyfriend threw her down the stairs when she was six months pregnant with her daughter Peace, now age three. McFarland ended up in a detoxification centre. A dedicated hospital discharge co-ordinator bent rules to have her admitted to various shelters, although she was still on methadone.

The turning point came in the autumn of 2006. McFarland got in a fight with another woman in a shelter, whom she accused of stealing her baby's clothes. She was charged with assault and jailed overnight. 'I was breastfeeding. The shelter kept my three-month-old daughter. I ran back when they let me out of jail. I felt my child depended on me.'

Community of Hope, a non-profit organisation, found housing for McFarland and her baby. In 2007, she enrolled in pre-nursing at UDC, and began to wean herself off methadone. 'I was almost suicidal,' she recalls. 'During withdrawal, I didn't sleep for two months. I was crazed. You feel cold and hot and sick. You don't want to be touched. My daughter was clinging to me.'

McFarland has a network of friends from Narcotics Anonymous and UDC. She earns $7.50 an hour working part time as a clerk in the UDC financial aid office. 'I'm still on the outside looking in, economically,' she says. 'I don't want a yacht or a plane or trips around the world. All I want is to be able to enjoy my kids without struggling.'

Kelly Sweeney McShane is the Irish-American executive director of Community of Hope, which saved Alyce McFarland. She has worked with homeless Americans for twenty years. 'What drives me are both the next family who need help, and individuals like McFarland, the ones who have taken it and run with it,' McShane says. 'I grew up Catholic, and I buy into the social justice component. I feel a call to do this work.' McShane started out as a Peace Corps volunteer in West Africa and later adopted a girl from Sierra Leone whose arms had been amputated. 'There is just as much need in the US, but it is a little harder to see. Here, people have cell phones, televisions and may be obese, but they are still poor.'

McShane disputes the right-wing stereotype of black welfare mothers milking the system. African-American women do not have more children so they can get more money: the payments are too small, and they love their children deeply, she says. The greatest fear of Louise Malloy, an African-American resident I interviewed in the Community's shelter at Colombia Heights, was losing custody of her two sons.

The story of homelessness in the US is both tragic and hopeful. The phenomenon took on major proportions in the recession in the early 1980s. 'People assumed that when the economy got better, the problem would go away, but it didn't,' says Steven Berg of the National Alliance to End Homelessness.

Between 600,000 and 700,000 Americans are homeless today, and the numbers are growing. 'No other developed country knows homelessness on this scale,' Berg adds. 'The basic, obvious solution would be to do what other countries do: have a safety net that says we're not going to allow people to lose their homes because they lose their jobs.'

It has taken three decades to learn how to deal with the problem. In the

1980s, city governments housed homeless people in hotels – at exorbitant cost. In the 1990s, the trend was to criminalise them, throwing them into jail for 'quality of life' offences. Finally, a political consensus emerged that the problem needed long term solutions, especially permanent, low income housing. States enacted programmes aimed at eradicating homelessness. The numbers began decreasing, until the recession started in 2007.

US unemployment has reached 10.2 percent, the highest rate since 1982, and millions of Americans are losing their homes in foreclosures. There are more than 6,200 homeless people in Washington alone, where 40,000 people are on waiting lists for public housing. Demand for beds in homeless shelters has risen an estimated 25 percent this year, and shelters are turning people away.

April Tillery, 39, stands forlornly outside the 'central intake' office for homeless families in northeast Washington. 'They have no openings. They say to come back every day,' Tillery tells me. She is going to pick up her two daughters at school, and doesn't know where they will sleep. Tillery worked in a fast food restaurant until she got pregnant for the first time. She blames only herself for her predicament. 'It's my fault, because I am not working. I could get a job in a fast food restaurant, for minimum wages ($7.25 an hour), but I wouldn't earn enough to pay rent.'

As Steve Binder, a public defender in San Diego and former chairman of the American Bar Association's commission on homelessness and poverty, notes: 'Homelessnees is the canary in the economic coal mine. If society could provide jobs and health care, we wouldn't have homelessness.' Binder's pioneering work with 'homeless courts' that enabled down-and-out veterans, then the homeless population at large, to extricate themselves from legal proceedings for vagrancy and drug use by enrolling in rehabilitation programmes, has become a model in California and much of the US.

The situation is especially dire for war veterans, who comprise approximately one-fifth of the homeless population in the US. The National Alliance reported this week that 131,000 veterans who served in the Second World War, Vietnam, Korea, Iraq and Afghanistan are homeless on any given night. This reality sits uneasily with President Barack Obama's Veterans' Day speech on 11 November. 'America will not let you down,' he told veterans. 'We will take care of our own . . . . When your tour ends, when you see our flag, when you touch our soil, you will be home in an America that is forever here for you.'

Washington's biggest shelter stands just three blocks from the Capitol building, on Mitch Snyder Place, named after the militant campaigner for the homeless who helped found the Community for Creative Non-Violence (CCNV) in the 1980s.

Some 1,200 men and women sleep in three shelters on the site every night. About one-third of CCNV's male homeless have jobs, but cannot afford rent. They sleep in bunk beds, nine to a cubicle. The inhabitants run the shelter themselves, and it has the feel of a derelict penitentiary. As payment for ensuring security in the complex, Erick Watkins, 40, a homeless former US Marine who fought in the 1991 Gulf War, has his own room. Watkins lost his job as a hotel banquet manager in 2005. His marriage broke up, and his wife took their three daughters to live in Baltimore. He wanted to start over, and bought a house near Howard, the African-American university. Then the interest sky-rocketed. The bank foreclosed in January and Watkins lost his house too.

It feels terribly lonely to be homeless, Watkins tells me. 'You lose what you're doing to try to build [your life] back up. It just leaves you very empty.' Yet the former Marine displays what Steve Binder, the public defender, called 'the rugged, cowboy, I-can-take-care-of-myself spirit' of many veterans. 'It's just hard luck,' Watkins continues. 'You keep getting up and you have to go forward.'

Few of the homeless men and women who mill around Mitch Snyder Place share Erick Watkins' determination to overcome hardship. All African-Americans, they do not answer when I speak to them, but stare back with blank, dejected eyes. One woman's lips move as she reads from a hymnal. Another woman drags a suitcase, saying only: 'It's horrible inside there.' On the far side of the street, a black man with matted hair and soiled clothes sits on a plastic crate, shouting gibberish, ignored by all. Human flotsam, washed up on the shore of the Capitol.

21 November 2009

When Reality of Afghan War Strikes Home

Tonight President Barack Obama will announce the deployment of some 30,000 more troops to Afghanistan. Almost 5,300 US soldiers have already perished in the Iraq and Afghan wars. One of them was an Irish-American of exceptional promise, Marine Sergeant Bill Cahir, who was felled by a bullet to the neck while on foot patrol in Helmand Province, Afghanistan, on 13 August.

Rene Browne, the attorney who married Bill in April 2006, is pregnant with twin daughters. In the only interview she has given since his death, Browne described to NBC's *Today Show* the moment dreaded by every soldier's family: 'When I saw them coming up my walk, all I could think was, "Please go away. Don't be coming to my house."'

But the uniformed men knocked on the door, and Rene opened it. 'And they told me that he was gone . . . . It took a very long time to sink in, and sometimes I'm still not sure it has.'

A few days before Bill's death, the couple spoke for the last time. 'Bill remembered that I had my doctor's appointment that day,' Rene said. 'He called to ask me how it went. They had told me we were having girls, and so I told him, and he was just ecstatic.' When the girls are born, before Bill's forty-first birthday on 20 December, those who loved him will be buffeted between joy and grief, life and death. 'We are all excited about the babies, but the reality of his absence will impact us tremendously,' predicts Bill's older sister Ellen, an assistant professor at Harvard Medical School.

I met Bill Cahir's father, John, a retired professor of meteorology and vice provost at Penn State University, and his sisters Ellen and Kathryn, at a coffee shop in Virginia, a few miles from Bill's grave at Arlington National Cemetery.

John told me how his father left County Clare and his mother left Galway for Boston almost a hundred years ago.

A postcard of Cahir Castle in County Tipperary was on display in the Cahir home when Bill was growing up. In 1990, after finishing his Bachelor's degree in English at Penn State, Bill visited Ireland, and a photograph of him on an Irish fishing boat is among those on the website created by his friends, *billcahirmemorialfund.org*.

The other Cahir children were good at maths and science, but Bill had a furious need to communicate. 'Bill was the writer, the one who could act and sing. He had all the talent,' says Ellen.

Their mother Mary Anne demanded that the Cahir children be home for supper every evening. The family discussed politics, and Bill was always the best informed. After university, he went to Washington to work as a staffer for Senator Ted Kennedy. The day before Kennedy died, Rene received a letter of condolence. 'Bill was a true Profile in Courage and his selfless dedication to our country will never be forgotten,' Kennedy wrote.

In 1995, Bill became a newspaper journalist, covering Washington for the Newhouse chain. After the atrocities of September 11, 2001, he decided to join the Marine Corps reserves. To some, it seemed a strange choice for a progressive Democrat. 'He felt pretty strongly that people who have choices and knowledge and background shouldn't be avoiding the military,' explains his sister Kathryn, a graduate student in architecture.

In 2003, around the time Bill began dating Rene, he went to boot camp. His family wondered at first whether an attractive, professional woman would stay with a man whose life was changing so dramatically at the age of thirty-four.

'Bill's sense of humour could be goofy,' says Kathryn. 'He was never as polished as some of the DC crowd, the movers and shakers. Rene appreciated the realness of him.' At boot camp and during his first tour in Iraq, Bill wrote letters to Rene in a spiral notebook, by flashlight, at night under a blanket. When he came home, he proposed.

'There were a few close calls in Iraq,' says Brett Lieberman, a close friend and journalist who worked with Bill at Newhouse. 'But you wouldn't know about it unless you asked. Other Marines told me more than he did. He wasn't a braggart.'

During his first tour, Bill participated in the November 2004 battle of Falluja. In his second tour, his civil affairs unit helped foster the Sunni 'awakening' that drove al-Qaeda out of Anbar province. There is something

Hemingway-esque about Bill in photographs of the period, with his moustache, cigar and pet dogs.

After his second tour in Iraq, Bill stood for Congress in Pennsylvania. Though he came second in the Democratic primary, his first steps in politics were promising. Then he was sent to Afghanistan.

Bill's last letter to his parents arrived two weeks after his death. 'It was probably the most optimistic of all,' says John. 'He said they were making progress and the Taliban were leaving the area,' adds Ellen.

Was it worth it? What does the heroism signified by three achievement medals, two combat action ribbons and a Purple Heart weigh compared to the fact that Bill Cahir will never hold his baby daughters? It's the hardest question of all, and Bill's family are reluctant to pass judgment on the escalating war in Afghanistan.

Bill Cahir wanted to be in the thick of things, not an observer on the sidelines. That desire to do, not watch, and the camaraderie of the Marine Corps, were perhaps equivalent to the 'lonely impulse of delight' that motivated Yeats's Irish airman. 'He really came alive in the Marines. He was passionate about it,' says Brett Lieberman. 'The bond he shared with the Marines was the byproduct of the risk he took,' says his sister Kathryn. 'He found meaning in his service.'

When Bill joined up, Ellen tried to convince him to stay in journalism. But, she says now, 'It was the best thing Bill ever did for himself. He grew into the man he wanted to be. It was unlucky for us. But he wouldn't have run for Congress . . . . He would have regretted it his whole life if he hadn't done it.'

1 December 2009

Bill Cahir and Rene Browne's daughters, Caroline Duggan Cahir and Elizabeth Curry Cahir, were born on 12 December 2009.

US Just Doesn't 'Get It' about Motivation for Suicide Attacks

In America, 2010 has been dominated so far by the aftermath of the failed Christmas Day bombing of Northwest Airlines Flight 253. Amid the flurry of recriminations and speeches, it was reported that a State Department official 'misspelled' the name of Umar Farouk Abdulmutallab, the Nigerian who attempted to bring down the aircraft with explosives sewn into his underwear, thus preventing data concerning him and al-Qaeda in the Arabian peninsula from being correlated.

The story fed the narrative of bureaucratic ineptitude, and received wide coverage. No one pointed out that there is no correct spelling of Arabic names transliterated into English. Umar is the same as Omar, and both spellings are correct, just as Mohamed can be written several ways. This footnote to the failed suicide bombing was symptomatic of a wider breakdown in understanding, as if the collective American psyche were preprogrammed by rigid mental software not to comprehend.

Any cop will tell you that the first thing one searches for when investigating a crime is a motive. The fact that two well educated young men, Abdulmutallab, a Nigerian, and Humam Khalil Abu-Mulal al-Balawi, a Jordanian, were ready to turn themselves into human bombs in the hope of killing Americans, just five days apart, ought to make us ask why. Abdulmutallab, 23, is from a rich family and studied engineering at University College London. Balawi, 32, was a medical doctor with a Turkish wife and two young daughters. On 30 December, he dealt the worst blow to the CIA in twenty-seven years by killing seven agents at its base in Khost, Afghanistan.

In a posthumously broadcast video, Balawi said his 'martyrdom' was to avenge the assassination by an unmanned US drone last August of Baitullah Mehsud, a Pakistani extremist leader.

It would be easy to dismiss Balawi's suicide bombing as merely another round in the cycle of revenge between the US and al-Qaeda. But clues to Abdulmutallab and Balawi's motives are there if you search for them. There was a photograph of the solemn, baby-faced Abdulmutallab, wearing a red polar fleece at what appeared to be a London demonstration against the Israeli bombing of Gaza. One of Balawi's brothers told the *New York Times* that Balawi was changed by the Israeli assault on Gaza, which killed 1,434 Palestinians.

Balawi's family, like that of Major Nidal Malik Hasan, the US army psychiatrist who killed thirteen US service members at Fort Hood in November, were Palestinians from what is now Israel. In 2008, the *Washington Post* reported, Balawi wrote on an Internet site that he wished to 'be a bomb' so he could punish Israel for its treatment of Palestinians.

You would think these events might spark a debate about the anger of Palestinians and Muslims towards Israel and the US. But to the extent that this anger is mentioned, it is portrayed as blind, fanatical hatred, with no reference to Israel's continued occupation of Arab land, the suffering of Palestinians still under siege in Gaza or the 1,434 Palestinians killed by Israel a year ago.

The *New York Times* published a one-and-a-quarter-page spread on 'The Terrorist Mind' in which the words 'Israeli' and 'Palestinian' appeared not once. It is as if a curtain, a de facto taboo, falls over these topics in the US. No wonder Americans 'don't get it'. President Barack Obama made six statements and speeches about the Christmas Day attack and ordered two policy reviews. House and Senate committees are gearing up for a string of hearings on the security lapses. I recall no comparable US interest in the Israeli onslaught on Gaza.

TIME Magazine reporters in Amman quoted senior Jordanian intelligence sources saying they believed Balawi turned on the CIA because so many civilian deaths resulted from the air strikes in Afghanistan for which he provided intelligence as a double agent.

The US has suffered 4,358 fatalities in Iraq and 943 in Afghanistan. In the same period, hundreds of thousands of Iraqis are believed to have been killed and thousands of Afghans. US officials say most die at the hands of their own countrymen. That doesn't change the perception that the US is ultimately responsible because it started both wars.

During a TV debate on profiling, MSNBC presenter Chris Matthews said: 'If Americans were going around killing Muslims, they'd be searched at airports too.' But Americans *are* killing Muslims – in far greater numbers than Muslims are killing Americans. A US federal judge's recent dismissal of charges against four Blackwater mercenaries who shot dead seventeen Iraqi civilians in a Baghdad traffic circle in 2007 was quickly forgotten by the US public. You can be sure it wasn't forgotten by Arabs.

MSNBC is supposed to be a politically liberal network. So I was surprised to hear one of its breakfast commentators suggest that prisoners at Guantánamo 'live better there than they did in their own countries'. A classified Pentagon report this month concluded that one in five prisoners released from Guantánamo then joined an extremist group. If you'd been waterboarded, subjected to sleep deprivation, loud music, extreme temperatures, threatening dogs and scantily clad women interrogators using sex to humiliate you, and seen your holy book flushed down the toilet, you'd probably join an extremist group too.

At a recent briefing, Obama's chief counterterrorism expert, John Brennan, was asked about the motivation of suicide bombers. Al-Qaeda, Brennan said, 'is dedicated to murder and wanton slaughter of innocents . . . has the agenda of destruction and death . . . is just determined to carry out attacks here against the homeland'. 'But you haven't explained why,' the journalist protested. Brennan ignored her, and went on to the next question.

The US 'failed to connect the dots', Obama and other officials repeated ad nauseam in the wake of the Abdulmutallab case. There is a dearth of co-ordination between the eighteen US intelligence agencies. They share no single database, and there are more than half a million names on an ineffectual 'terrorist watchlist'.

Yet nothing has been said about the equally dangerous failure to provide Muslims appalled by US policies with an alternative to suicide bombing. Obama hinted at this in a speech on 7 January. 'We must communicate clearly to Muslims around the world that al-Qaeda offers nothing except a bankrupt vision of misery and death,' he said, 'while the United States stands with those who seek justice and progress.'

One thing would convince Muslims that the US seeks justice: the creation of a viable, independent state for the Palestinians. After more than half a century of skewed US Middle East policies, peace between Israelis and Palestinians would not stop attacks on the US overnight. But the injustice done to Palestinians remains a festering wound and, even more than Guantánamo, the best recruitment tool for al-Qaeda.

Obama knows this but seems powerless to do anything about it.

13 January 2010

First the Storm, Now the Spill

The Storm. The Exodus. The Return. The Spill. Residents of New Orleans sum up their plight in one-word titles with Biblical resonance. In an ironic linguistic twist, oil spills, like hurricanes, 'make landfall'.

When James McKay, an appellate court judge and Ireland's honorary consul in New Orleans, heard about the BP oil spill that is still gushing an estimated 210,000 gallons of crude into the Gulf of Mexico each day, he said: 'My God, what next? I was wondering if pestilence was going to be around the corner.'

A new city government took office this week, and Kristin Gisleson Palmer is the councilwoman for District C, which comprises the French Quarter, Algiers, Marigny, Bywater and Treme – the birthplace of jazz and the setting for a new, highly acclaimed television series about a musician returning to the city in late 2005, after Hurricane Katrina.

'When I heard about the Spill, I said to my sister, "Sometimes I feel like we're the toilet bowl of America",' Palmer recounts as she paints her own office in City Hall. 'Thirty percent of US oil and natural gas and seafood come from our coastline, not to mention the shipping up the Mississippi. We've allowed this country to grow.'

Film-maker Michelle Benoit pauses to talk at a café in the Marigny district. 'It's like that other big thing that happened,' she says, holding her hands wide, as if to show the enormity of Katrina. 'It's just out there, and we don't know . . . I see Lloyd is over there eating oysters. Maybe I should do the same.'

Fishing was banned east of the Mississippi river on 30 April, out of fear of contamination by the oil spill. The *Times Picayune* newspaper reports 'a local feeding frenzy' as Louisianans rush to consume seafood while they can. Lawyers monopolise television advertising time, offering shrimpers and oyster-men assistance in suing BP. Catholic charities and a group called 'Santa on the

Bayou' have been handing out food packages and cash gift cards to fishermen who have lost their livelihood. And yet, as McKay notes: 'This is the city that care forgot. We didn't really worry about the Spill until it was right at our doorstep.'

While millions of gallons of petrol swirl in choppy seas off the coast, the Jazzfest ended with its usual clamour. In the French quarter, Bourbon Street is still loud, sexy and careless. New Orleans remains true to its nickname, the Big Easy, and to its unofficial slogan, *laissez les bons temps rouler* (let the good times roll).

'There was always a party atmosphere in New Orleans,' McKay says when we talk in the Stanley and Stella café, downstairs from the Pontalba Apartments where Tennessee Williams once wrote. 'The planters came here to sell their crops. They partied between Twelfth Night and Ash Wednesday. It was a big port, and the sailors drank and cavorted. It became a naughty town for professional ladies.'

But there's a price paid for all that *joie de vivre*. New Orleans ignored the erosion of its marshes, which could no longer protect it from the ravages of Katrina. 'There is no philanthropic tradition, because the city pours everything into Carnival,' McKay observes. Five years after Katrina, the Orpheum and Saenger theatres, the Loew and Joy picture palaces, are still boarded up. There are 61,000 blighted buildings, which have become havens for drug addicts and squatters.

This week it felt almost as if Louisiana, the state that smokes, drinks, eats and gambles to excess, might dodge the bullet. Winds and tides kept pushing the oil slick east, towards Mississippi and Alabama. BP stopped one of three leaks, though the Coast Guard emphasised that this didn't reduce the amount of oil gushing into the Gulf. And BP held out hopes that a four-storey concrete dome it began lowering over the fissured pipe might stop the haemorrhage by the beginning of next week. It seemed too good to be true, and it probably was. *Laissez les bons temps rouler.*

The full impact of the hurricane is most evident in the lower ninth ward, where the majority of the 1,800 people who died in Katrina perished. Vegetation and graffiti cover derelict buildings. Many houses have been demolished, leaving only weeds and cement porch steps. A few dozen state-of-the-art ecological designer houses, financed by the actor Brad Pitt, are the only visual relief.

The lower ninth had the highest ratio of black home ownership in the US. In the middle of an August night, when the storm was abating, a loose barge crashed into the wall of the industrial canal that borders the district. The bank was breached and a 7.5-metre-high wall of water swept away houses and lives.

Like many of the lower ninth's residents, Robert Lynn Green, a fifty-five-year-old tax accountant, moved to the ward as a child, when he, his mother and three brothers were flooded out of the Desire housing project by Hurricane Betsy in 1965.

On the night the levee broke in 2005, Green and his family climbed on to the roof of their house, which was torn off its moorings and transported several blocks.

'The house started breaking up,' Green recalls, sitting under a wall covered with Barack Obama memorabilia in his new home. 'I saw my small grand-daughter Shanai washed away in twenty-five feet of water. We climbed on top a truck, which started tipping over. Then we pulled ourselves on to the roof of a house. My brother Jonathan and I were holding our mother's hands. Three times she was sucked down into the water, and three times we pulled her out. We resuscitated her, but we stayed five hours on that roof, and by the end of the ordeal she was dead. We had to leave her body there . . . we thought they would retrieve her body.'

Green was one of the first residents to move back into the lower ninth, where he and his family lived for three years in trailers provided by the Federal Emergency Management Agency (FEMA). The sign in front of the trailer, which is still there, says: 'I am home. I will rebuild. I am New Orleans.' The trailers had formaldehyde in the insulation, and many of those living in them suffered headaches and respiratory ailments. In another FEMA blunder, Chinese-made plasterboard used in reconstruction projects propagated mould and rust and interfered with the hard drives of computers. It was made from recycled refuse.

In the autumn of 2007, the New York visual artist Paul Chan came to the lower ninth to stage a production of Beckett's *Waiting for Godot*, which 6,000 people attended. Green quotes from the play and speaks of Didi, Gogo and Pozzo as if they were intimate acquaintances.

'*Waiting for Godot* was the experience of everybody who went through Hurricane Katrina,' Green explains. 'We waited for FEMA. We waited for President Bush to keep his promises. We waited for the National Guard to show up. We waited four months for them to find my mother's body.'

When Chan staged *Godot* in the wasteland next to Green's trailer, people were still waiting – for electricity and lights, for the insurance companies to pay. But sometimes, says Green, 'waiting is what gets you what you need'. By staying on in his formaldehyde-coated trailer, he met the actors Brad Pitt and Danny Glover, and a host of politicians and officials, and became the neighbourhood's most effective advocate.

Like many New Orleans residents, despite the oil spill, Green is still riding the surge of hope which started with two events in February. The New Orleans Saints (whom New Orleanians used to deride as 'the Ain'ts') won the Superbowl. Mitch Landrieu was elected mayor, along with a new cabinet and district attorney. Ray Nagin, his predecessor, was overwhelmed by Katrina, and earned a reputation for gaffes and hiding in the bathroom.

When Landrieu was inaugurated this week, New Orleans declared the day a holiday. One of Landrieu's first actions was to appeal to the US Department of Justice to put the city police under its direct control. New Orleans has the highest homicide rate in the US. 'I personally have known five women who were murdered, three in their own homes,' says Madeleine Molyneaux, a freelance film producer.

The election results were interpreted as a sign of improved race relations. Landrieu, who is white, won a landslide victory in a city that is two-thirds black. All the blacks I met in the lower ninth told me they voted for Landrieu.

'The difference between the oil spill and Katrina is we didn't have people stepping up to the plate and saying "I'm responsible",' says Robert Green. 'In Katrina, you didn't have the federal government, the governor and the mayor all saying what should be done. We have leadership now.'

A few blocks away, in Tupelo Street, Ronald Lewis, a retired streetcar repairman and union organiser, presides over the House of Dance and Feathers, a small museum dedicated to elaborately beaded and embroidered Mardi Gras Indian costumes. Lewis seems older than his fifty-eight years.

'I worked hard all my life,' he explains. 'Young people used to say hard work never killed anybody. It may not kill you, but it damn sure wears you down.' Although Lewis's discourse is one of racial harmony and hope for the new New Orleans, the story that emerges in the small museum that university students built for him post-Katrina is the more nuanced reality of a city whose half-life of trauma will not be spent for generations.

'Tell the world you visited the lower ninth, and five years after there are still empty lots and empty houses, that a couple of miles from the French Quarter you still see helplessness,' says Lewis. He keeps an album of obituaries of friends who died too young, from suicide or heart attacks, after Katrina.

'This thing is so deep in our lives, you can fill every page of your notebook with the emotion of Katrina. The world was snatched from under us.'

Lewis's museum is a sort of social club for those who have returned to the neighbourhood. Alvin Seymore, fifty-five, wanders in and sits cross-legged on the floor, drinking beer from a bottle in a paper bag. Seymore is emaciated, and Lewis is made visibly uncomfortable by his tragic, disjointed monologue – a life story of loss and racial discrimination.

'We didn't have gas money. We walked ten miles to the Convention Centre. There was raping and robbing, and nobody did crap. I lost my wife after thirty-four years and she didn't die. I am not going to sugar-coat this. I was a police officer and a teacher and a ditch-digger. When I was a child in the Desire projects, the cops came in with their cars with the cherry top and I wanted to be one. But when I put the uniform on, people couldn't see me because I wore the suit of oppression. After Katrina, they wouldn't allow us to clean up our own city. They brought Mexicans to do it. Now BP is paying fishermen $1,200 a day to clean the oil spill. What about us? I'm not afraid to work. I'm not afraid of dying. It's living that's hell.'

Back at City Hall, Kristin Gisleson Palmer, who heads the council's recovery committee, says she is determined to improve life for men like Alvin Seymore. Despite its trials, New Orleans is a proud and beautiful city, founded in 1718. Until the War of Secession, it was the richest city in America. But nearly a quarter of its population, a hundred thousand people, never returned after Katrina. 'To all those who have gone away, it is time, it is time for you to come home,' Mayor Landrieu said in his inauguration address this week.

Palmer had an Irish boyfriend at university, and something from a holiday in Ireland has stayed in her mind. 'Mary Robinson was president,' she recalls. 'She hung a light in the window, for the Irish to come home. I think we should do that in New Orleans.'

8 May 2010

Rogue Sheriff Investigated

What kind of law enforcement officer boasts of using 'the world's only female chain gang' to bury dead indigents? Of housing convicts in furnace temperatures next to the city dump? Of feeding his prisoners twenty-cent meals and forcing them to write home on postcards bearing his picture?

Joe Arpaio is the rogue sheriff of Maricopa County, the largest in Arizona, encompassing the state capital, Phoenix. He has been elected five times since 1993. Two weeks ago, he decided not to stand for governor because he is involved in a dispute with his own board of supervisors, two of whom he has had arrested. He did not want to give the board the satisfaction of replacing him.

Arpaio says the federal government is investigating him 'for alleged civil-rights violations, abuse of power, all that. Do you think I'm worried? Why would you be worried if you did nothing wrong?' Meanwhile, the Sheriff remains the most prominent figure in Arizona's crusade to rid itself of undocumented Mexicans.

If he had entered the gubernatorial race, he might well have won. Candidates from all over the country seek Arpaio's endorsement. The right-wing Tea Party love him, and his local ally, J. D. Hayworth, could defeat Senator John McCain in the Republican primary.

The Sheriff thinks SB1070, the immigration law that is turning Arizona into a pariah, is great. But it won't change much for him, he says, ensconced in his fortress-like nineteenth floor office in downtown Phoenix.

In certain circumstances, a legal exception known as 287g enables local law enforcement to act in place of federal agents. Late last year, the Obama administration yanked Arpaio's 287g authorisation. 'Under the 287g programme, we arrested and charged 318,000 people, starting in April 2007,' Arpaio says.

'Out of that, we detected that 35,000 were here illegally, which means they have to stay in jail.'

Arpaio spews statistics: 'We average 8,000 to 10,000 prisoners on a given day. About 30 percent of them are Hispanic; 19 percent of the people in jail are here illegally. If they weren't here, we wouldn't have those crimes. Fifty-five illegals in jail have been charged with murder.'

The Obama administration's assault on Arpaio's authority 'doesn't make any difference', he says, 'because I'm still doing the same thing'.

Two state laws – one on human smuggling, the other on employer sanctions – enable him to get round the loss of 287g. 'Under the human smuggling law, we just arrested sixty-one people in the last twenty-four hours, coming into this county,' Arpaio says. 'We charged them with smuggling and co-conspiracy. We're the only ones doing that. We've arrested more than two thousand people in the last two or three years [in addition to the above-mentioned 318,000]. It's a class four felony, which means they can't get out on bond. We arrest the people in the vehicle that [sic] have paid the smuggler and we charge them with the same crime.'

On 28 May, the Obama administration asked the Supreme Court to void Arizona's two-year-old law on employer sanctions, on the grounds that it infringes federal prerogatives. Law SB1070 may fall on the same grounds. So the feds don't want Arpaio to do it? 'Well, Sheriff Arpaio is doing it anyway,' he says.

The sanctions law has given Arpaio the pretext to raid thirty-five workplaces. He arrested eighteen illegals in two recent raids on McDonald's, and more at the Burlington coat factory last week.

'It had nothing to do with employer sanctions, but we still accomplished the same mission, because we arrested people who were working illegally,' he says.

Arpaio uses his 2,700-strong 'posse' on raids. 'When you watch the old Western movies,' he explains, 'the sheriff would swear in private citizens and make a posse, and they'd go catch the horse thief. Under the constitution, I have the authority to swear in private citizens to help me do my job. I have fifty-seven different posse organisations: airplanes, jeeps, motorcycles, horses . . . . We train them, five hundred with guns."

The sheriff shrugs off allegations about contacts with neo-Nazi white supremacists. A photographer once took a picture of him talking to a young man he didn't know, he says. However, video on the Internet, from a May 2009 rally of Arpaio supporters, shows demonstrators shouting 'Heil' as they give Nazi salutes and stamp on a Mexican flag. 'Deport all illegal scum', says one placard.

Arpaio bristles when I suggest that even with 10 percent unemployment, Americans won't do the low-paying jobs performed by undocumented Mexicans. 'I don't want to get into racial stuff, but if you go down South, if you look at who's cleaning hotels, what race do you think is cleaning in these southern areas?' he asks. 'The black people are doing that. *They're* even US citizens.'

Arizona's chief persecutor seems to have a persecution complex. Arpaio says his earlier career, as a soldier in Korea, as a cop, then working for two decades with the Drug Enforcement Agency, endowed him with invaluable experience. 'It's sad [that] after spending thirty years dedicating my life . . . as a federal official, . . . they're going after me as the elected sheriff because they don't like me enforcing the immigration laws,' he sighs.

Woe betide Arpaio's prisoners. 'I'm the only one who uses the word "punishment",' Arpaio says. 'Everybody else wants to "rehabilitate" and "educate".'

One of his first acts as sheriff was to buy surplus Korean war tents to house prisoners. 'They're next to the dump and the dog pound and the waste disposal plant,' he says with relish, admitting that the stench can be overpowering. 'It gets to be 140 degrees in the summer. I've had a half million people come through the tents, and none of 'em died yet. I shut everybody up when they complain. I tell them our men and women are fighting for our country and they're living in tents.'

Arpaio is particularly proud of his ten-year-old female chain gang, 'the first in the history of the world'. The women wear striped prison uniforms. 'I hook women together and put them on the streets where everybody can see them. They bury the dead bodies at the county cemetery [he chuckles in mid-sentence] once a week.'

Last November, Mexican television broadcast an interview with Alma Minerva Chacon, a deported migrant who said she gave birth shackled to a hospital bed in Phoenix. 'I think she was just [shackled by] one leg,' Arpaio says, adding that 'there's nothing unconstitutional to restraining people when they're in hospital under guard.'

Arpaio's male prisoners must wear pink boxer shorts. 'They were stealing the white ones, to sell when they got out,' he says, 'and they hate pink.' A souvenir version, with his sheriff's badge and signature stamped on them, goes for $15 a pair to help finance Arpaio's 'posse'.

Arpaio's parents immigrated from Naples, Italy, in 1917. Why does a nation of immigrants now view new arrivals as criminals? I ask him. 'Because they violate the law,' Arpaio snaps. 'My mother and father came here legally.'

I mention the Jesuit priest who a few days ago quoted Matthew 25 to me, about helping the poor, hungry, sick and imprisoned. Arpaio is a Catholic who has refused to transport female prisoners to the abortion clinic, but he doesn't like me bringing religion into our discussion. 'I think there's something in the Bible that says you should obey the laws too,' he snarls.

11 June 2010

IX
HAITI

'We dug for five hours . . . we no longer heard him'

'*Ça commence ici,*' says Claude, the Haitian driver. It starts here, at Ganthier, fifty kilometres from the Haitian capital. Just one roof caved in, glimpsed behind a garden wall. Lush vines and banana groves, bougainvillea, framed by the stark mountain range to the north. Every few minutes, another collapsed wall, a staircase that has fallen off a building.

Brightly painted pick-ups, lorries, and buses known as 'taxis tap-tap' with names like 'Jesus Saves' and 'God Be Praised' still ply the highway, an impossible number of passengers clinging to the sides. Then more and more houses, as if they'd been bombed from the air, or dynamited.

Claude thinks a curse has fallen upon his country. '*If not, why us and not the others? It's because Haitians have no conscience. After Baby Doc left, we did terrible things. We threw petrol on people and burned them alive, because they'd been Tontons Macoutes* [agents of Duvalier's secret police]. *God must do his work. This is the anger of God.*'

We have reached the outskirts of the city, and there is more and more devastation. A crowd presses in around a water tanker, brandishing jerricans. People pace the streets, purposefully, as if they had somewhere to go. But not one of them is smiling. About a third of them wear surgical face masks or bandanas, to keep out the cement dust and the smell of rotting flesh.

Those who do not wear masks smear a stripe of white toothpaste on their upper lip, to attenuate the stench.

'*We're a people who resign themselves, who accept everything, like innocent children. I was educated by Salesian Fathers in Pétionville. I am the oldest in my family. I understand things,*' Claude continues wearily.

Buildings in every stage of demolition. Some appear untouched. Others are piles of rubble. No rhyme or reason. The arbitrariness of it. '*Why us and not the others?*'

At an intersection, the hand-painted sign over the ground floor shop can still be read: 'Where the customer is king'. Upstairs, the shopkeeper's apartment has been shaved off like a doll's house. A red armchair faces the television. A floral picture hangs in a gilt frame. The wrought iron gates on the ground floor are twisted and tossed into the street, bound by an irrelevant padlock.

A crowd has formed on the slanting slabs of a collapsed building. Two men wear hard hats, and they are hack away uselessly at the concrete with sledgehammers. That smell again, of decomposing flesh.

Cars in driveways crushed by fallen balconies. A man sits on the back fender of a 'tap-tap', his head dropped between his knees in despair.

At the sector known as Delmas thirty-three, the road is closed because they're clearing the ruins of the police commissariat, where some thirty policemen died. A girl hobbles by on a crutch. A child sits on the ground, her right hand wrapped in a bandage the size of a football.

From a distance, it looks like a colourful picnic. But closer up, one reads only desolation on the faces of these thousand or more Haitians who have crowded onto the lawn of the School of the Brothers of Saint Louis de Gonzague. The Collège Dieudonné l'Hérisson, the top sliced off and leaning backwards, opened like an oyster, a flag fluttering from the top.

At an intersection in Delmas, two Haitians play cards at a folding table on the pavement. A shiny, brand new bus, sparkling clean, glides by, surreal. It is filled with US Marines in full combat gear, wearing Ray-Bans, from a contingent of five thousand, just landed.

But the heroes are the Mexican rescue team I meet in their dust-covered red jumpsuits, exhausted from a day of battling broken buildings. They throw their shovels on the ground, sink down, exhausted, to smoke a cigarette. Oscar Oliva, 36, from Cancun, is a giant of a man, with arms and a neck as thick as tree trunks.

'*The nuns asked us to go to the archbishop's office, next to the cathedral. This morning we heard Father Benedict's voice – Father Benedict, like the Pope – from under the rubble. We dug for five hours, and we couldn't get to him. This afternoon we no longer heard him.*' Oscar Oliva is crying.

16 January 2010

The Agony of Faimi Lamy

Five-year-old Faimi Lamy's screams pierce the morning air as a Cuban nun, a trained nurse, draws needle and thread through the raw meat that is the stub of the little girl's left arm.

'*Aiee, aiee*. Give me water so it will stop hurting. Stop, stop,' Faimi cries.

Sister Lazal Guevara cleans and sutures the infected wound without anaesthesia, and the pain is more than the child can bear. 'Give me a knife. Give me a knife so I can kill the devil,' Faimi screams, writhing as her aunt and godmother, Sandra Oscar, holds the child on her lap. The little girl's hair is plaited, and she is wrapped in a grimy floral sheet. She seems delirious. 'Let me go. I want to go to school . . . . *Marraine, marraine, marraine*' she cries, using the French word for godmother. Tears flood down Sandra Oscar's cheeks.

It was 9 AM in the small garden in front of what had been the *Centre Hospitalier de la Renaissance*, across the road from the ruins of Port-au-Prince Cathedral. '*Brigada Medica Cubana*' says the flag hanging from the building. While Western aid agencies continue to be stymied by logistics and security hurdles, a handful of Cuban and Mexican nuns and doctors heroically care for victims of the earthquake, working on a folding table in the open air, beneath dusty eucalyptus trees, with little or no equipment.

A few feet from Faimi, a small boy sits on a wooden stool, his arms wrapped tightly around his mother's waist. A nurse wearing a mask and plastic gloves pours disinfectant on the deep, six-inch gash on the boy's ankle. 'It burns. It hurts. Heal me Jesus,' the boy cries. His mother pleads: 'You have to do it or you'll lose your foot.'

Another boy with a bandaged head screams at the top of his lungs as a doctor pulls on his twisted legs to straighten them. While the operation continues, Faimi's mother, Sajine, and her father, Manuel, explain that their children lived with their aunt and grandmother in the Poste Marchand neighbourhood. (A second child, a boy, survived the earthquake unscathed.)

Faimi formed a special bond with her Aunt Sandra, a childless spinster in her thirties. When Faimi was buried under the rubble, it was Sandra, her god-mother, whom she called for. When she was freed, it was Sandra who took the child in her arms.

'It took almost three hours for my brother and father to reach Faimi,' Sandra Oscar recounts. 'Her arm was already cut off, and the bone stuck out. That first night, we could do nothing. The wound bled, but she was calm because she was in shock.'

The following day, Cuban doctors sawed the protruding bone from Faimi's arm. They still had anaesthetics then. They gave the child ampicillin and amoxycillin, and paracetamol for pain. Sandra and Faimi went 'home' to a tent where twenty family members now live in Poste Marchand. But the wound became infected.

Earlier in the morning, at the Catholic Relief Services' compound in Delmas, a German doctor with the Order of Malta told me there would be a 'second wave of deaths' from the earthquake 'in about a week's time'. 'Thousands more will die because their wounds are infected, and we cannot get to them,' said Dr Georg Nothelle. 'These people are living in camps. Some have been running around for days, trying to find treatment. It is horribly frustrating.'

The Cuban open-air clinic is in Belair, one of the worst neighbourhoods of Port-au-Prince, where police have played cat and mouse with looters for the past week. We hear shooting once or twice, and police cars speed by with sirens blaring.

About three hundred injured Haitians, most with amputation wounds, are stranded in this small public garden, where a wrought iron fence provides an illusion of shelter. Unspeakable suffering goes side by side with routine domestic chores. A woman washes clothes in a plastic tub. A white-haired granny sorts black beans on a cloth. A man with one leg amputated at the knee, the other splinted with a broken board, lies on the ground. In every direction, there are only crumbling buildings. Two corpses rot on the street corner, just beyond the enclosure.

Dr Gaston Bob Edem, a Haitian who trained in Cuba, stops to speak for a moment. He has been treating the injured since the night of the earthquake. 'I've seen such horrific things, I couldn't begin to list them. Mangled people . . . I never thought I would see such things. We are used to seeing dead animals in the streets, but not people, it is inhuman . . . .'

The doctor is glad that the Americans, Europeans and other foreigners are in Haiti, 'but they're taking too long. They should do like us.' Yet he understands their fears about security. 'There are thieves. We can't even go out to help people. There are wounded people in the neighbourhood outside. Everyone is afraid. All of Port-au-Prince is unsafe.'

Manuel Lamy, little Faimi's father, interrupts Dr Edem. He believes there is honour among Haitan thieves, that looters attack only shops destroyed in the earthquake, not aid workers. 'The foreigners shouldn't be afraid,' Lamy says. 'They must jump over the barriers. When they come to help, people will make sure they get through.'

As I wander through the garden-turned-clinic, the suffering and injured raise hands towards me, begging for food or money. A woman lies on a metal hospital trolley that has been cranked down to the ground. Her torn gauze bandages are stained yellow and brown, and the wound is black with swarming flies. 'I'm in the sun. Get me out of the sun,' the woman pleads, glassy-eyed.

My driver and interpreter and I attempt to move the trolley, but it is too heavy. We call out for help, but no one comes.

Emanise Zamy, 66, follows me through this raft of misery. She is a skinny woman in a long black T-shirt and flip-flops. Her plastic carrier bag says 'Paris' and bears a garish photograph of the Arc de Triomphe.

'The Lord is good to us,' she shouts. No one pays attention. At first I think Zamy is being ironic, but then I realise she is unhinged with grief. 'The Lord does wonders for us,' she continues. 'I want to sing his praises. God gave us commandments. We didn't obey them.'

There were six people in her family, Zamy tells me. She is the only one who survived. She sinks to her knees on the pavement in front of the Cuban clinic, under the blazing sun, and raises both hands to the sky.

19 January 2010

The Salvation of Faimi Lamy

The little Haitian girl in pigtails and a lime-green playsuit stood on the far side of Delmas Boulevard, clutching her aunt's hand with her own right hand. I recognised the child immediately, from the stub that ended just below her left elbow.

Five-year-old Faimi Lamy had survived the three-part, salami-style amputation of her arm last January. She smiled radiantly. It was a good omen for Haiti.

The last time I saw Faimi, a Cuban nurse was suturing the raw meat of the child's lower left arm, in an open-air clinic next to Port-au-Prince's ruined cathedral. There was no anaesthetic, and the child raved deliriously about wanting to kill the devil. 'Godmother, make them stop, please,' she begged Sandra Oscar, who is raising Faimi. Sandra held Faimi on her lap throughout the operation, with tears streaming down her face.

'It's a miracle. I thought she would die,' Sandra recounts joyously. Faimi's arm was crushed when the upper storey of the Oscar family's cinder-block house in the Poste Marchand neighbourhood collapsed on her. The wound from a first amputation was infected. The operation I witnessed was her second without anaesthesia. The wound became infected again, Sandra told me. Despairing of saving the child, Sandra found volunteer American doctors working *with* anaesthesia, and the third operation succeeded.

Sandra took two weeks off from her job assembling electronic parts in a Port-au-Prince factory to nurse Faimi back to health. From the one-room shack they have built with boards, corrugated steel and cinder blocks, the family can see their former home, less than ten metres away. It, too, was a poor dwelling, but with its three rooms up and three rooms down, it seems palatial now.

When I ask Faimi what happened, she whispers her self-censored child's version of events to me: 'I was asleep and I woke up because the house was shaking. It fell on top of me. My father got me out with a hammer. My father was crying and crying. He rolled on the ground. My aunt and mother took me to a hospital. Nothing happened after that. I didn't hurt. I didn't cry.'

An open sewer runs down the winding alley that leads to the shack where Faimi lives. The heat is sweltering, the stench overwhelming. Faimi's family must walk nearly half a kilometre through the labyrinth of houses, which are in various states of collapse, to reach the neighbourhood's only water taps, then carry buckets back up the hill. Rubble that people have cleared from their homes mixes with rotting garbage in the main street.

Three adults and five children share the shack that Faimi's family cobbled together after the earthquake. Two more adults – Faimi's mother and father – sleep elsewhere.

Her mother Sajine and aunt Sandra are the only family members with salaried jobs. Her grandfather, Louis-Jacob, brings in a little money as a plumber. The entire family of ten gets by on the equivalent of $250 a month.

Aside from the three operations which Sandra organised, no one has offered Faimi's family any kind of assistance. Sandra would like to obtain a prosthesis for Faimi but doesn't know where to go.

Faimi returned to Le Bocage kindergarten on 7 April, but now her school is demanding back tuition for the three months she was absent because of the earthquake. All schools were closed from 13 January until April, but many Haitian schools are trying to raise money in the same way. 'We can't leave Faimi there; we'll have to send her to the Sisters of St Anne,' says Sandra.

Faimi seems blissfully unaware of her family's travails. She has her best friends at school, Lid and Jildana. She has not yet reached an age where children are cruel enough to tease amputees, where some men would shun a one-armed woman.

No one has told Faimi that her ambition of becoming a nurse may not be realistic. 'She tries to do everything, comb her hair, wash, as if she had two arms. She can't manage but she never complains,' says another aunt.

Faimi plays the clown, wriggling the little nub of flesh with her elbow joint, to make the other children laugh. She dances in the dusty path in front of the shanty, waving her stunted arm as if in triumph.

Someone – Sandra thinks it was the Haitian government – surveyed all the houses in Poste Marchand and marked them with paint. Red means the house is in danger of collapsing and must be torn down. Green equals safe for habitation. Yellow – the colour daubed on the house where Faimi lost her arm – means it can be salvaged.

'It's hard to start over from scratch,' Sandra sighs, 'but we have a plan for next year. I told my father last week: "We're going to rebuild the house."'

Louis-Jacob Oscar, 66, stands nearby, skinny and shirtless, nodding in approval. It was he who built the damaged house. 'Every month we'll save a little money to buy sand, cinder blocks and cement,' says Sandra.

Faimi was the only one injured, and no one in the family was killed. 'We were very lucky,' Sandra says, 'but three of my best friends died.'

Sandra Oscar is cheerful, despite circumstances that a European or American would find unbearable. She says she is happier now than before the earthquake, because 'God gave Faimi back to me. She is so brave. She gave me hope for Haiti. I want her to be a lesson for the world, that Haiti is alive.'

6 July 2010

Aftershock

It started with a strange noise that I mistook for machinery, perhaps an electrical generator. At 6 AM yesterday, Haiti was rocked by the worst aftershock since the earthquake that killed up to two hundred thousand souls and displaced 1.5 million people on 12 January. This one, I would learn a few hours later, measured 6.1 on the Richter scale, compared to just over 7 for the cataclysm of eight days before.

But I wasn't thinking about magnitudes or Richter scales as my room, on the third and top floor of the Kinam Hotel in Pétionville, on the heights above Port-au-Prince, began to move. The mind works rationally at such moments.

The Kinam is an old, Caribbean-style wooden gingerbread building, and I remembered a Haitian woman telling me that concrete buildings are safe for hurricanes but death traps in earthquakes, whereas wood is safer in earthquakes but offers no protection against hurricanes.

Lesson number one, I thought: you're lucky to be in a wooden building. Two: what should I do? I was dressing to go to down to breakfast when the tremor started. I mentally ran through the options. I could run on to the landing and downstairs – but that would put me in the courtyard of the U-shaped hotel, which might fall on me. Better to stay on the top floor, where it would be easier to dig me out if the building collapsed.

I grew up in California, where earthquakes are a frequent occurrence. My childhood education kicked in. Seek shelter under a table or a heavy piece of furniture or, failing that, a door jamb.

So I stood between bathroom and bedroom, watching the walls sway back and forth. I swear I felt seasick. Time seemed to stop. It lasted perhaps thirty seconds, certainly less than a minute. But it felt much longer. I didn't expect to die, but I feared being pinned under wreckage. A short, eerie silence followed the tremor, then screams from the Place Saint-Pierre across the street, where hundreds of homeless Haitians are living.

Until yesterday, I didn't share the Haitians' fear of aftershocks. Even those whose houses were unscathed by the first quake prefer to sleep in the street rather than risk death or entombment in further tremors.

On Haitian radio, 'experts' tell us that aftershocks are a good thing, because they relieve pressure on tectonic plates. One seismologist has sown panic in the north by predicting an imminent quake measuring more than 8 on the Richter scale in Cap-Haïtien, Haiti's second city.

21 January 2010

Catholicism and Voodoo:
Rival Faiths

The voices rise up in the middle of the night, from the darkened streets and public parks that are now home to more than a million Haitians. '*Chanter, c'est prier deux fois,*' Haitians say. Singing is like praying twice. A lone voice launches a hymn. Others join in. I have heard them every night, and it's the same in other parts of the city. The prayers, in Creole, often mixed with what sound like voodoo chants, continue for an hour or two, then subside before dawn.

Faith and mysticism have shaped Haitians' response to the cataclysm of 12 January. The US Secretary of State, Hillary Clinton, called it an event of Biblical proportions. I've heard Haitians evoke Noah and the Flood, Jonah and the Whale, the destruction of Sodom and Gomorrah.

Intellectual, French-educated Haitians, including Bishop Pierre Dumas, object to the popular wisdom that portrays the catastrophe as divine retribution. That's an Old Testament interpretation, Bishop Dumas told me: the Christ of the Gospel does not judge and punish; he suffers with people.

The televangelist Pat Robertson created a scandal in the US by saying that God had punished Haiti for its centuries-old pact with the devil. Shocking and politically incorrect as it is, Robertson's belief is shared by some Haitians.

In 1791, at the start of the slave rebellion against the French, a voodoo *houngan* (priest) called Boukman held a ritual ceremony where worshippers drank the warm blood of a sacrificed black pig and prayed to their African gods to free them.

The French practised a particularly virulent form of slavery in Haiti, where the average life expectancy was seven years after arrival in the colony. Because the stock of slaves was continuously replenished from Africa, Haitians remained closer to their original culture and religion than slaves elsewhere in the Americas.

Haiti's early leaders knew first-hand the rallying power of voodoo drums and ceremonies, and tried to suppress the religion. Faustin Soulouque, the fourth illiterate black general to rule the country, claimed that the Virgin Mary told him he should be emperor, was crowned with gilded cardboard, then openly embraced voodoo in the mid-nineteenth century. The Catholic Church turned its back on Haiti from independence in 1804 until 1860, thus allowing voodoo to become deeply entrenched.

Haiti's modern history has seen a constant struggle between Christianity and the African religion, with its *houngans, mambos* (priestesses) and *peristyles* (chapels). The American military tried to stamp out voodoo during its occupation of the island from 1915 to 1934.

François 'Papa Doc' Duvalier, whose family terrorised the island from 1957 until 1986, concluded a Boukman-style pact with the *loas* (spirits), bringing them en masse from the cave they were said to inhabit at Trou Foban to the presidential palace. No living human could overthrow Duvalier, Haitians believed, because he was protected by the *loas*.

Duvalier persecuted the church, expelling priests and bishops and even sending a *houngan* to perform a voodoo ceremony on the steps of Port-au-Prince's now-ruined cathedral. When his son Jean-Claude was overthrown, *houngans* and *mambos* were tracked down and murdered, along with Duvalier's infamous *Tontons Macoutes*.

In recent decades, Haitian Catholicism has also been challenged by evangelical missionaries. Catholic sources say that 65 percent of Haitians are practising Catholics, 35 percent Evangelical Protestants. Though Christian leaders condemn voodoo, many Haitians practise both religions. France's slaves resisted imposed Catholicism by attributing the identity of a *loa* to each saint. When a Haitian sees an image of the Virgin Mary, he also sees the *loa* Ersulie Dantord.

In a gesture of solidarity towards his Christian counterparts, Max Beauvoir, the French-educated head of the association of voodoo *houngans*, promised to give shelter to any priest or pastor displaced by the earthquake. They have not taken up the offer.

'When the earthquake started, I thought it was the end of the world,' Father Fernand Pierre told parishioners at Altagrace Church in the Delmas neighbourhood. 'When I learned it was only Haiti, and not the whole world, I knew it was God's will. God does with us as he pleases.' Haitians are so terrified of aftershocks that many worshippers listened from outside the church building.

More Haitians survived than perished, Father Fernand noted. 'Haiti will survive. The same God that protects the US, France and Britain, the rich and powerful countries of the world, also protects Haiti.'

26 January 2010

Whims of the West
Will Shape Future for Haiti

One can only marvel at the outpouring of sympathy for Haiti. The country's tragic history is one reason we find the catastrophe so compelling. The sheer scale of the destruction reminds us of the capriciousness of nature, the fragility of all civilisation. Two hundred thousand lives lost, a capital city destroyed in seconds, many thousands of survivors in agony, their limbs snapped like twigs. From the vantage of our own good fortune, we contemplate, in the words of T. S. Eliot, some 'infinitely suffering thing'.

The Haitian earthquake poses the big questions of the human condition. Life and death. Hope and despair. The good of doctors and rescue workers versus the evil of thugs who raid orphanages in Port-au-Prince. 'Why?' is the most obvious question; neither God's will nor science seem adequate responses. Albert Camus' belief in the absurd comes closest to it, but also fails to satisfy our need for answers.

My flight from Santo Domingo the other morning was filled with volunteer relief workers and journalists, heading back to the land of hot showers and cooked meals. The stewardess called for a round of applause for the aid workers. Problem solved. We can go home now. Our short attention span is the biggest threat to Haiti's recovery.

I'll bet my bottom dollar that the poorest country in the Western hemisphere will remain so, that in a year, or two, or three, most of the 2 million Haitians whose lives have been shattered by the quake will still be poor, jobless and homeless. Urgent appeals have gone out for proper tents. But the rainy season will start in March. Even if tents arrive in the meantime, they'll be washed down the hillside or mired in mud. We should have the foresight to start building houses on a massive scale, now.

A year after Israel killed 1,434 Palestinians in Gaza, the enclave is still under siege, and little of the $4.5 billion (€3.2 billion) pledged to rebuild has materialised. A year and a half after the August 2008 war, Russia still occupies part of Georgia, and refugees cannot go home. I could give many more examples, but you get the idea. The lack of messy political issues comparable to the Arab-Israeli conflict or Russian irredentism made it easy for the world to agree on Haiti. Let's hope that consensus continues.

The needs of our own countries militate against a sustained effort for Haiti. A young woman with the face of a black madonna, Francina Renard, followed me to the rope that separates US soldiers from Haitians at a camp for the displaced. 'Can you give me a job?' she pleaded shyly. During the ten days I spent in Port-au-Prince, I lost track of the number of Haitians who asked me for employment – not money, employment.

But how will the US government create jobs in Haiti, with 17 million jobless at home? Is America going to build shelter for 1 million Haitians, when 600,000 Americans are homeless?

Fortunately, Concern, Goal, Trócaire, MSF and the Red Cross will be there to nag our conscience. Their heroism in Haiti has been impressive. I distinguish between those with a commando attitude, who don't let security worries prevent them from rushing to help those in need, and the bureaucrats who waited in compounds for assessments, instructions and escorts. One often finds both attitudes within the same agency. It's a question of character, and leadership.

Reconstruction will be complicated by the fabled corruption of the Haitian government, and the need to respect Haitian sovereignty, but neither must be allowed to prevent help reaching people. John O'Shea, the head of Goal, tells how his agency redirected its post-tsunami efforts from Indonesia to Sri Lanka because of the unhelpful attitude of the Indonesian military. Aid agencies owe it to donors to impose conditionality and accountability, says O'Shea.

We should be aware of the colour-blindness that affects our scorn for corruption. The biggest thieves in Baghdad after the 2003 US invasion were US contractors, who made off with hundreds of millions of dollars. Dealing with 'our sons of bitches' (as Teddy Roosevelt called US-backed despots) does not preclude corruption either. Remember the Shah of Iran, Ferdinand Marcos, Saddam Hussein (before we turned against him), Hamid Karzai's administration in Afghanistan . . . .

Endowing Haiti with effective, democratic government may be the greatest challenge. On the night of the earthquake, what was left of President René Préval's government got on motorcycles and rode up the hill to the US ambassador's residence. But the Obama administration and international donors would rather deal with a strong government than a helpless client state.

'The only institutions that function throughout the Caribbean and Latin America are the Catholic Church and the gangs,' notes Patrick Moynihan, an Irish-American who runs a school in Port-au-Prince. I rode around Port-au-Prince in a 'tap-tap', a Toyota pick-up with benches in the back for passengers. As we headed down the hill one morning, coasting without power to save petrol, a middle-aged man dressed like a clerk or office worker jumped in. Jean-Claude, the tap-tap driver, explained that we weren't taking passengers, and asked him to leave. The man clutched his document folder to his chest and refused to budge.

There was no public transport, he said, and he had somewhere to go. The determination of the man in the tap-tap gave me hope for Haiti. So did the calm, dignity and resilience of the earthquake survivors.

Haiti is a state founded on two genocides – the native indigenous Indians, exterminated by the Spanish, followed by the slow deaths of up to 1 million African slaves at the hands of the French. In the nineteenth century, France demanded reparations from the world's first black republic. Fearful that the example of rebellion would spread to slaves on its own territory, the US imposed a crippling trade embargo on the former 'pearl of the Antilles'.

In Haiti, the evil done by men, including the island's home grown tyrants, has lived on. It will take tremendous determination, commensurate with the effort of the past two weeks, to prove that the chains of history can be broken.

28 January 2010

EPILOGUE:
FURRY FRIENDS

Walter the Beirut Puss

Articles about cats may seem a frivolous way to end a book on such serious topics. But judging from the response from readers, these have been among my best-received pieces. Shortly after the 2003 invasion of Iraq, a reader in Dublin wrote saying: 'I enjoyed your reporting of the war, but couldn't you write another piece about your cat?'

For the week that our cat Walter, a female despite the name, spent in the Marais veterinary clinic, Dr Flachaire was businesslike. But on the day she broke the news to me, the French vet was full of compassion.

She had thought she could treat Walter's heart disease, but her condition worsened and the cat's liver and kidneys no longer functioned. Our pet of eleven years suffered, and risked going into convulsions. Dr Flachaire used the word I'd always heard applied to terminally ill humans: 'euthanasia'.

I held Walter on my lap while the vet injected lethal pink liquid into her. 'A cat represents a whole period of one's life,' Dr Flachaire philosophised. 'People who don't have pets can't understand.' I stroked Walter's velvety fur as her body went limp. 'Bye bye Walter,' the vet said sadly. Before I left, she snipped a tuft from one of Walter's tiger stripes and put it in a glass vial for me.

Who says Parisians are heartless? Before taking the métro at St Paul station, I stopped to buy *Le Monde*. 'Where's the pussy cat?' the woman newspaper vendor asked, peering into Walter's empty wicker basket.

'She's dead,' I blurted out.

'It's been ten years since my dog died,' the woman commiserated. 'I still haven't got over it,' she added, holding out a handful of tissues.

I returned to the clinic the next day to fetch Walter's body. A long-faced assistant handed me a cold cardboard box, sealed with tape. At the end of her life Walter weighed almost nothing, so I was surprised how heavy it felt.

The first driver in the taxi queue, an African, did not want to take me to the suburb of Vanves on the pretext that he didn't have a map. By law, Paris taxi drivers cannot refuse you, but they hate trips to the *banlieue* because they don't want to return with an empty cab. I managed to dissuade the second driver, a Moroccan, from arguing with the African. 'What's in the box?' he asked suspiciously, reaching for it as he said, 'I'll put it in the boot.' Guessing that he would not want to transport a dead cat to the pet crematorium, I ignored his question and insisted that I keep the box with me on the back seat.

During the fifty-minute drive out to Vanves, I wrote down pages of memories of Walter. Our Beirut driver Abed brought her to us between bombardments, late in the summer of 1989. She was a frightened little kitten, an alley cat from Mosseitbeh, covered in fleas, with a yellow ribbon around her neck.

We named Walter after an editor at the *International Herald Tribune*. When the US navy had complained about a freelance piece I wrote on a naval exercise in the Mediterranean, Walter Wells cravenly failed to defend me. Naming our cat for him was a journalist's revenge, but the name suited her, and like T. S. Eliot's cats, she would soon have many others: Wally, the Wal, WTP (for Walter The Puss).

When we threw fake mice covered in rabbit fur, Walter ran after them and retrieved them, earning another nickname: 'Cadog'. She liked to sleep on the telex machine, and more than once I had to ask newspapers to resend messages that were garbled because she blocked the paper. During that long drive to Vanves, it was hard to believe that I would never again feel her tap my cheek with her paw, or gently nibble my forearm to wake me early in the morning, that she would never again sit on our suitcase in protest at our departure, butt her head against me to show affection, or roll on her back with pleasure.

The pet crematorium is in a leafy street, indistinguishable from other houses save for a discreet sign. In the waiting room, the owner's ageing bulldog snored on an armchair and a blonde French woman in a fluffy sweater burst into sobs as she received a plastic jar containing the ashes of her Yorkshire terrier. 'Give your companion a dignified end,' said a poster bearing the silhouettes of cats and dogs. 'Spare him the rendering plant.'

I handed over the cardboard box holding Walter, and a thoughtful young man filled out her certificate of cremation. 'There's always a lot of paperwork in France,' he said apologetically. 'By law, you must wait one year and one day before spreading the ashes. You must keep these papers in case there is an inspection.'

Inspection? I asked incredulously. In theory, the police could call any time and ask to see Walter's ashes, but he didn't know of it ever happening.

We scattered Walter's ashes on the Mediterranean, in front of the Beirut balcony where she spent so many years.

7 June 2000

An Irish Cat in Paris

When I wrote about the death of my cat Walter, several readers sent condolences, so I thought they should have an update.

Carmel Courtney of Dundrum encouraged me to get a kitten. At first the idea seemed disloyal, but before Christmas I began looking for a new pet. I was in Ireland, and a Bray vet put me in touch with Belinda Caulfield, who gave me Spike.

At Christmas-time we put a door-sized plank across the kitchen entry, in the naive hope that Spike could be confined to the most functional part of the house. He was still chubby, with down-soft kitten fur and a bushy raccoon tail, but he was already a fearless, breakneck puss with a sense of humour.

Spike jumped to hook his paws over the top edge of the plank. His little hind legs scrambled madly to lever himself over the top. When he tumbled on to the dining room side of the barrier, he looked at us as if to say: 'So you thought you could pen me in?' Then he repeated the escape in reverse.

Air France is the only airline that lets you carry a pet in the cabin from Dublin to Paris. Before leaving for the airport, I tried, unsuccessfully, to force an animal tranquilliser down Spike's throat. He wailed all the way to Paris.

One of Spike's first outings was to Dr Vigneron, the vet in the rue du Cherche-Midi. She tattooed his right ear. If he ever got lost, the Ministry of Agriculture would in theory contact me. In a country where you can buy eau de cologne and cashmere sweaters for pets, four thousand cats and a hundred thousand dogs are discarded every summer.

Brigitte Bardot, France's most famous animal rights activist, has purchased colour advertisements in magazines and newspapers, featuring a heartbreaking photo of an emaciated dog. 'Your family takes you on holiday?' asks the caption. 'Mine shamefully abandoned me.'

Dr Vigneron also told me about the 'parachute cat syndrome'. Every summer she treats several Paris felines who fall or jump from upper-floor apartments. Knowing Spike's penchant for acrobatics, I wired green netting to the wrought iron balconies.

Now I understand why the French call alley cats *chats de gouttière*. My Paris neighbours have a tabby named Frimousse, with continents of milk-white fur mapped over her striped body. Frimousse's owners don't worry about parachute cat syndrome, and she is given free run of the sixth-floor rain gutter.

While Spike is imprisoned behind the green netting, Frimousse struts by to taunt him. Sometimes they kiss, Eskimo-style. Or lay their ears back and swat at one another. Usually Spike hunches down and coos like a turtle dove when Frimousse approaches.

French cats have delicious and musical names. Frimousse means 'pert little face'. I know a cat in Bordeaux called Clafoutis, after the fruit tart, and a tabby near Morlaix who answers to Galipette (Somersault).

But friends are perplexed when I tell them Spike's name, which they almost invariably pronounce 'Speek'. The best translation I have come up with is '*pointe de fer*', and I have yet to find a French person who hears the poetry in it.

Most evenings Spike embarks on what my goddaughter's mother calls his *quart d'heure colonial*. Suddenly, as if he had taken a jolt of 220-volt current, Spike races at high speed through the apartment, ricocheting off walls, crashing into any obstacle in his path, overturning waste bins and the laundry basket, sliding on rugs.

Unlike Walter, who hung back fearfully when the front door opened, Spike plunges into frontier territory. He grasps the door latch with his paws, swings from it and miaows when he wants out now. In the early morning and late evening, when he's least likely to encounter the concierge, postman or neighbours, I let him roam the staircase.

Although Spike has adjusted to Parisian life, his character is Irish: always cheerful, without an ounce of pretension. How else do you explain that the only visitor he boldly kissed at first meeting, with a wet nuzzle on the forehead, was the Irish ambassador's wife?

He is the only cat I've known who shows no fear of water – a fact I attribute to early months in the rain. He sticks his paws under the tap and dips into soap suds when I wash dishes.

And when he sits on the balcony contemplating the lady feeding pigeons two floors below, I suspect he's dreaming of field mice in Wicklow. But alas, unless the Department of Agriculture lifts quarantine restrictions, my brave Irish puss will stay in Paris.

11 July 2001

Paris–Washington

Every time the Japanese artist Hokusai moved, he walked out of his house, set it alight and burned it to the ground. Having just moved from Paris to Washington, I may follow Hokusai's example next time.

For a while, I was on a roll. I was appointed to the Washington job, which I'd coveted for some time, and spent the last week of July house-hunting in the US capital.

After Paris, the efficiency and friendliness of America seemed stunning. Despite Barack Obama's woes over Afghanistan and health care reform, the capital still seems to bask in the glow of his election. At a building in downtown Penn Quarter, a young black receptionist told me with obvious relish, 'My name is Michelle.' The estate agent who found my lovely apartment in Georgetown is a retired US navy officer who targeted cruise missiles at Baghdad during the 2003 war. I heard and saw the explosions. Small world.

My luck turned the moment I returned to Paris to undo thirteen years of life there. It was probably folly to attempt such a thing in the month of August. Each day brought a new crisis.

First, the moving company refused to take my most prized possession, a Pleyel baby grand piano which I bought to reward myself for surviving the Iraq war. American customs officers take very seriously the international convention banning the export of ivory, and my eighty-nine-year-old piano has an ivory keyboard.

If the piano were a hundred, I could bring it in, but the serial number doesn't lie. If you're caught trying to sneak ivory into the US, I was warned, your whole shipment is blocked, the item is confiscated and you're hit with a massive fine.

In my mind, the piano saga came to represent the New World keeping out the Old. A dear friend, a composer, has agreed to look after my beloved piano for me.

Then my bank of twenty years, the Société Générale, informed me there had been $1,400 worth of fraud on my French credit card while I was house-hunting in Washington. I blocked the card and filled out the forms. But my new credit card didn't arrive, and I received a letter from Soc Gén threatening me with legal proceedings.

'You ticked the wrong box,' my bank manager said in an accusatory tone. (I'd ticked the box that said 'The card is in my possession', which was true.) 'If the card is in your possession, and there was fraud on your card, then you committed fraud,' he said with flawless Cartesian logic. Remember, this is the bank that let a junior trader named Jérôme Kerviel lose €5 billion on the derivatives market . . . .

The very word *l'administration*, meaning government bureaucracy, sends dread through the average Frenchman. When I telephoned the tax authorities to give them my new address, a civil servant told me they were reimbursing my 2008 income tax, because I hadn't earned anything. 'But I did. I received a monthly salary. Please don't transfer any money till we sort it out,' I pleaded. Three days later, the funds landed in my account. Ten days later, the *trésor public* admitted they'd made an error entering my tax return into their computer. I count myself lucky. My best friend received a notice she owed an extra €53,000 in back taxes – also an error.

France Télécom cut my landline a week earlier than I requested. I protested for two days, but wearied of being insulted by harridans. By comparison, the woman at AT&T who (unsuccessfully) tried to help me receive e-mails on my Blackberry in Washington was an angel.

My Paris cleaning lady asked me to 'go to social security' to ensure she received benefits for having worked three hours a week for three years. There ensued a heated discussion during which I asked her to obtain a name, phone number or application form for me, because I was swamped with the movers, Soc Gén and tax authorities, and didn't have time to embark on a wild-goose chase through *l'administration*. She kept using phrases like '*J'ai le droit*' and '*C'est votre responsabilité*'. We played an unpleasant game of Jacobins and aristocrats for a week until we located the right form.

Whatever my frustrations, the move was far more traumatic for Spike, the Irish moggy from Bray. He endured the injection of a microchip between his shoulder blades, a rabies vaccination and a veterinarian's house call for a health cert and tranquilliser on the morning of our departure. Drugged though he was, Spike escaped from his carrier in the staircase of our Paris building, and I chased him up five flights while the taxi waited.

Air France graciously gave Spike and me two seats so I wouldn't have to sit for eight hours with my feet on his cage. The Customs man at Dulles Airport waved us through without a glance at Spike's papers. Now the poor, jet-lagged puss wanders through the apartment at odd hours, wailing and literally trying to climb the walls. He spends much of his time hiding behind the washing machine, but has taken a liking to American cat food.

8 September 2009

In Praise of Cats

I have venerated cats since early childhood. For more than two decades, Walter the Beirut Puss, and now Spike the Irish Moggy, have enriched my life. There are people and possessions I could live without. But a cat is indispensable.

Rosita Boland remains a cherished friend and colleague. But I could not allow her attack on the feline species (Irishwoman's Diary, 14 June) to go unanswered. Reading it here in Washington, I relived the disappointment – not to say sense of betrayal – that I felt years ago when on a pilgrimage to Edith Wharton's home in Lenox, Massachusetts, I discovered that the novelist regarded cats as 'snakes in fur'.

I cannot say why reading a book is more pleasurable with a cat sitting in teapot mode at one's side, or why I sleep better with Spike curled up at the foot of the bed, but it is so. I understand why the ancient Egyptians worshipped cats, and why medieval man burned them as witches. Something in cats surpasses their status as household pets; they are a mystery that eludes us. Victor Hugo wrote that 'God invented the cat to give man the pleasure of caressing a tiger.'

Every day, Spike makes me laugh. Some readers may recall his traumatic move from Paris, ten months ago. On the day our furniture was finally delivered, Spike purred triumphantly from the top of the sofa and rolled on his back on the living room carpet.

Now we enjoy watching the sparrows, orioles, cardinals and doves that cavort in the ginkgo and magnolia trees surrounding our third floor terrace in Georgetown. The pastime has its perils: when birds land on the balustrade, Spike's haunches quiver as he prepares to leap. I clap and scream to break his launch into the void.

When I work, I recall the eighth century Irish monk who hunted words while his cat, Pangur Bán, hunted mice. The mouse in our apartment is attached to my computer, and Spike has an unfortunate habit of walking on the keyboard and obscuring the screen, just when I'm most desperately seeking the right phrase.

Consider how much felines have given to art and literature. Foujita and Steinlen immortalised them on canvas. Colette pampered cats in her Palais Royal apartment. Ernest Hemingway kept thirty of them. Irène Némirovsky's posthumous masterpiece, *Suite Française*, contains a jewel of a chapter in which Albert, the pet cat of bourgeois Parisian refugees, goes hunting on a warm night in German-occupied France.

Baudelaire's 'The Cat', as translated by Ulick O'Connor, explains how humans identify with felines: 'He returns my gaze, careless what I discover/ And what do I find there, I find myself.'

Like me, Spike loves the feather duvet and fireside in winter. But like me, he's chronically restless. We zigzag between boundless energy and exhaustion, and we share the journalist's most important characteristic, curiosity.

Last week, I attended a Bloomsday celebration at the home of the Irish ambassador, Michael Collins, and his wife Marie. Actors from the Irish arts group Solas Nua read excerpts from *Ulysses*. I love the passage where Leopold Bloom prepares breakfast for Molly. 'I never saw such a stupid pussens as the pussens,' Bloom says. 'Silly cat. You silly cat,' I tell Spike several times daily.

The Joycean professor Declan Kiberd understood the meaning of Bloom's encounter with the pussens. 'The cat already offers an antidote to a puffed-up, self-important humanity,' Kiberd writes in *Ulysses and Us*. Bloom's ability to empathise with the cat is one of his most human, if not, indeed, 'godlike' qualities, says Kiberd.

Years ago, Zeinab, my Arabic teacher in Beirut, glanced at her Siamese cat Feyrouz, who liked to sit in on my lessons. 'Sometimes, you'd almost think they were thinking,' Zeinab said. 'Of *course* they are thinking!' I blurted out. I never doubted it for a moment.

'They call them stupid,' Joyce wrote of cats. 'They understand what we say better than we understand them.'

If I was sad or discouraged, my previous cat, Walter, would sit quietly nearby. Perhaps it's his gender (Walter, despite her name, was female), but Spike is a good-time cat who has no patience for brooding. When I'm cheerful, his eyes light up. He performs celebratory leaps, makes a gurgling sound from the throat, and runs to the toy basket in the hope of a game of mousing.

My favourite T-shirt bears a cat face drawn by Jean Cocteau, and the words '*Club des amis des chats*'. It's true we cat-lovers recognise one another, exchange news of our moggies. Back in Paris, my relations with a stern administrator at the Élysée Palace improved after I ran into her in the pet food section of La Grande Épicerie one Saturday morning.

I don't discriminate against non-cat-lovers, though I must admit I had second thoughts about a recent visitor whom Spike hissed at. Tactful friends greet Spike with respect on arrival. Nothing so elaborate as 'Hail, *Majesté*'; 'Hello, Spike' is sufficient.

22 June 2010

Index